Handbook for Youth Sports Coaches

Vern Seefeldt, Editor

sponsored by the
**National Association of
Sport and Physical Education**

an association of the
**American Alliance for Health, Physical
Education, Recreation, and Dance**

THE STATE UNIVERSITY OF NEW JERSEY

RUTGERS

During the 1940s and '50s, organized sports were virtually always thought to have a positive influence on our youth. During the 1960s and '70s, however, youth sports went through a period in which competitive pressure and physical stresses were often harshly criticized. By the 1980s, the question had become, "Under what conditions are organized youth sports healthy and appropriate for children, and under what conditions are they not?" Now, as we move into the 1990s, the focus is on the most critical factor distinguishing healthy youth sports programs: **The quality of the adult leadership.**

On May 12, 1986, New Jersey became the nation's first state to enact legislation protecting volunteer coaches from lawsuits. This law, which required safety education training for coaches, was improved and expanded in August, 1988, with six amendments developed and advocated by the Rutgers Sports Council (Public Law 1988, c. 87, 2A:62A-6.2). In January, 1990, these amendments led to the development of minimum standards regarding course content.

Since 1986, the Youth Sports Research Council, in cooperation with the **New Jersey Recreation and Park Association,** has offered safety training to tens of thousands of youth sports volunteers. The current "SAFETY" Course--"**S**ports **A**wareness **F**or **E**ducating **T**oday's **Y**outh" --is administered by recreation departments and youth sports agencies and was designed to meet the stipulations of New Jersey's law. It is equally appropriate for the more than 20 states which have enacted similar legislation to protect volunteer coaches (e.g., Maryland, Pennsylvania, Delaware, Connecticut, Rhode Island, Massachusetts).

Those who believe that youth sports can have a profound effect upon the youth of our nation must also realize that such influence is heavily dependent upon the quality of the coaches to whom our youth are entrusted. Coaches need not only the skills to teach their sports safely, but also the value systems that allow them to realize that development of their athletes, not the outcome of the competitions, is the most important part of their sports programs.

For additional information, please contact:

Dr. David A. Feigley, Director
Gregg S. Heinzmann, Administrator

YOUTH SPORTS RESEARCH COUNCIL
Rutgers, The State University of New Jersey
Department of Exercise Science and Sport Studies
Room 206, College Avenue Gymnasium
New Brunswick, New Jersey 08903
(908) 932-7178; (908) 932-6537

Preface

The *Handbook for Youth Sports Coaches* is a project of the Youth Sports Coalition of the National Association for Sport and Physical Education (NASPE). In an attempt to identify the specific needs of the coaching community, a survey was sent to 100 individuals selected because of their diverse roles in children's sports. The results of the survey revealed that the handbook should focus on information that addresses the needs of beginning level, volunteer coaches. The editorial committee heeded this advice and proposed twenty chapters of content that should be available to every youth sports coach. At that time invitations were extended to writers who had first-hand knowledge and experience in the trials and delights of teaching sports to children. To the editor's gratification, 20 of 21 designated authors accepted the invitation to contribute to this volume and completed their obligation with dispatch.

The phenomenon of children's sports continues to provide information to scientists, educators, and physicians as they study the benefits and detrimental effects of athletic participation. The authors of these twenty chapters have incorporated the latest information into content which we hope will be sought and digested by those who teach sports to children.

Vern D. Seefeldt
Editor

List of Authors

Marjorie Albohm
International Institute of Sports
   Science and Medicine

Eugene Brown
Michigan State University

Linda Bunker
University of Virginia

John Drowatzky
University of Toledo

John Dunn
Oregon State University

Martha Ewing
Michigan State University

Deborah Feltz
Michigan State University

Jeanne Foley
Michigan State University

Daniel Gould
University of Illinois

John Haubenstricker
Michigan State University

Thelma Horn
Miami University

Richard Magill
Louisiana State University

Vern Seefeldt
Michigan State University

Ronald Smith
University of Washington

Frank Smoll
University of Washington

Jerry Thomas
Louisiana State University

Paul Vogel
Michigan State University

Maureen Weiss
University of Oregon

Holly Wilson Greene
San Leandro, California

Table of Contents

Section I: Introduction

Section II: Foundations of Coaching

Section III: Fundamental Skills of Coaching

Section IV: Special Considerations

SECTION I:
INTRODUCTION

■ **Benefits of Competitive Sports for Children**

■ **Your Role as a Youth Sports Coach**

■ **The Coach as Teacher**

chapter one

Benefits of Competitive Sports For Children And Youth

Vern Seefeldt
Michigan State University

Questions to consider. . .

☐ *What are the benefits of sports for children and youth?*

☐ *Do the benefits of sports apply equally to boys and girls?*

☐ *Do the benefits of sports apply equally across the age range for children and youth?*

☐ *How can you, as the coach, ensure that these benefits are available to your athletes?*

☐ *What should you do if your ability to provide certain of these benefits is deficient or undeveloped?*

S ports for children and youth are so popular in the United States that they have become a part of the American culture. Each year, an estimated 20 million children between the ages of 6 and 16 years are involved in sports that are organized and supervised by adults. The unusual part of this sporting experience is that the adult volunteer who is designated to lead and teach these teams or groups may have had little or no professional education or competence for the tasks involved in coaching. The trust that parents commonly place in their childrens' coaches is testimony to the belief that parents have in the values of organized sports. Whether this trust is justified or misplaced depends to a large degree on the characteristics of the coach.

What are the potential values that children may gain or acquire in organized sports? A survey of the literature devoted to children's sports identifies 20 objectives of agencies that sponsor youth sports (Martens and Seefeldt, 1979). They include:

- development of motoric competencies
- development of physical fitness
- learning how to cooperate
- developing a sense of achievement, which then leads to a positive self-image
- development of an interest in and a desire to continue participation in sports during adulthood
- development of healthy, strong identities
- development of independence through interdependent activities
- acquiring the values of our society
- learning moral reasoning
- having fun
- developing social competencies
- enhancing family unity
- providing opportunities for physical-affective learning, including learning to understand and express emotion, imagination, and appreciation for what the body can do
- developing speed, strength, endurance, coordination, flexibility, and agility
- developing leadership skills
- developing self-reliance and emotional stability by learning to make decisions and accept responsibilities
- learning sportsmanship
- developing initiative
- learning how to compete
- learning of one's capabilities by comparing them with others

For the purposes of this chapter, these objectives have been summarized into the following areas: learning motor skills; health related and motor fitness; participating and belonging; learning socially acceptable values and behaviors; long-

Figure 1.   As the coach you must ensure that the benefits of sports are available to all your athletes.

term skills for leisure; and enhancing child-adult relationships. Because of the special role that sports have in the lives of young girls, a section has also been devoted to this topic.

Learning Motor Skills

There is agreement among parents and coaches that one of the benefits to be gained through youth sports is learning the physical skills associated with a specific sport. As a coach, you are expected to assume many roles and possess many competencies, but none of them is more important than being an excellent teacher of motor skills. In fact, even though you possess many of the competencies required of a coach, none of them will be sufficient to overcome an inability to teach the motor skills of the sport for which you have been designated as "coach." Children's perception that they are improving in their physical skills is such a strong motivation for their continued participation that they will often tolerate physical and mental discomfort, or even abuse, in return for good instruction in motor skills.

Perceived improvement in motor skills also provides the foundation for many other "teachable moments." For example, persistence in a task, team play, enhancement of self-esteem, improvement in self-confidence, physical fitness, and goal setting are all more easily taught when the learning of physical skills is the basis of your instructional program. Conversely, children who know that they are not making progress in motor skill development seldom continue their participation in that sport. Clearly, being able to teach so that all of your athletes improve in their motor skills is one of your essential tasks as a coach.

Health-Related and Motor Fitness

When children are asked to list the benefits of being involved in sports they commonly include "physical fitness." Although they do not always use the term as it is used by adults, there is abundant evidence that children who are active in sports also have the desirable characteristics that we classify under the term "physical fitness." In fact, the term "physical fitness" is now usually divided into two categories, depending on the kind of effects that the activities have on the body. The two categories are called *health-related fitness* and *motor fitness*. Some activities are more directly related to health, and others are more directly related to developing the traits or components that are important in performing certain skills successfully, such as power, agility, and balance.

Health-Related Fitness

Some of the health-related benefits of youth sports include increased cardiorespiratory capacity, greater flexibility, stronger muscles of the stomach and back, and less body fat. Each of these health-related benefits is described briefly in the following.

Cardiorespiratory capacity refers to the ability of the heart, lungs, and circulatory system to function more efficiently for longer periods of time. Among these benefits are having the heart pump more blood per beat, being able to recover from strenuous exercise more quickly, being able to withstand more strenuous exercise for a longer period of time, and being able to do a specific amount of exercise more efficiently by having a lower heart and respiratory rate.

Flexibility refers to the ability of various joints, primarily the ankles, knees, hip, back, shoulders, elbows, wrists, and neck, to function better in specific sports because of an increase in their range of motion. This increased range of motion allows the body to produce more force, absorb more force over greater time and distance, and generally to adjust to the demands of specific skills with less strain to the muscles and skeleton.

Body fat. Loss of fat is due primarily to the expenditure of energy as children practice and compete in a sport. The more strenuous the activity, in terms of cardiorespiratory demands, the greater is its contribution to energy expenditure and weight loss.

Motor Fitness

There is general agreement that certain sports require specific amounts of muscular strength, muscular endurance, power, balance, coordination, agility, and anaerobic capacity in order for an athlete to perform successfully. These re-

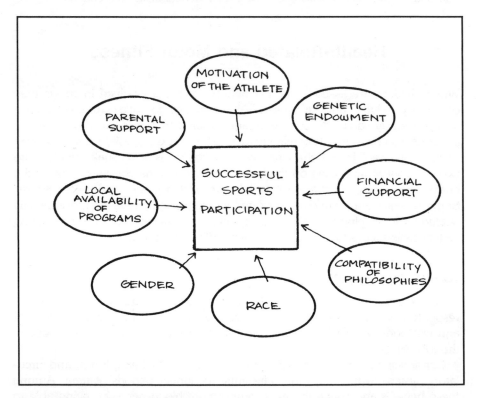

Figure 2.   Successful sports participation depends on the interaction of many events and the cooperation of many individuals.

quirements are called *components* of skills because they are required to some degree in many skills and therefore belong in the category of *motor fitness*. The components of motor fitness are defined as follows.

Muscular strength is a force that is exerted against moveable or immoveable objects by muscular contraction. When the object moves as a result of contraction the result is called an *isotonic* movement; when the force is applied and the object does not move, the effort is call *isometric*. Most muscular efforts in children's sports involve isotonic contractions.

Muscular endurance refers to the performance of repetitive movements through a designated distance or for a specific amount of time. Common examples of muscular endurance are doing sit-ups, pull-ups, push-ups, or throwing a baseball repeatedly as pitchers do in game conditions.

Power is the ability to provide a maximum force in a small amount of time. Examples of skills that involve power include the vertical jump to retrieve a basketball from the backboard, the standing long jump for distance, and swinging a baseball bat in an attempt to strike a ball. Many of the skills in which an object is thrown or struck or in which the body is projected involve power.

Agility involves the ability to change the body's direction rapidly and accurately. Agility is a common component in skills such as ice hockey, football, soccer, and basketball.

Balance is measured in two situations; when the body is stationary (static) or when it is moving (dynamic). Some sports such as gymnastics require the ability to maintain both static and dynamic balance, but generally the games, dances, and sports of the American culture place a greater emphasis on maintaining one's balance while moving.

Reaction time and movement time are commonly combined and are called *speed* or *quickness* by coaches. Generally, the objective is to move one's body, a body part, or an object such as a tennis racquet as quickly as possible from one point to another. The ability to react and move quickly is an important component of many sports, including tennis, badminton, baseball, and basketball.

Anaerobic capacity. Many activities in children's sports require a short, intense effort. Activities such as running from home plate to first base, running from one end of the basketball court to the other, or dribbling a soccer ball and then passing to a teammate are classified as *anaerobic* activities because they are usually accomplished without oxygen or by using the body's stored supply of oxygen. Activities that require anaerobic fitness are classified in the category of *motor fitness* because they are usually closely associated with the skill being developed, rather than contributing to cardiorespiratory health.

Although the components of motor fitness are partially determined by genetic endowment, gender, and chronological age, each child should have ample opportunities to develop his or her capacities for each component. Some children will be more successful in specific sports because their characteristics match those that are required by the sport. For this reason coaches and parents should permit children to experiment with numerous positions within a sport and to try playing various sports. Restricting the opportunities of young athletes, whether by position or sport, is a short-sighted and questionable practice.

Participation and Belonging

For many children, organized sports are a natural transition from the independent play of infancy and early childhood to a form of activity that is organized by adults. This transition from independent to structured play is usually pleasant when the fundamental skills which underlie sports have been learned early in life.

Children learn to run, throw, catch, kick, strike, balance, roll, and dribble at different rates. As a coach, you are likely to have athletes in the same age group who have a wide range of abilities. The younger the age group, the more likely that you will have to teach separate, fundamental skills before these skills can be combined into the skills of your sport. However, children and youth of all ages establish their reputations and status within the group based on their abilities to perform the skills of their sport. Children who have deficiencies are not likely to be highly valued as team members. As a coach you must be able to detect those who are delayed in motor skills and provide the kind of instruction that will improve their performance. The ability of children to perform physical skills on an equal basis with others of the same age is essential if they are to have a feeling of belonging. This feeling of being part of a team or unit is an important reason why children continue to participate in sports.

Learning Socially Acceptable
Values and Behaviors

Many adults believe that involvement in sports is not an end in itself but that sports are an avenue through which many other lessons can be taught and values can be learned. As indicated in Chapter 9, "Teaching Sportsmanship and Values" and in Chapter 14, "Principles of Effective Coach-Athlete Interactions," whether or not these lessons are learned and values incorporated into the child's life depends, in part, on how much you emphasize them as a coach. Your team members will attend to your words only if they are consistent with your actions. This means that you must not only plan to teach physical skills, but you must plan and conduct the practices so that fairness, equality of opportunity, respect for the dignity of each person, whether teammate or opponent, and respect for authority are part of every practice plan. In other words, the values and actions

Figure 3. The frustration of failing to meet the unreasonable expectations of adults may erase many of the potential benefits of sports.

that children must acquire in order to be good citizens must also be practiced when they play organized sports. When the actions and values condoned in sport are at odds with those of society, we must re-examine the purpose of sports for children.

Long-term Skills for Leisure

Unfortunately, many of the sports that we promote for children and youth are only popular with them during childhood and adolescence. The vast majority of competitors drop out of their favorite sports by the time they reach 15 years of age. This tremendous attrition has many causes, but one of the primary reasons is the great emphasis that we place on excellence of performance—at the expense of opportunities for all who wish to compete. Although slogans such as "everyone plays" and "sports for all" are popular throughout children's programs, often they are only catchy phrases that have little relation to what occurs once the competition begins. The more intense the competition, the more exclusive is the selection of participants. By the time children reach high school, the emphasis is generally on supporting one "best" team rather than on the continued development of many athletes, regardless of ability. Despite our attempts to make sports generally available to all children, there are many who have been denied an opportunity to improve their skills because their initial skill level was inadequate or because they did not progress rapidly enough to keep pace with their peer group.

As a youth sports coach, you must strive to promote the skill development of each individual, regardless of that person's initial competence or potential. If each coach supports such a goal, then the accumulated experiences will provide for the ultimate development of all individuals. Even if there is a period of time during the high school years when competition at one's level of ability is not readily available, the basic skill development that has been acquired prior to this time may serve as a foundation for re-entry into recreative sports during adulthood, when the emphasis on competition may have given way to an emphasis on participation.

Enhancing Child-Adult Relationships

One of the special benefits of children's sports is the relationships that can develop between coaches and athletes. Because many of your athletes may be growing up in single-parent families, you may be called upon to provide the kind of support that is customarily provided by the missing parent. Perhaps your role will be that of friend, counselor, teacher, intermediary between the child and another adult, or advocate for the child's welfare. Athletes have historically stated that the greatest benefits they obtained from sports were not necessarily the physical skills or physical fitness that are so commonly mentioned, but the lessons and values they learned because their coach took the time to place athletics into a proper perspective. This perspective of sports as a vehicle through which important lessons are learned was of value to them far beyond their days on the field, floor, court, or pool. Successful coaches must prepare themselves for the special and challenging relationship that can exist between a coach and athlete.

When opportunities arise for you to assume the role of counselor, parent, or teacher, you are in a position to either respond or to ignore the opportunity. Your response will depend greatly on your personality, philosophy of coaching, and how much you have thought about the alternatives to solving the specific problems of young athletes. Remember that players of all ages are apt to need support from the coach, even though the older athletes may not show their needs as clearly as those below high school age. The calls for your guidance may be clear or subtle, loud or barely audible, or perhaps even disguised to suggest that everything is going well. A thorough knowledge of each player's environment will help you to recognize opportunities to develop the many special roles that a coach may play.

Girls' Sports: A Special Opportunity

Children's sports have historically provided opportunities for boys to learn the skills and teamwork that are necessary for success at interscholastic, intercollegiate, and adult levels of participation. Only recently have such opportunities become available to girls. Even though public laws require equal opportunities for boys and girls in the public supported non-school sports and at interscholastic levels, the rate of participation for girls in each of these categories is far below that of boys. (For a detailed account of some issues involved in sports for boys and girls, see Chapter 19, "What About Co-ed Competition?") If youth sports are truly the place where fundamental motor skills and strategies are learned, then girls must be encouraged to participate at the same level of intensity and to begin their exposure to sports at the same ages as boys. The disparity between the skill level of boys and girls may be at least partially due to the increased years of experience that boys have at any given chronological age.

A major problem in children's sports, with the possible exceptions of gymnastics, swimming, figure skating, and softball, is an acute shortage of women coaches. This lack of women coaches presents problems that extend beyond the lessons to be learned during practices and competitions. The absence of women coaches may carry a message to young girls that athletics are the domain of boys and men; that coaching is not a suitable activity for women; or that a total commitment to sports is inappropriate for girls and women.

Although we do not know whether an increase in the number of women coaches would increase the initial entry rates of girls into sports and encourage their continued participation, both of these outcomes are possible. Both men and women coaches must encourage young girls to become involved in sports and to ensure that their participation is rewarding by providing an environment which supports psychological and physical development. If girls are to derive the benefits that seem to be so readily available to boys who participate in sports, then they must be encouraged and nurtured during their early sporting experiences.

Summary

The benefits of sports competition for children and youth are numerous, but whether or not they are realized by the young athletes depends on the kind of adult leadership that sports programs provide. The many roles of the youth sports coach will demand much time and provide many challenges. Frequently the obstacles may seem overwhelming, just as they sometimes appear beyond the control of teachers, counselors, and parents in their day-to-day associations with children. The only recourse that you have as a coach is to prepare as thoroughly as possible for the situations that may arise and then call for assistance in circumstances where the solution to a problem is not within your reach.

Each of the remaining 19 chapters of this handbook is devoted to a specific category of problems that commonly occur in children's sports. Select the chapters that pertain to the areas in which you need the most assistance now and read those first. Then proceed systematically through the remaining chapters until you have read them all. This process will introduce you to most of the problems that you are likely to encounter in your coaching experience. Even though you may not be able to recall all of the suggested solutions at a later date, this overview will provide a source of reference for future study. As your coaching experience increases, you will be able to incorporate more of the potential benefits into your practices and games. You may also be able to anticipate and avoid some of the problems. The combination of practical experience and knowledge of your sport will also increase your enjoyment of coaching young athletes.

References

Martens, R. & Seefeldt, V. (1979). (Eds.) *Guidelines for children's sports.* Washington, DC: American Alliance for Health, Physical Education, Recreation and Dance.

Suggested Readings

Guidelines for coaching education: Youth sports. (1986). Reston, VA: National Association for Sport and Physical Education.
Sports medicine for children and youth. (1979). Columbus, OH: Ross Laboratories.
Smith, N., Smith, R., & Smoll, F. (1983). *Kids' sports.* Reading, MA: Addison-Wesley Publishing Company.
Smoll, F., Magill, R. & Ash, M. (1987). *Children in sport* (3rd ed.). Champaign, IL: Human Kinetics Publishers, Inc.

2

chapter two

Your Role As A Youth Sports Coach

Daniel Gould
University of Illinois

Questions to consider. . .

☐ *What are the roles of the youth sport coach?*

☐ *What is my role as a coach in providing quality adult leadership for young athletes?*

☐ *How do I put my coaching role priorities into action?*

☐ *How do I provide quality sport experiences for my young athletes?*

K aren is eleven years old and has always enjoyed playing soccer with her older brothers. The park district now offers coed soccer and she is elated. She can't wait to come to practice and improve her soccer skills.

Kevin is nine years old and has never participated in organized sport. In fact, he doesn't even enjoy sports. His mother and father, however, are worried about his lack of physical activity and preoccupation with MTV. They sign him up for the new soccer league.

Michael is twelve and has been in and out of juvenile court several times for shoplifting and disorderly conduct. In Michael's last appearance before the bench, Judge Holt (an ex-college athlete) recommended that Michael get involved in sport. His hope is that sports participation will help Mike build the qualities that he has not yet developed.

Sue and Brad are both ten years old and have been playing organized sports for several years. Their mother and father both have highly successful professional careers and want Sue and Brad involved in sports so that they will learn to compete. In essence, they want to prepare their children for the "dog-eat-dog" competition of adult life by giving them an edge—knowing how to win!

Billy is your son . . . your pride and joy. He is eleven years old and enjoyed playing baseball during the last two summers. He thought he would give soccer a try this fall. It looks like a lot of fun, besides, the uniforms are neat!

Finally, you are Billy's parent and played some high school sports, but never participated in soccer. You came home from work the other night and received a call from the park district. Cheryl, the district's youth sports director, informed you that the sign-up for soccer was overwhelming. In fact, they had fifteen extra teams—none of which had coaches. The league is to begin next Saturday and she had to have coaches for all of these teams. If not, several hundred children (including your son Billy) will be turned away.

You told Cheryl that you would be glad to help, but that you had never played soccer. She said that's OK, most of the mothers and fathers who are coaching had not played the sport. Besides, the park district would hold a clinic and teach you the basics of the game. You reluctantly agreed to coach.

Two weeks have passed since you agreed to coach. You have attended the Saturday morning soccer coaching clinic and received your team roster. In addition to Billy, you also have Karen, Kevin, Mike, Sue, Brad and nine other boys and girls between the ages of 9 and 12 assigned to your team. You have held your first practice and are driving home.

While driving home you begin thinking about the talk given on the role of the youth sport coach during the soccer clinic. You recall that during the talk, the speaker indicated the youth sports are not automatically beneficial for children. In fact, many times children's sports can have negative effects by placing children under too much stress, by creating environments where children are pushed so hard they sustain injuries, or by destroying children's feelings of self-worth through constant negative evaluation. You were surprised by this statement because you had always felt that sports were good for kids. They were good for you!

You were glad when the speaker concluded that youth sports can have a tremendously positive impact on children. Positive results only occur through positive experiences, however, and the key factor in determining if quality experiences occur is *quality adult leadership*.

As you continue your drive, you decide that you agree with the speaker. For youth sports to be beneficial, quality experiences are needed. The questions that you ask are, "How do I create quality experiences for my players? What is my role as a youth sport coach?"

While some of the circumstances in the above story may be different from your coaching situation, many of the elements of the setting will be similar. You will have a number of children on your team. The children will be similar in many ways, but they will also each be unique, with different needs and reasons for being out for the team. Your main responsibility is to provide quality experiences for these children and in so doing help ensure the benefits of sports participation. Few youth sport coaches would disagree that this is their major responsibility. However, like the coach in the story, they ask "What is my role in providing quality adult leadership?"

What is my role in providing quality adult leadership?

This chapter is designed to address the issue of adult leadership in youth sports. Its overall purpose is to help you identify the different roles of the coach. In addition, emphasis will be placed on helping you determine what roles are most appropriate to adopt in your situation with your players. Lastly, the chapter will focus on helping you implement your chosen roles and priorities as a coach.

As a youth sport coach, you will play many different roles in your effort to provide quality adult leadership. These may range from being a teacher of fundamental sport skills to that of a disciplinarian. Some of the more important roles you may play are discussed in the following sections.

The Coach As An Organizer-Planner

One of the most important, but least recognized, roles played by the youth sport coach is that of an organizer-planner. As a coach you are responsible for the development, health, and safety of a group of children. You must be organized to meet this responsibility.

The first step in becoming an effective organizer-planner is to divide the season into three phases: the preseason; the season itself; and the postseason. Make a list of what needs to be accomplished during each phase of the season. For example, Chapter 11, "Planning For The Season," outlines a number of factors to be considered in preseason planning. Similarly, Chapter 15, "Conducting A Sport Orientation Meeting For Parents," outlines critical factors to consider when conducting a preseason sport orientation meeting. Planning does not stop with the preseason, however. Chapter 12, "How To Conduct Effective Practices," outlines a number of organizational principles for conducting effective practices during the season. Chapter 20, "Post Season Evaluation: What Did We Accomplish?" discusses the essential elements of a postseason evaluation. Key points from all of these chapters should be incorporated into your three-phase seasonal plan.

Planning and organization make life much easier for everyone involved. The children learn more because the coach has planned practices and determined what to teach. In turn, the young athletes are more motivated and behave better because the organized coach plans practices so that all of the athletes are actively involved. Finally, unexpected conditions like rained-out games are handled more effectively because the coach has developed procedures for dealing with these situations.

The Coach As A Teacher

Every coach is a teacher and is responsible for teaching the skills of the game. However, every coach is not an effective teacher! Too many coaches assume that mere practice makes perfect and fail to properly plan and organize practices. Little is learned in unorganized and unplanned practices. Athletes become bored and disinterested in such settings. Thus, it is important to remember that practice does not necessarily make perfect—planned, purposeful practices are needed if optimal learning is to result (Martens, Christina, Harvey, and Sharkey, 1981).

As outlined in Chapter 3, "The Coach As A Teacher," teaching is more than putting on the coaching cap and blowing a whistle. You must decide what to teach, when to teach it, and what method of instruction is most effective. You must also know how to give effective demonstrations, provide clear and constructive feedback, and construct practice environments that promote learning. In short, teaching involves a concerted effort on the part of the coach.

The Coach As A Winner

Our society places tremendous emphasis on competition, success, and winning. This is not necessarily bad. After all, striving to win is a primary goal of sports competition. What often happens, however, is that winning is viewed as the only objective of sport participation—and winning is often defined in a very limited way.

Winning is not the primary goal of youth sport. Sure, we all want our teams and children to win, but the youth sport coach must be more concerned with

Figure 1. Teaching the skills of the sport is a major responsibility of the coach.

the total development of the child—physically, socially, and emotionally. Most young athletes indicate that they would rather play on a losing team and participate than sit the bench on a winning team. When coaching young athletes, we cannot let defeating one's opponents override the other important objectives of sports such as participation, skill development, fun, and friendship.

Winning is not the primary goal of youth sports.

It is also important to recognize that winning is often defined in a very limited way in youth sports—as defeating one's opponent. Defining winning solely in this fashion guarantees that most children will not succeed because for *every* winner of a contest there are many more losers. A better way to look at winning is to expand the definition and emphasize that winning means surpassing one's own previous performance and giving a maximum effort (Martens et al., 1981). In this way every child can be a winner (Orlick and Botterill, 1975)!

The Coach As A First Aid And Medical Consultant

"What do you mean a first aid and medical consultant—I am not a doctor!" This is the reaction of many coaches when they learn that they must fill this role, too. They have no specialized medical training and feel they are not qualified to give medical treatment and advice.

The fact of the matter is, however, that the coach is often the first on the scene in many sports related medical emergencies and, like it or not, must assume this role. In addition, coaches are often asked questions by athletes and their parents about the appropriate medical treatment for recurring injuries.

An increased knowledge of athletic injuries also allows the coach to understand why these injuries occur. Moreover, as discussed in Chapter 6, "Preventing Common Athletic Injuries," many injuries can easily be prevented through forethought and preplanning.

Many common injuries can be prevented through forethought and preplanning!

While the coach plays a vital role in the first aid and emergency treatment of athletic injuries, it is important to recognize that no one expects the coach to do things he or she is not qualified to do. In fact, Chapter 16, "Emergency Procedures Every Coach Should Know," indicates that it is just as important for a coach to know what not to do in an emergency situation as it is to know what to do.

An appreciation and knowledge of first aid and emergency procedures is a must for every coach! It is only with this knowledge that the coach can help ensure that sports participation occurs in a safe and healthy environment.

The Coach As A Motivator

Most of us assume that children are naturally motivated to play sports. If not, why would they come out for the team in the first place? The examples of Kevin, Sue, and Brad given at the beginning of this chapter show that this is not always the case. Children have many reasons for coming out for the team. They also vary in their levels of motivation. The coach must recognize these differences and act accordingly. For some children, this means increasing their level of motivation. For others it means helping them avoid becoming overmotivated. For still others it may mean helping them to maintain their healthy enthusiasm.

Coaches must also understand how their actions directly and indirectly influence the levels of motivation of their young athletes, what goals to set, and the relationship between intrinsic and extrinsic motivation. These and other important strategies influencing motivation are discussed in detail in Chapters 7, "Goal-setting: Principles For The Coach And Athlete" and 8, "Motivating Young Athletes For Optimal Performance."

The Coach As A Developer of Fitness

Many coaches think that physical fitness is automatically improved anytime someone participates in sport. Others feel they must continually push their athletes to the limit if fitness is to be achieved. Both of these assumptions are wrong!

Mere participation in sport does not guarantee that fitness will be developed. Coaches must understand some basic principles of fitness and employ them on a regular basis, if fitness goals are to be realized. Chapter 6, "Preventing Common Athletic Injuries," addresses the attainment of physical fitness.

Mere participation in sport does not guarantee the development of physical fitness.

Coaches must also recognize that too much emphasis on fitness can be just as bad as too little. In fact, basic principles of fitness include allowing for intervals of work and rest, and alternating difficult workouts with easier ones. Too often coaches forget these important principles and overtrain their young athletes. This can lead to injury, poor performance, and loss of motivation.

The Coach As A Disciplinarian
And Developer Of Character

One of the most difficult roles for the volunteer coach is that of a disciplinarian. Constantly disciplining athletes and dealing with unsportsmanlike behavior is an unpleasant task. This role must be assumed, however. If not, the unsportsmanlike behaviors and disciplinary problems spread and lead to additional problems both in and out of the sport setting.

It is much easier to start children off on the right foot or correct minor disciplinary problems when they are young than to wait and try to develop good habits or change ingrained attitudes later in life. Sport does not build character or develop sportsmanship by itself. Coaches develop these attributes by employing the specific strategies outlined in Chapter 9, "Teaching Sportsmanship And Values."

The Coach As A Parent

This role of the coach-parent is twofold. Approximately 60% of youth sports parents serve as coaches of their own children. In addition, many coaches end up being substitute parents for some of the other children on the team who come from single-parent families.

Coaching your own child is a difficult task. On one hand, you are probably coaching because you want to spend time with your child and help him or her improve and have a rewarding sports experience. On the other hand, you want to be impartial and show no favoritism to your child. In many ways, you end up in a "no win" situation and either overreact by being tougher on your child that you are with the others, or unknowingly spend more time with your child and neglect the others.

Coaching your own child does not have to a "no win" situation. A good strategy for solving this dilemma is to have an impartial third party observe your practices and games from time to time and let you know if you are being fair and impartial. This strategy works especially well when some parents on the team begin to unfairly criticize you and accuse you of favoritism.

Coaches influence young athletes both on and off the field.

Because of the importance of sport in American society, children have a natural tendency to look up to their coaches. In fact, coaches sometimes act as substitute parents without knowing it. Because of this, it is important for the coaches to remember that they will be influencing some of their young athletes both on and off the field. If you use alcohol or drugs, swear, smoke, or argue with officials, it is likely that your players will learn from your actions and view drinking, swearing, smoking, and arguing with officials as desirable behaviors. The key, then, is to model what you believe is best for children. As a substitute parent, your behavior will have an enormous influence on the young athletes.

Figure 2. As a coach you may be called upon to be a substitute parent.

The Coach As A Friend

A few months ago I received a letter from a volunteer coach who had been criticized by a fan as not being effective because he was a friend to the children on his team. The fan thought it was not "coachlike" to be a friend.

Criticizing coaches for being the friends of the children on their team is unjust. The most effective volunteer coaches are friends with the children on the team. They have the characteristics of a good friend—they are good listeners, for the children are not afraid to confide in them. They "tell it like it is", but in a way that will not put their athletes down. They are respected, and they are there when the children need them. The coach who is a friend, however, does not forget about his or her responsibilities. A coach must discipline the children when it is appropriate, run organized and controlled practices, and do what is best for the children—even if the children do not like it at the time. In short, don't be afraid to be a friend to your players. You will enjoy it and friendship will make you a more effective coach.

The Many Roles Of The Youth Sports Coach

- Organizer-Planner
- Teacher
- Winner
- First Aid-Medical Consultant
- Motivator

- Developer of Fitness
- Disciplinarian-Character Developer
- Parent
- Friend

Evaluating Your Coaching Priorities

The youth sport coach can play a number of different roles. What roles you adopt depend on a number of different factors. One factor of particular importance is your own system of priorities.

While a coach's priorities are an important determinant of which coaching roles are adopted, coaches seldom take time to sit down and establish a list of priorities. Instead, these priorities emerge haphazardly as the season progresses. Therefore, it is important that a coach identify his or her priorities before the season begins.

Table 1 contains a priority assessment of the various coaching roles discussed in the previous section. Take a few minutes to rate the importance of the various roles for you. Then examine your ratings. What roles received the highest ratings? Don't worry if you gave them all high ratings. This is a typical response. Most coaches feel that all the different roles of the coach are important.

Unfortunately, there are times when the various roles of the coach conflict. For example, a coach may feel that it is important to win the game, but to develop sportsmanlike behavior he or she must keep the star player out of the contest because this was the agreed upon penalty for violating a team rule. The coach is faced with a dilemma. Is winning the game or developing sportsmanship the most important objective? Keeping the star player on the bench may result in defeat, but playing him or her will convey to the athlete and the other team members that it is OK to be unsportsmanlike if you are the star player. Which role is of higher priority to you?

Table 1.   Priority assessment of possible coaching roles.

Directions: Rate from 1 to 5 the importance of the following nine possible roles of the coach. A rating of one signifies low importance and five high importance. Be sure to rate each item.

	Rating	Rank
The coach as an Organizer-Planner	_____	_____
The coach as a Teacher of Sport Skills	_____	_____
The coach as a Winner	_____	_____
The coach as a First Aid and Medical Consultant	_____	_____
The coach as a Motivator	_____	_____
The coach as a Developer of Fitness	_____	_____
The coach as a Disciplinarian And Developer of Character	_____	_____
The coach as a Parent	_____	_____
The coach as a Friend	_____	_____

To obtain a better understanding of the relative importance of the various coaching roles for yourself, go back to Table 1. In the blank next to your ratings of importance, rank from 1 to 9 the importance of each role, with 1 being the most important role and 9 the least important. This will be difficult, but try to make these tough decisions. It will show you what roles are of greatest importance to you.

Finally, take a good look at your rankings and ratings. Do you feel your ratings and rankings reflect the most important benefits children receive from participation in sport? Can you live with these decisions? That is, if being a winner is not the highest ranked objective for you at this time, will your behavior match this decision when you are on the field or in the gym when the team title is on the line and the fans are yelling for victory? Will you still be able to focus on skill development and sportsmanship in the heat of competition?

Putting Your Coaching Role
Priorities Into Action

At this point, you probably feel that only Superman or Wonderwoman could assume all these roles and be a successful youth sport coach. In fact, these have been my exact feelings after reading chapters on the role of the coach. I kept asking, "How can one mere mortal do all this?"

Figure 3. Every coach must make decisions about the many important roles to be assumed.

Relax. You do not have to be superhuman to be a successful coach—no coach is perfect! Years of research have shown sport scientists that there is no one best method of coaching, no one perfect teaching method, and no one personality type of the great coach. Instead, it has been found that great coaches assume different roles and use different methods of coaching in different situations with different children.

Coaches must assume different roles in different situations with different children.

Your responsibility, then, is to employ the various roles discussed in this chapter at the appropriate times, with the appropriate young athletes. A case in point would be coaching the youth soccer team discussed at the beginning of this chapter. As a coach, you would first try to do what was best for the entire team. You would plan for your season, get organized, and then focus on what the team needs most. In this case you would focus on skill instruction, fitness development, teaching sportsmanlike behavior, and enhancing motivation by making soccer enjoyable. However, certain children on your team would have special needs which would signal that more attention be given to a particular coaching role.

Karen, for example, is a very skill-oriented and is one of the better players on the team. Therefore, you might want to present more advanced skills to her. This would not only meet her need to excel, but also help maintain her motivation.

Kevin is the boy whose parents made him come out for the team, so watch him carefully and try to ensure that he is involved and having fun. His motivation level may initially be low, but by making sure he is involved and having fun, you can increase his motivation.

Michael, who has spent time in juvenile court, may need special attention regarding the development of sportsmanship. Be careful, however, not to single him out from the group as a behavior problem. Instead, meet with him individually and discuss appropriate behavior. Moreover, make sure you reward him for demonstrating good sportsmanship.

Sue and Brad are normal ten year old children, but their parents seem to place excessive pressure on them to win. Make sure their mother and father attend the parent orientation meetings, where the nature and role of winning is stressed. In addition, do not be afraid to talk to your players about the meaning of success. Teach them to view improving relative to their own goals and giving maximum effort as the important components of success.

Finally, be careful to remain impartial with your own son, Billy. Don't get on his case in an effort to appear impartial. It would also be useful to have a friend (perhaps an assistant coach) observe you throughout the season and let you know if you are treating your son differently from the rest of the team.

Figure 4. You are not required to be superhuman to be a great coach.

Summary

The youth sports coach is not a professional. Coaching is not a full-time job for you. This fact does not detract from the important role that you as a coach have in providing quality sports experiences for children, however. In many ways, youth sport coaches are the most important coaches in the sport system. After all, it is the youth sport coach who starts children off in sport, and who has the potential to unintentionally end a child's athletic career. The critical question for the youth sports coach, then, is "How do I provide quality experiences that will ensure that participation is beneficial for the young athletes?"

The best way to provide quality sports experiences for young athletes is to be aware of the diverse roles that coaches play and to know your own coaching priorities. Effective coaches get to know their young athletes, consider the purposes of the program, and assume different roles with different players in different coaching situations. Finally, the effective coach should evaluate his or her behavior in an effort to provide quality sports experiences for all the children involved.

References

Martens, R., Christina, R. W., Harvey, J. S., & Sharkey, B. J. (1981). *Coaching young athletes*. Champaign, IL: Human Kinetics.

Orlick, T., & Botterill, C. (1975). *Every kid can win*. Chicago, IL: Nelson-Hall.

Suggested Readings

Martens, R. (Ed.). (1978). *Joy and sadness in children's sports*. Champaign, IL: Human Kinetics.

Martens, R., Christina, R. W., Harvey, J. S. & Sharkey, B. J. (1981). *Coaching young athletes*. Champaign, IL: Human Kinetics.

Martens, R., & Seefeldt, V. (Eds.). (1979). *Guidelines for children's sports*. Washington, D.C.: AAHPERD.

Smoll, F. L., & Smith, R. E. (1979). *Improving relationship skills in youth sports coaches*. East Lansing, MI: Institute for the Study of Youth Sports, State of Michigan.

3

chapter three

The Coach As Teacher

Richard A. Magill
Louisiana State University

Questions to Consider. . .

☐ *Why is an opportunity to learn and improve skills an important objective in youth sports?*

☐ *What are some important characteristics of good instruction?*

☐ *How can a coach use demonstrations effectively?*

☐ *What can we do in practice sessions that will help young athletes learn skills more efficiently?*

☐ *What kinds of feedback can a coach give players?*

☐ *How should instructions be given to young athletes for maximum effectiveness?*

A common objective of youth sports programs is to provide participants with an opportunity to learn and improve skills. How important is this objective? Three key points can be considered to demonstrate why this objective is critical for any youth sports program.

First, in order to be successful, an athlete must be able to perform a large number of different skills. All sports, whether team or individual, are complex activities and are made up of many "subskills" or fundamental skills. For example, baseball requires participants to be able to throw, hit, run, and catch. Each of these subskills of baseball must be learned by the athletes. A critical question here is, "Where will athletes learn these important and necessary subskills?" One of the key places for this learning to take place is in youth sports programs.

Compare this learning of sports subskills to what occurs in the learning of other skills in the classroom. If a student is to be successful in mathematics, for example, there are a number of mathematics subskills that must be learned. To be able to successfully divide one number into another number, the student must be able to distinguish one number from another, and to be able to add, subtract, and multiply. These critical subskills must be learned before success in division can be experienced.

Being an effective teacher is an important characteristic of a successful coach.

Just as it is essential that subskills of math are taught in the elementary schools, it is also important that the subskills of baseball, football, or any sport, be taught in youth sports. Because of this, the youth sport coach is a key person in providing the opportunity for these subskills to be learned.

The second point to consider is the importance of learning fundamental sports skills to the athletes themselves. Both research and personal experience indicate that a common reason given by young athletes for dropping out of sports is that they weren't learning anything or that they weren't experiencing satisfactory improvement in their own skills. When you consider that another important objective of youth sports programs is to encourage youth to stay involved in sports, it becomes essential that they continue to learn the skills that will lead to long-term involvement.

Finally, consider what characterizes successful coaches. If you read almost any book discussing what made a coach successful at any level of competition, you will find that a common characteristic among these people is that they were all skillful teachers. For example, one of the most successful college basketball coaches in history was John Wooden, who led many of his UCLA teams to national championships. It is common knowledge that one of John Wooden's greatest assets as a coach was that he was an outstanding teacher. It seems

Figure 1.   In order to keep children involved in sports, the coach must be a good teacher.

logical that if a coach at the major college level of competition concentrates on being a good teacher, then a coach at the youth sports level should be even more concerned about this role.

Historically, the best coaches at all levels of competition have also been good teachers.

Clearly, teaching fundamental skills is an important job for the youth sports coach. This means that as a coach, you will be expected to be a teacher. How successfully you fulfill this role will determine your level of success as a coach.

Guidelines presented in this chapter will help you define and carry out your role as a teacher. Successful teachers act differently than unsuccessful teachers. The guidelines presented here are based on what we know about the characteristics of successful teachers and how they teach their students.

Giving Instructions

One of the essential ingredients for successful learning is knowing what to do. The young athlete wants and needs to know what must be done to perform a skill correctly. Providing this information is at the heart of giving instructions. Effective instructions are those that make clear to the athlete what is to be done and how it should be done. The following suggestions can be used to guide you in providing instructions to your athletes. Giving instructions in this manner will increase the likelihood that your athletes will learn what they need to know to be successful.

Providing clear instructions is an essential part of effective teaching.

Gain Their Attention

It won't matter how good your instructions are if you cannot get your athletes to pay attention to what you say or demonstrate to them. You must be certain that every one of your team members is giving you his or her undivided attention before you begin telling or showing them what you want them to do. There are several ways to be sure that this occurs.

Make sure that the athletes are seated, standing, or kneeling in such a way that every one can see you. Check this before you begin talking or demonstrating. Also, make certain that they are arranged in such away that you have minimized distractions from other parts of the practice area. For example, you may be coaching baseball on a field that is a part of a large complex where there are several teams practicing at the same time. To help minimize distractions from these other teams, arrange your team for instruction sessions in such a way that they face away from the other fields. If you are going to give instructions to just one or a few of your team members while the others keep practicing, have them face you so that they won't be able to see the other team members. In these ways, you can help keep your athletes from being distracted by outside interference and increase the chances that they will focus their attention on what you have to tell them.

Give Your Athletes Appropriate Information

Now that you have their attention, what you tell them or show them becomes critical. An important point to keep in mind here is that what you tell them or show them directs their attention to what it is that you want them to know or to do. To accomplish this, here are some key points to keep in mind.

Let your athletes know the goal of your instructions. If you are giving instructions about how to pass a football, let your athletes know that this is what you want them to accomplish. Be as specific about your objectives as you can. For example, you can let them know that the goal is to learn to pass the football to a receiver who is standing still and only a few yards away. Other goals might be to learn to pass the ball to a receiver who is running away from you or who is running from left to right in front of you. Rather than saying that they are going to learn to throw the football in different ways, be specific with what they will actually learn. Tell them the category or event about which you will be giving them instructions before you give the instructions.

Effective instructions make it clear to the athlete what he or she is supposed to do.

Don't tell them too many things at once. One of the common problems for beginning coaches is to give too much verbal information when they are teaching. Even though all of what you say is correct, it may be a waste of time because your athletes will not remember all of it. As human beings, we can handle only a limited amount of information at one time. The implication of this characteristic for the coach is that he or she should make certain not to overload the athletes with information.

As human beings, we can handle only a limited amount of information at one time.

Suppose you are giving instructions about batting. It is tempting to tell your athletes everything they will ever need to know about how to successfully hit a ball. It is not uncommon to hear a coach tell young athletes during one instruction session about where their feet should be, how their weight should be distributed, how and when to step toward the pitch, how to hold the bat, and so on. While all of these points are important, they provide much more information than the athletes can handle at one time. The result is that they will remember none of what you have said, or they will pick and choose at random from the points that you have made. Whether these points coincide with what you want them to remember or pay attention to is left to chance.

Instructions should be simple and to the point.

Emphasize what should be done. When you give instructions, it is not only important for you to consider how much you say, it is also important to consider *what* you say. It will be helpful to evaluate your instructions with the following question in mind: *Do my instructions tell the athlete what to do in order to perform the skill correctly?* For example, if you are teaching your team how to shoot a basketball and you want them to concentrate on the release of the ball, then your instructions should let them know how to the release should be done. Don't assume that they can figure it out on their own.

This point is especially critical if you are coaching beginners or teaching a new skill. Learning theorists agree that the first step in learning a new skill is to try to "get the idea" of what should be done to successfully perform the skill. Once students get through that phase of learning, they can concentrate on refining the skill, and doing it as correctly as possible in whatever situation requires its use. This means that when you teach something new to your athletes, your instructions must provide sufficient information to help them get the idea of what they are supposed to do as they perform the skill.

Instructions must help beginners "get the idea" of what they are supposed to do to perform the skill you are teaching them.

Use images where possible as a supplement to your instructions. Often a coach provides too much information in his or her instructions by trying to verbally describe the movements that must take place to successfully perform the skill being taught. One way to reduce the information is to avoid the lengthy verbal description and instead present an "image" or analogy of the skill. For example, it is not easy to describe the action of the hand, wrist, and arm for the proper release of a basketball shot. A useful image might be, "When you finish the shot, your hand and arm should look like a goose neck." With this image, you have presented a minimum amount of information and you have helped the athletes "get the idea" of what they are supposed to do by relating this new skill to something with which they are familiar. Try to incorporate images in your instructions as often as you can. Imagery works well for all age levels.

Guidelines for Giving Instructions

- *Gain the athletes' attention*
- *Give the athletes appropriate information*
- *Don't overload them with information*
- *Emphasize exactly what should be done and how to do it*
- *Use visual images to supplement your demonstration wherever possible*

Use Demonstrations Effectively

One of the most common means of providing information about how to do a skill is to demonstrate that skill. While this may sound easy, especially if you can do the skill yourself, there are some important guidelines that should be followed when using demonstrations as a means of giving instruction.

> *Demonstrating the skill being taught is one way to increase your effectiveness as a teacher.*

Make sure everyone can see the demonstration. Demonstrate the skill so that your athletes can see the part or parts of the skill that you want them to see. While the skill may be easy to demonstrate, be certain that the part you really want them to see is not hidden from their view. Plan your demonstrations ahead of time so that you know where to begin the demonstration. Be sure that what you want them to see will be in their line of sight when you come to that part of the skill. Remember that some skills, if started while you are facing the athletes, will finish while your back is toward them.

Tell your athletes what to look for in your demonstration. Make sure that you tell your athletes *before you begin* your demonstration what they should be looking for while you demonstrate. This is especially important when you demonstrate the entire skill and you only want them to pay attention to a particular part of it. By giving them this information in advance, you direct their attention to what is important in the demonstration. The benefit here is that you will help your athletes get the idea of what they are supposed to do when they try the skill themselves.

Demonstrate the skill correctly. It is important when you demonstrate a skill to your athletes that you demonstrate it correctly. Exactly how correct and to

Figure 2. Be sure your athletes can see your demonstrations.

what level of precision you need to perform the demonstration will depend on the skill level of your athletes. For beginners, your demonstration should be sufficiently correct to help the athletes "get the idea" of what they should do. Remember that when you demonstrate a skill, you set up the situation where the athletes will try to imitate exactly what you did. If you can't demonstrate the skill correctly, find someone who can. Often, one of your team members will be able to provide an excellent demonstration. Video tapes or films also are a useful means of providing a correct demonstration of a skill.

Directing Practice

Giving instructions is only one part of the teaching process. Providing the best instructions possible is no guarantee that your athletes will learn to perform the skill successfully. Instructions must be followed by a sufficient amount of practice by the athletes themselves. However, you must remember that it is not just practice by itself that leads to successful learning, it is the *right kind of practice* that brings about desirable changes. This is where you, as the coach, play a critical role. You are the person responsible for directing the kind of practice in which your athletes will engage.

In this section, some guidelines will be presented that will help you direct your athletes to engage in the right kind of practice. Because Chapter 12 is devoted to conducting effective practices, the guidelines presented here will be related to your role as a teacher, helping your athletes practice the skills you are teaching.

Provide Sufficient Practice Time

One of the most important points you can remember about conducting a practice session is that the degree to which a skill is learned is directly related to how much time is spent in specific practice of that skill. It seems that it is impossible to practice a skill too much. However, it is very easy to practice a skill too little.

The key to helping your athletes learn skills is to give them as much of the right kind of practice as possible.

Be sure your athletes have plenty of time to practice each skill you teach. Repetition is a very powerful tool in learning sports skills. Explaining this fact will help you to motivate your team members to try the skill over and over again. Be careful, however, to limit the repetition you allow in a single practice session.

There is a point at which too much repetition at one time can be detrimental to learning. Learning is hindered when athletes become bored. You can increase the amount of practice for a specific skill by providing opportunities for practicing that skill on different days of practice or within different contexts of the same practice session.

For example, suppose you are teaching a young athlete to bat a ball. This is a very difficult skill to learn and will require a lot of practice. Even professional athletes continue to practice and to receive instruction about batting after many years of playing experience. While you cannot really provide too much practice time for batting, you can overdo it with how much you provide at any one time. Specify a number of swings or pitches for the athletes each time it is their turn for batting practice. Following these attempts, move the player to some other type of activity in the field. In this rotation each player can take several turns at bat, but each turn is rather short and other skills are being practiced between turns at bat.

Practice Complex Skills By Parts

Many of the skills that must be learned in sports are very complex. For example, the tennis serve can be broken down into many parts. To serve, players must correctly hold the ball, hold the racket, stand at the baseline, toss the ball, bring the racket back into position, swing forward, contact the ball, and follow through. The serve can even be divided further as necessary. One of the reasons that the tennis serve is a difficult skill to learn is that it is so complex.

When teaching a skill as complex as the tennis serve, it is helpful to practice its parts before actually practicing the whole serve. While this sounds easy enough, implementing this type of practice can be tricky. A good rule of thumb is to practice a part separately only when that part can be naturally separated from the rest of the action. Otherwise, keep parts together to maintain the natural relationship critical to performing the skill.

The rule of thumb for practicing parts of a skill is to only practice parts that can be naturally separated from the whole skill.

The parts of the serve that are relatively independent from other parts are holding the ball, holding the racket, the stance, and the ball toss. Even the ball toss is not totally independent because it is done together with the backswing of the racket. However, it can be done alone as well as together with the backswing. The backswing, forward swing, and followthrough should always be practiced as a unit because they are so interdependent.

Even though you may choose to have your athletes practice individual parts

Figure 3. Adjust your practice sessions according to the ages of your athletes.

of a skill, be sure to demonstrate the whole skill to them before they begin this type of practice. They must get the idea of how each part fits into the whole picture. You may even wish to have them practice the whole skill for a little while before you break it down into its parts.

Use Game-Like Conditions in Your Practice Sessions

After an athlete shows a basic level of proficiency in the skill he or she has been practicing, it is important to provide practice situations that mimic game conditions. Two important guidelines must be followed when using this type of practice. First, only use this type of practice after a basic level of proficiency has been achieved. Second, this type of practice should not be a substitute for other types of practice. It should be used in addition to other practice routines.

Situation drills are effective ways to imitate game conditions.

Some types of skills lend themselves to being practiced in game-like conditions more readily than others. For example, the free throw in basketball or the penalty kick in soccer can be practiced exactly as the player will be required to perform the skill in a game. However, other skills, such as the basketball or soccer pass or shot from the field, cannot be so precisely imitated. The goal here is to have the drill be as similar as possible to game conditions. Situation drills or scrimmages are effective ways to accomplish this goal.

Instructional Aids Should Be Used In Practice

An effective way to teach a sport skill is to use devices that help the athletes focus their attention on specific parts of the skill that are critical to performing the whole skill correctly. For example, the batting tee is useful to teach the correct batting technique because it requires the athlete to focus attention on the ball and on the swing. There is no possibility for being distracted by directing attention to the pitcher, to the kind of pitch, or the trajectory of the ball.

Other instructional devices help the coach to incorporate game-like conditions into practice sessions without having to depend on another coach or player to set them up. For example, if a coach wants the team to practice rebounding in a game-like situation, a rebounder ring in the basket will turn every shot at the basket into a rebounding situation. The coach doesn't have to hope that a shot will result in a rebound.

Guidelines for Conducting Effective Practices

- *Provide sufficient time to master the skills*
- *Divide complex skills into their subparts*
- *Use practice sessions to simulate game-like conditions*
- *Use instructional aids to hasten learning*

Giving Feedback

The final part of this chapter completes a three-part cycle. The first part of the cycle focuses on giving instructions, which begins the practice of a skill by letting the athlete know what is to be done. The second part of the cycle provides the opportunity for actually practicing the skill, which allows the athlete to experience how to do the skill. The final part of the cycle occurs after the athlete has practiced the skill. Here, the coach provides feedback to the athlete concerning the attempt that has just occurred, which provides information to the athlete about what must be done the next time to improve his or her performance. The cycle then begins all over again.

The guidelines presented in this section are designed to help you provide effective feedback to your athletes.

Providing useful feedback is an essential part of effective teaching.

Give Feedback That Will Help The Athlete

Feedback is being used here to denote the information that a coach gives an athlete about the athlete's practice attempt. This information can take several forms. It can be *evaluative,* as when the coach says, "You did that dive very well." Feedback can also be *corrective,* as when the coach says, "You need to tuck your chin sooner the next time." Or, the feedback can be *neutral,* that is, neither evaluative or corrective, but simply informative about the outcome of the performance. Here the coach might say to the athlete, "Your score was a 6.0."

Regardless of the type of feedback given to the athlete, it is important that this information helps the athlete. The type of assistance to the athlete may take several forms. It might help him or her to improve on the next practice attempt, or it might encourage the athlete to do the same thing again. The feedback may tell the athletes how they are doing in relation to some performance goal.

Do Not Give Too Much Feedback

As in the situation of giving effective instructions, feedback should not overload the athlete with information. This problem seems to be particularly related to the use of corrective feedback. Because a beginner will typically make many mistakes on a practice attempt, the coach is often tempted to identify and discuss all of these errors. The coach should avoid this temptation and pick out one or two important mistakes, and then have the athlete work on these in the next few practice attempts.

The difficulty is to pick out the most important one or two mistakes from all the mistakes that have been made. A useful guideline is to determine from your analysis of the skill what part or parts of the skill are the most critical for success. What parts of the skill must be done correctly if there is any possibility that the skill is to be successful? As coach, focus your attention on these parts when your athletes are practicing and provide corrective feedback about these parts only.

Figure 4. Don't overload your athletes with information.

> *Limit corrective feedback to one or two critical mistakes the athlete has just made.*

For example, if your shortstop is having trouble throwing the ball to the first baseman, what would you consider to be a critical part of this skill? One possibility is the shortstop's visual focus. If the athlete's visual focus is not on the glove of the first baseman, it won't matter how well he or she performs the rest of the throwing action; there will be little chance of the throw being accurate.

Use All Three Forms of Feedback

Just because a particular athlete is still not doing a skill correctly doesn't mean that you must continually bombard him or her with corrective feedback. Use liberal amounts of positive evaluative feedback. It is important that the athlete know that at least some of what he or she is doing is being done correctly. You can even put two forms of feedback together in the same statement. For example, you could say, "You had your chin tucked just right that time, but you still had your knees bent." This type of statement lets the athlete know that the practice time spent has been beneficial and, specifically, what parts still need additional practice.

Summary

Teaching young athletes the fundamentals of the sport is one of the most important parts of your job as a coach. This chapter has provided guidelines designed to help you carry out this role as effectively as possible. Teaching has been divided into three parts: giving instructions, directing practice, and giving feedback. Your instructions let your athletes know what to do; their practice enables them to do what they are supposed to; your feedback provides them information about the success of their practice and can serve as instructions for their next attempts.

Successful coaches are successful teachers. Successful teachers employ effective teaching techniques. The guidelines that have been presented in this chapter should help you to employ some of the techniques that successful teachers use.

Suggested Readings

AAHPERD. (1981). *Motor learning.* (Basic Stuff Series I, Volume 3). Reston, VA: AAH-
    PERD.
Magill, R.A. (1985). *Motor Learning: Concepts and applications* (2nd ed.). Dubuque,
    IA: W.C. Brown Publishers.
Martens, R., Christina, R.W., Harvey, J.S., & Sharkey, B.J. (1981). *Coaching young
    athletes.* Champaign, IL: Human Kinetics Publishers. (See Part 3: Sport Pedagogy.)
Stallings, L.M. (1982). *Motor learning: From theory to practice.* St. Louis: C.V. Mosby.

SECTION II:

FOUNDATIONS OF COACHING

- **How Children Grow and Develop**
- **Guidelines for Selecting Skills, Rules, and Strategies**
- **Preventing Common Athletic Injuries**
- **Goalsetting: Principles for the Coach And Athlete**
- **Motivating Young Athletes for Optimum Performance**
- **Teaching Sportsmanship and Values**
- **Observing and Analyzing Sports Skills**

chapter four

How Children Grow and Develop

John L. Haubenstricker
Michigan State University

4

Questions to consider. . .

☐ *Why should a coach be concerned about the growth and development of children?*

☐ *How are children different from adults?*

☐ *What are the growth patterns of children?*

☐ *Are there differences in the growth and development of boys and girls?*

☐ *How do body size, body shape, and tissue composition influence the performance of young athletes?*

☐ *How can you apply knowledge about growth and development to your coaching situation?*

O ne of the biggest challenges for you, as a coach, will be to adapt the knowledge and skills you have in the sport you are coaching into forms that can be understood and learned by the children you plan to coach. Your ability to do this will have a direct bearing on at least six of the ten rights specified in the *Bill of Rights for Young Athletes* (Martens & Seefeldt, 1979), namely:

- right of the opportunity to participate in sports regardless of ability level
- right to participate at a level that is commensurate with (one's) developmental level
- right to play as a child and not as an adult
- right to proper preparation for participation in the sport
- right to an equal opportunity to strive for success
- right to have fun through sport

Knowledge of how children grow and develop is an important key to becoming an effective coach in youth sports. It can mean the difference between success and failure in learning skills and in winning games; between increasing and decreasing the risk of injury; and between enjoyment of and disappointment in sport participation. The purpose of this chapter is to provide some basic information about how children grow and develop. For some of you, it may serve as a review of what you already know; for others, it may provide the foundation for a successful coaching experience with children and youth.

Knowledge of how children grow and develop is an important key to becoming an effective coach.

Children versus Adults

There is a tendency for inexperienced coaches to treat children as miniature adults. That is, they expect children to learn, perform, and behave like adult participants in a sports setting. To a certain extent, this is to be expected. Most coaches of youth had their last experience in sports as adults, and tend to coach from that base of experience. In addition, many coaches have had little, if any, formal education in child growth and development. Even coaches who are parents, aware of physical and behavioral changes taking place in their own children, do not understand all of the implications of these changes for participation in youth sports. Coaching a squad of 15 to 20 growing nine-year-old children can be quite different from coaching a similar sized group of young mature adults.

Children differ from adults physically, cognitively and socially.

How are children different from adults? To say that they are smaller and younger than adults is obvious, but even the obvious has important implications for you as a coach. For example, because children are smaller, should you expect them to run as fast, throw as far, endure as long, and handle adult-sized equipment as well as adults? Certainly not! Yet some coaches have these expectations. Because children are younger than adults, should you assume that they are as skillful, have the same knowledge of a sport, have the same motive(s) for participating, possess the same strategies, handle critical situations as effectively, and respond to the coach in the same manner as do adult athletes? In most instances, no!

Major differences between child athletes and adult athletes are summarized as follows:

Figure 1.   Children within an age group come in various sizes and shapes.

- Child athletes are still growing physically; adult athletes are mature. Children are changing not only in terms of body size, but also in terms of body proportions, body shape, and body tissue composition.
- The various systems of the child's body (muscular, skeletal, nervous, cardiorespiratory, endocrine, and sensory) are changing, structurally and functionally, at a much faster rate than in adults. The level of maturity of these systems greatly influences the strength, coordination, and endurance of children as well as their capacity to learn new skills, rules, and strategies.
- Young athletes have less cognitive capacity and less experience in processing information vital for learning skills and participating successfully in competitive sports. This means that children, mentally, cannot process the same amount of information or deal with the same complexity of information as adults. They also benefit less from previous experience than adults because they have less experience to draw from and are less able to apply what is available to new situations.
- Child athletes are less able to function successfully in complex group activities than adults. Young children, in particular, have difficulty learning complex offensive and defensive plays that require a high level of teamwork. Thus, such behaviors must be acquired through rote memory, rather than through understanding.
- Young athletes are more apt than adults to idolize and copy the values and behaviors of their coach. Therefore, what you say, how you say it, how you interact with your players, with officials, with parents, and with other coaches and their players will have an impact on the behavior of your athletes.

Patterns of Physical Growth

Although children and adults are different in many dimensions of growth and development, the remainder of this chapter will be limited to a description of how children grow, physically. Other dimensions, such as the mental, personal, and social aspects of growth are discussed in chapters 2, 3, 5, 8, and 9.

General Patterns of Growth

The most common means for determining the physical growth of children are measures of height and weight. When taken with care, they provide valuable information about the pattern of an individual athlete's growth so that it can be understood and compared with that of peers. Measures of height and weight, in some instances, can be useful for grouping children for instruction and/or competition.

The general pattern of physical growth is similar for all individuals whose growth processes have not been interrupted by disease, injury, or genetic defects. The typical pattern for growth in standing height is shown in Figure 2.

There are four general phases in the growth pattern. The first phase, from birth to two or three years, consists of a rapid, but declining, rate of growth in which the child gains less height each successive year. For example, during the first year after birth, boys grow about 10 inches and gain about 15 pounds. During the third year, they grow a little less than four inches and gain about five pounds. (The values for girls are slightly lower.)

The second phase of the growth pattern represents a steady period of growth. It extends from approximately three years of age until puberty, the time when the adolescent growth spurt begins. During this phase, both boys and girls grow, annually, from 2.0 to 2.5 inches and gain from 5.0 to 7.0 pounds.

The third phase of growth is comprised of the pubertal or adolescent growth spurt. During this period of accelerated growth, the annual gains in height and weight may be more than double those of the immediately preceding years. This spurt occurs earlier in girls, but is generally not as intense as that of the boys.

The last phase of the growth pattern represents a gradual decline in the rate of growth until final stature has been attained. On the average, this occurs around age 15 for girls and just after age 17 for boys. The more intense growth spurt of the boys, plus the extra years for growth, account for most of the difference

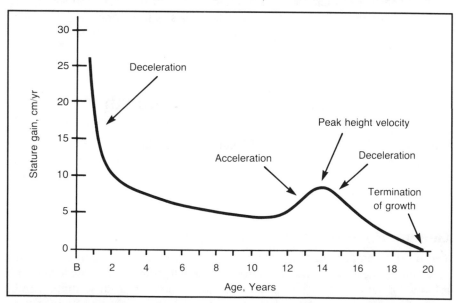

Figure 2.   The general growth pattern for standing height. From *Growth and development: The first twenty years in man* (p. 21) by R.M. Malina. Copyright 1975 by Burgess Publishing Company. Reprinted by permission.

in the final stature of boys and girls. The pattern for annual gains in weight is similar to that for height, except that weight gains, mostly in the form of fatty tissue growth, generally continue into the adult years.

You can obtain valuable information about your athletes by accurately measuring their height and weight at least twice a year—once before training for a sport begins and once after the season is over. The first measure can be helpful in your planning for instruction and competition. The post season measure can tell you what impact the program has had on the participant during the course of the season.

Height can be measured by having the athlete stand barefoot on a level, hard surface with his or her back against a doorpost to which a steel tape measure has been attached. A 10-inch square or right triangle wooden block is held against the doorpost and slowly lowered until the top of the head is contacted. The measurement should be read to the nearest ⅛th inch. Devices for measuring height that are attached to some weight scales are not recommended because they are not very accurate. Weight measures should be obtained from a calibrated beam or digital scale and recorded to the nearest ½ pound. The athlete should be lightly clothed (e.g. t-shirt and shorts or swimming suit, no shoes and socks). Ideally, the pre- and post-season measures should be taken at the same location, during the same time of the day, using the same instruments and procedures.

Height and weight should be measured twice yearly, just before and just after the season.

Individual Differences

Although physical growth follows a predictable pattern, it is essential that the coach recognize that not all children follow this pattern at the same pace. Some children will pass through some (or even all) phases of the pattern at a faster pace than others. Some children are genetically destined to be taller, shorter, heavier, or lighter than others. The interaction of these factors may present you with a dilemma, for in any given age group you will be confronted with young athletes of differing body dimensions. You may have team members who are tall and heavy, tall and light, short and light, short and heavy, and all sizes in between. There also will be those who mature early and those who mature late. Thus, some children who are genetically large, but late maturers, may not be as strong and coordinated as you might expect. Conversely, genetically smaller children who are early maturers may be stronger and more skillful than you anticipated.

The differences in height and weight that you can expect to find among boys and girls at various ages during the growing years are presented in Tables 1 and 2, respectively. Note that the "difference" column only lists the difference be-

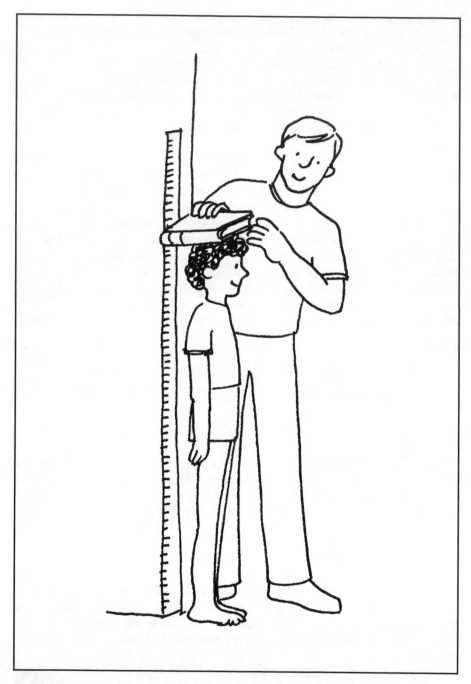

Figure 3.   A suggested procedure for measuring standing height.

tween the 5th and the 95th percentile points. It is possible that you may find even greater differences in height and weight among the children you are coaching. To insure fairness and to protect the rights of all the participants in your charge, you will need to allow for extreme differences in height and weight in the instructional and competitive phases of your program. (The role of physical growth factors in equating children for competition is addressed in Chapter 13, "Equating Children for Sports Competition.")

At any given chronological age you will be confronted with young athletes of differing body sizes and shapes.

Young athletes also will differ in their body shape and body tissue composition. Body shape can be determined by measuring the breadth of the shoulders and the width of the hips, and by examining their relationship to each other. More

Table 1. Standing height (inches) of males and females at selected age percentiles. Adapted from "NCHS growth curves for children, birth - 18 years, United States," National Center for Health Statistics, 1977, *Vital and Health Statistics*, p. 37, Series 11-Number 165. DHEW Pub. No. (PHS) 78-1650. Public Health Service. Washington DC: U.S. Government Printing Office.

	Males Percentile				Females Percentile			
C.A.	5th[a]	50th	95th[b]	Diff.[c]	5th	50th	95th	Diff.
3.0	35.0	37.4	40.2	5.2	34.8	37.0	39.6	4.8
4.0	37.7	40.5	43.3	5.6	37.4	40.0	42.6	5.2
5.0	40.2	43.3	46.1	5.9	39.8	42.7	45.5	5.7
6.0	42.4	45.7	48.6	6.2	42.0	45.1	48.3	6.3
7.0	44.5	47.9	51.1	6.6	44.0	47.5	51.0	7.0
8.0	46.5	50.0	53.4	6.9	46.0	49.8	53.6	7.6
9.0	48.4	52.0	55.8	7.4	48.1	52.0	56.3	8.2
10.0	50.3	54.1	58.3	8.0	50.2	54.4	58.9	8.7
11.0	52.2	56.4	61.0	8.8	52.6	57.0	61.5	8.9
12.0	54.2	58.9	63.9	9.7	55.0	59.6	64.1	9.1
13.0	56.3	61.6	66.9	10.6	57.2	61.9	66.2	9.0
14.0	58.6	64.2	69.6	11.0	58.5	63.1	67.4	8.9
15.0	61.1	66.5	71.6	10.5	59.3	63.7	68.0	8.7
16.0	63.4	68.3	73.0	9.6	59.7	63.9	68.2	8.5
17.0	64.9	69.4	73.7	8.8	60.1	64.2	68.3	8.2
18.0	65.2	69.6	73.9	8.7	60.5	64.4	68.3	7.8

[a]Four percent of the children in any age group are expected to be shorter than the height listed in this column. [b]Four percent of the children in any age group are expected to be taller than the height listed in this column. [c]The value in this column is the difference in inches betwen the 5th and 95th percentile scores.

Table 2. Weight (pounds) of males and females at selected age percentiles. Adapted from "NCHS growth curves for children, birth - 18 years, United States," National Center for Health Statistics, 1977, *Vital and Health Statistics*. p. 38, Series 11-Number 165. DHEW Pub. No. (PHS) 78-1650. Public Health Service. Washington DC: U.S. Government Printing Office.

	Males Percentile				Females Percentile			
C.A.	5th[a]	50th	95th[b]	Diff.[c]	5th	50th	95th	Diff.
3.0	26.6	32.2	39.2	12.6	25.6	31.1	38.0	12.4
4.0	30.1	36.8	44.7	14.6	28.9	35.2	43.9	15.0
5.0	33.7	41.2	50.9	17.2	32.1	38.9	49.9	17.8
6.0	37.3	45.6	58.1	20.8	35.4	43.0	56.8	21.4
7.0	41.1	50.4	66.4	25.3	39.0	48.1	65.4	26.4
8.0	45.0	55.8	76.1	31.1	43.3	54.8	76.5	33.2
9.0	49.1	62.0	87.3	38.2	48.1	62.7	89.6	41.5
10.0	53.6	69.3	99.8	46.2	53.7	71.8	104.0	50.3
11.0	59.1	77.8	113.5	54.4	60.1	81.5	119.0	58.9
12.0	65.8	87.7	128.1	62.3	67.3	91.6	134.1	66.8
13.0	74.2	99.1	143.3	69.1	75.3	101.6	148.4	73.1
14.0	84.3	111.9	159.0	74.7	83.2	110.8	161.1	77.9
15.0	95.0	125.0	174.4	79.4	90.4	118.3	171.5	81.1
16.0	105.2	136.9	188.8	83.6	95.7	123.2	178.6	82.9
17.0	113.5	146.2	201.3	87.8	98.6	125.0	181.8	83.2
18.0	119.0	151.9	211.1	92.1	99.8	124.8	181.8	82.0

[a]Four percent of the children in any age group are expected to be lighter than the weight listed in this column. [b]Four percent of the children in any age group are expected to be heavier than the weight listed in this column. [c]The value in this column is the difference in pounds betwen the 5th and 95th percentile scores.

often, however, body shape is estimated through visual inspection. Individuals who have a linear (narrow) body frame, limited muscle mass, and little fat are classified as *ectomorphs*. They generally are of medium height or taller, but a few may be genetically short. Ectomorphs generally are considered good candidates for endurance type activities such as distance running.

Persons with sturdy body frames, broad shoulders, greater than average amounts of muscle tissue, and limited amounts of fat are referred to as *mesomorphs*. Visually, they look like athletes and perform well in activities requiring speed, power, strength, and agility.

Endomorphs are relatively large individuals, whose hips appear to be large when compared to their shoulders. Endomorphs often are quite strong, due to a large amount of muscle tissue, but it is hidden under an excessive amount of fatty tissue. Because of this extra fat and large viscera, they generally have difficulty with activities that place high demands on agility and cardiovascular endurance.

Most children have a physique that represents a combination of the three

Figure 4. The three types of physique: a) ectomorph, b) mesomorph, and c) endomorph.

characteristic types described above, with one or two of the types more dominant than the third. Thus, you may classify a child as a meso-ectomorph or an ecto-mesomorph, depending on which type is most evident. You might type another child as an endo-mesomorph if the endomorphic component seems most dominant. It is the extreme ectomorph or extreme endomorph that you must recognize and for whom you must be ready to provide extra assistance.

Tissue composition of the body usually is examined to determine how much is lean body mass (muscle and bone) and how much is fat and viscera. Although underwater weighing is the most accurate and valid method of obtaining estimates of lean body mass and body fat, a more practical way is to get estimates of body fat from skinfold measures taken at two or more body sites. When taken carefully, these measures can help you identify children with excessive body fat that may hinder the learning and performance of motor skills in which they are interested. (Some references for obtaining skinfold measures are listed in the Suggested Readings at the end of the chapter.)

Disproportionate Growth

One of the reasons that children should not be treated like miniature adults is that they have different body proportions. That is, the relative size and length of various body segments in children are not the same as those in adults. For example, because the head and trunk of the unborn child develop much faster than its limbs, the arms and legs must grow at a faster rate after birth in order to achieve adult proportions. Thus, children have proportionately shorter legs, compared to their standing height, than do adults. The effect is that children, especially infants and young children, tend to be "top-heavy" and are at a disadvantage in activities that require dynamic balance (i.e. balance while moving), agility (e.g. dodging) and body control (e.g. stunts and tumbling).

The rate of growth of various body segments is not constant during the growing years.

Even though some body segments must grow at a faster pace than others in order to reach their adult dimensions, their rate of growth is not constant during the growing years. Instead, body segments grow faster at certain times during the growth cycle than at others. Estimates of when, and how much, body segments change from birth to maturity are shown in Figure 5. Note that leg growth accounts for about two-thirds of the growth that occurs between age one year and the start of the pubertal growth spurt.

The rapid growth of the arms and legs during childhood often results in the appearance of oversized arms and legs during puberty, especially in late maturing children. Although the longer limbs have the potential to allow children to run faster and throw farther, they also place greater demands on the nervous system and musculature to control and move these oversized body segments. Consequently, many youth may have less coordination and balance during puberty than they had during the earlier childhood years. As a coach, you need to be aware of these changes so that you can give extra encouragement when needed and assist your athletes to set reasonable goals during this "awkard" phase of the growth cycle.

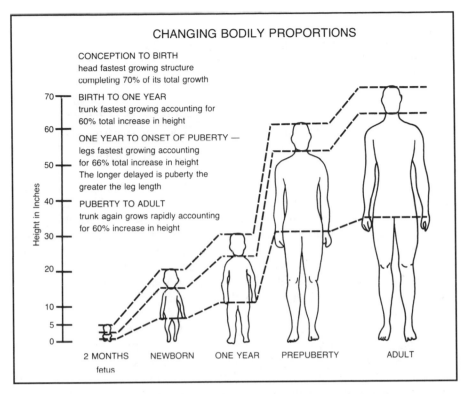

Figure 5. Changing body proportions from conception to adulthood. From *Dynamics of development: Euthenic pediatrics* (p. 122) by D. Whipple, 1966, New York: McGraw-Hall. Copyright 1966 by McGraw-Hill, Inc. Reprinted by permission.

Gender Differences

Although boys and girls follow similar growth patterns, girls generally achieve maturity several years before boys. Biologically, the average girl already is a year more mature than the average boy upon entering first grade. This difference increases to nearly two years by the time she enters puberty. Moreover, the average female reaches adult height two years before the average male. This earlier rate of maturation permits girls to approximate the heights and weights of boys during childhood and even exceed them when they enter puberty, despite the fact that they are, on the average, genetically smaller than the boys.

Gender differences in height and weight can be identified from Tables 1 and 2. By examining the 50th percentile values for boys and girls across the various age categories, you can see that boys are only slightly taller and heavier than girls until age nine. From age 9 through age 13, girls are, on the average, taller and heavier than boys. Once the boys enter their growth spurt, they regain the advantage in height and weight.

Prior to age nine, gender differences in height and weight are not meaningful from a practical standpoint. In other words, on the basis of physical size alone, there is little reason to separate boys and girls in physical activities. In fact, height and weight differences within each gender group before age nine are much greater than the differences between the two gender groups.

Prior to age nine, there is little reason to separate boys and girls in physical activities on the basis of physical size and shape.

Gender differences in body shape, segmental lengths, and body tissue composition also are minimal during childhood until the time that girls enter puberty. Ratios of shoulder breadth to hip width and of standing height to sitting height are similar for boys and girls prior to age nine. However, boys do have longer arms and more muscle mass than girls from early in life and therefore have an advantage in activities such as running, jumping, throwing, and kicking. This advantage is offset, somewhat, by the relatively more mature neuromuscular system of the girls. The latter gives girls the advantage in activities that require balance and fine motor coordination.

After girls and boys enter puberty, gender differences in body size, shape, and tissue composition become marked (Figure 6). After girls enter puberty, their hips grow at a relatively faster rate than the shoulders, and leg growth begins to diminish in comparison to that of the trunk. In addition, the growth of fatty tissue is stimulated with the release of a hormone (estrogen) and is deposited primarily in the breasts, hips, and thighs.

Upon entering puberty, boys experience accelerated growth in the shoulders and make large gains in muscle tissue. Moreover, because they enter puberty later than girls, boys have a longer period for arm and leg growth. Thus, with longer limbs and a larger body frame, and with more muscle mass, particularly around the shoulders, adolescent boys have a substantial advantage over most girls in skills that require strength and power. These advantages, plus those of a psychological and cultural nature, suggest that after age nine boys and girls generally should not be required to compete against each other in highly competitive youth sports activities. Additional discussion concerning co-ed competition, especially the sociocultural issues, is found in Chapter 19, "What About Co-ed Competition?"

Physical Growth and Motor Skill Performance

The physical growth of children is related to their performance of motor skills. In some activities, the actual physical size of children (e.g. height and weight) has a direct bearing on success or failure in performing specific skills. For example,

Figure 6. Changes in body size and shape from childhood to adolescence.

you would not expect a short player to rebound basketballs better than a much taller player. Nor would you expect a 75 pound boy to wrestle successfully against one who weighs 125 pounds, even if they are both the same chronological age. In other activities, such as skiing, archery, and golf physical size *per se,* may not be a critical factor in performance.

Although we attempt to reduce size differences by limiting youth sports competition to narrow age groupings, substantial differences in body size and biological maturation still exist. To illustrate, a nine-year-old boy at the 5th percentile in weight (49 lbs.) weighs only half as much as a ten-year-old boy at the 95th percentile (100 lbs.); yet, we often combine nine- and ten-year-old boys for competition.

Even more important is the fact that most boys and girls who enjoy a size advantage over other children their age also are more mature, biologically. Thus, they are not only bigger in size, they also are stronger and better coordinated.

As a result, they tend to excel in nearly all motor skills when compared to their smaller, less mature peers (assuming that motivation, opportunity for practice, health status, and other factors are similar for both groups).

> *Most boys and girls who are taller and heavier than other children their age also are more mature, biologically, making them stronger and better coordinated.*

Children with endomorphic and mesomorphic body builds generally are the early maturers and enjoy the most success in youth sports (except for the extreme endomorph with too much body fat). As a coach, you must be careful that the late maturing children, mostly ectomorphs who are generally smaller and weaker, are not placed in practice or competitive situations where they constantly experience frustration and failure. Ironically, many of these late maturers have the potential to be the best athletes during the late high school and college years because they characteristically are taller at maturity than their earlier maturing peers. Therefore, you must protect these young athletes from too much discouragement and keep them interested in sports activities until they are ready to compete successfully.

This book provides you with numerous suggestions on how to accommodate children of various sizes and abilities through proper goal-setting, practice organization, motivational techniques, levels of competition and other means. One of the most satisfying experiences for a coach at the end of a season is to have children say, "Thanks, coach, it was fun. I'll be back next year."

Summary

This chapter contains basic information about the growth and development of children which you, as a coach, should know in order to provide a wholesome experience in youth sports for all your participants. Attention is focused on how children differ from adults. This is followed by a discussion of: (a) the general growth cycle; (b) individual differences in body size, shape, and tissue composition; (c) the unequal growth of various body segments; and (d) gender differences in growth and maturation. Implications for the youth sports setting are included for each of these topics. Finally, the relationship of physical growth and biological maturation to motor skill performance is addressed.

References

Malina, R. M. (1975). *Growth and development: The first twenty years in man.* Minneapolis: Burgess Publishing Company.

Martens, R., & Seefeldt, V. (1979). *Guidelines for children's sports.* Washington, DC: American Alliance for Health, Physical Education, Recreation and Dance.

National Center for Health Statistics. (1977). *NCHS growth curves for children, birth - 18 years, United States,* Vital and Health Statistics, Series 11, Number 165. DHEW Pub. No. (PHS) 78-1650. Public Health Service. Washington, DC: U.S. Government Printing Office.

Whipple, D. (1966). *Dynamics of development: Euthenic pediatrics.* New York: McGraw-Hill.

Suggested Readings

AAHPERD. (1980). *AAHPERD health related physical fitness test manual.* Reston, VA: American Alliance for Health, Physical Education, Recreation and Dance.

Durnin, J., & Rahaman, M. (1967). The assessment of the amount of fat in the human body from measurements of skinfold thickness. *British Journal of Nutrition, 21,* 681-689.

Katchadourian, H. (1976). Somatic changes of puberty. *The Biology of Adolescence* (pp. 22–51). San Francisco: W. H. Freeman and Company.

Lohman, T. G. (1982). Measurement of body composition in children. *Journal of Physical Education, Recreation and Dance, 53,* 67–70.

Zaichkowsky, L. D., Zaichkowsky, L. B., & Martinek, T. J. (1980). Physical growth and development. *Growth and development: The child and physical activity* (pp. 14–29). St. Louis: The C. V. Mosby Company.

Zaichkowsky, L. D., Zaichkowsky, L. B., & Martinek, T. J. (1980). Development of motor skills. *Growth and development: The child and physical activity* (pp. 30–51). St. Louis: The C. V. Mosby Company.

chapter five

Guidelines for Selecting Skills, Rules, and Strategies

Jerry R. Thomas
Louisiana State University

Questions to Consider . . .

☐ *How do children learn sport skills?*

☐ *What types of cues and feedback should the coach provide to young athletes?*

☐ *Does knowledge about skills and strategies by young athletes result in a more skillful performance?*

☐ *How can the coach promote improvement in skills and in skillful performance?*

☐ *Should your coaching behavior differ from practices to contests?*

E very coach wants to help children become more skillful in sport and perform skills more successfully during contests. To achieve this goal, you must understand how skills are learned and how the memory of children develops. These principles provide direction for your behavior during practice and contests. Although this chapter is related to other chapters in this book, the reader will find that it is most closely associated with the content of the two previous chapters, "The Coach as a Teacher," and "How Children Grow and Develop." The reasons for this close relationship may seem apparent but they are worth repeating. First, the coach cannot be a successful teacher unless he or she understands how sport skills are learned, developed, and performed. Second, the young athlete's growth and development are important features of skillful performance because as height, weight, and body proportions change (e.g., arms and legs grow longer), the ratio of muscle and fat changes (especially with puberty), the nervous system becomes increasingly better organized, and gender differences develop. Obviously, children are not "little adults" who think and perform as we do, but in a scaled-down way. Children are, in fact, different in the way they think about and perform sport skills, and the successful coach understands these differences and can adjust to them.

The movement plan for a specific sport skill is developed through practice and is stored in the young athlete's memory.

Developing Sport Skills

Movements (in this instance specific sport movements) are represented in an abstract way in a child's memory. This representation is called a *movement plan.* The representation of the skill is developed as the child practices the skill. Some parts or patterns of skills become very constant so they are done nearly the same way every time. Thus, the coach can always recognize the overhand throw in baseball. Other parts of the movement are varied each time the child performs the skill (Schmidt, 1985). For example, the angle at which the ball is released and the force applied in the overhand throw differs depending on how far or hard the ball is to be thrown. This becomes especially obvious in the situation where a baseball pitcher tries to make the throwing motion for a fast ball and a change-up appear exactly the same.

As children learn sport skills such as throwing, the coach encourages them to use a sound mechanical motion but provides a lot of practice at varying the location and size of the target as well as the force with which the ball is thrown. The same idea applies to kicking a soccer ball, shooting a basketball, hitting a tennis ball, and many other skills. The coach is attempting to aid the young athlete in developing a good movement plan that the child can use effectively in various sport situations.

The types of skills that were just mentioned are called *open skills,* which means the movement plan is basically the same, but the movement is used in response to differing game situations. Other types of sport involve *closed skills.* For example, the swimming coach wants the swimmer to perform a stroke the same way every time, and the gymnastics coach wants the performer to execute a routine in the same way on every attempt. Of course, this is true only when the movement is correct. Some sports involve both open and closed skills. For example, in tennis, the serve is a closed skill, while the return of serve is an open skill.

Whether skills are open or closed, the idea of the movement (movement plan) is represented in the child's memory. When skills are open, certain aspects of how the movement will be performed are decided at the last moment. For example, will the shortstop throw the ball to second base for the double play, or to first for the easy out? When skills are closed, the performer attempts to add nothing: he or she wants to perform the skill the same every time. Skills are also open or closed to varying degrees. The tennis serve is not completely closed. For example, the server may try to hit the serve to the receiver's forehand or backhand, or with a lot of spin or less spin. The server's movement pattern varies slightly to allow for the different objectives of the serve.

The movement plan is represented in memory and practice sessions should be designed to help the athlete learn the movement skill (develop a more effective and efficient plan) and then concentrate on applying the skill as it will be used in games and contests. As the skill is practiced over and over, the movement becomes more automatic. That is, the child does not need to think very much about the movement as it is being performed. Instead, the child can concentrate on the situation in which the skill is to be used. Effective youth sport coaches teach children the basic sport skills and then spend considerable time in situations that mimic game conditions.

Coaches should encourage young athletes to practice the skills associated with all of the positions or events in the sport. Children need to acquire a variety of skills and experiences prior to specialization. As athletes master the skills of the sport and become more mature, increasing specialization is appropriate. It seems unfair that a chunky young boy should be placed as a guard in football at 8 years of age and have to play guard forever. Maybe he will eventually become a guard, but everyone wants to be the quarterback, or running back, or receiver. Young athletes should be given this variety of opportunities. One reason young athletes are sometimes denied this opportunity is that the outcome of the contest is more important to the coach than developing skills and allowing the children to have fun.

Physical growth influences sport skill performance.

Physical Growth and Sport Skill

As the previous chapter indicated, children grow considerably from year to year, with large growth spurts at the time of puberty. While we often think of growth as increases in height and weight, we should also consider that arms and legs grow longer and body proportions change. For example, the proportion of total height made up by the legs increases each year up to adult stature. Boys have slightly larger shoulder/hip ratios (boys shoulders are wider than their hips) than girls prior to puberty and considerably larger shoulder/hip ratios after puberty (Malina, 1984).

Structural changes such as these influence children's performance of sport skills. How would you like to try and strike a baseball with a bat if your arms had grown two inches longer since the last time you tried to hit the ball? An increase in arm length of two inches frequently occurs during a year for boys in the 13-15 year age range. Thus, a young athlete may initially have difficulty in making adjustments in seasonal sports where considerable time has passed since the last season. Coaches should be particularly alert to this problem because it is very frustrating for the young athlete to be unable to perform a skill as effectively as he or she did in the previous season.

Initial practices should always review and provide plenty of practice for previously learned skills, not only for the value of review, but to aid the young athlete in making adjustments for changes in size. This problem does not appear to be as great for sports that involve year-round practice (e.g., swimming, gymnastics). While the same amount of growth still occurs, the continual practice sessions allow the athlete to make gradual adjustments.

Gender Differences in Sports Performance

While the growth differences between boys and girls prior to puberty are minimal, boys generally are more skillful in performing sports (Thomas & French, 1985). Before puberty, few reasons exist for these differences, other than that boys are more frequently encouraged to participate and practice sports skills. This encouragement comes from parents, peers, teachers, and coaches. When you have both boys and girls on your team (and there are few reasons to separate them prior to puberty), you should make special efforts to teach girls the important sport skills and encourage them to practice these skills. You must be careful to

Figure 1. Annual gains in growth may cause temporary problems with established motors patterns.

provide equal practice opportunities for girls and boys. For instance, youth sport coaches will frequently ask a boy to practice a skill over and over when he makes an error. The same coach may be concerned that a girl in a similar situation might be embarrassed at having to perform the skill repeatedly.

Coaches also frequently provide unequal opportunities to skilled and unskilled players. When the skilled player makes an error, the coach asks him or her to repeat the skill over and over, while the unskilled player will be allowed to make one or two mistakes and then stop practicing. Unskillful children immediately get the message that they are not as important as the more skilled players. How can less skilled boys or girls become more skilled unless the coach insists that they practice? Other chapters in this book deal with this topic in more detail (see Chapter 13, "Equating Children for Sports Competition," and Chapter 19, "What About Co-Ed Competition?"). Because skill acquisition is involved, the coach should recognize the importance of this issue as he or she thinks about how children learn and perform skills.

Providing Cues and Feedback

Cues are information provided the young athlete prior to attempts at skill performance, while *feedback* is information the athlete receives after the performance of a skill (Thomas, 1984). Cues are usually attempts to aid the athlete in selecting and executing a movement plan that is appropriate for the situation. Cues may be provided by the coach, other performers, or the nature of the situation. Feedback is used to reinforce a correct movement or to adjust an incorrect movement. Feedback may be obtained when the athlete observes what happened, or may be provided by the coach or another player in the form of a suggested correction.

One characteristic of young athletes is that they do not think as rapidly as adults. Thus, when cues and feedback are given, younger performers need more time to consider the information relative to the performance (Gallagher & Thomas, 1980). If the player does not appear to be taking sufficient time to consider cues and feedback, forcing him or her to take additional time may improve performance (Newell & Kennedy, 1978).

Cues about sport skills and how to use them can aid the young athlete's performance.

Cues

Cues can focus either on the movement itself or on how to use the movement. Modeling is one of the best ways to focus a young athlete's attention on important aspects of the sport skill. Having an athlete observe someone performing the skill correctly provides many cues for the observer. However, the child's age and skill will influence how much of the behavior should be modeled (Weiss, 1983). Young and poorly skilled athletes will only get the general idea of the movement from watching the model, while older and more skilled players may be able to learn refined movements. For young or less skilled players, the coach should use verbal cues to point out the important features of the skill. If the athlete is older or has more skill, verbal cues can be used to point out specific details of the skill that the athlete needs to practice. While some coaches can serve as good skill models, choosing some of the more skillful players as demonstrators may be more effective because they are similar in size and proportion to the athletes who are observing them.

Coaches can also give verbal cues that will aid a player's skill performance. For instance, checking the child's grip on the baseball bat, reminding the swimmer not to breathe on every stroke, and cueing the child on where the ball should be when shooting a jump shot are all examples of how verbal cues could be used. However, cues are not effective during the actual performance of the skill. If the coach yells cues while the athlete is trying to perform, only two things can happen, both of which are bad. If the athlete listens to the coach, he or she will be distracted from concentrating on the skill and performance will deteriorate. The other choice is for the athlete to ignore the coach.

Cues should be given prior to the performance. Giving cues is more easily accomplished in some sports than in others. Sports that are discontinuous, where a play occurs and then there is a break in the action (e.g., between pitches in baseball, between plays in football), allow the coach to give many cues because they can be delivered during the breaks. Other sports such as soccer, swimming, and gymnastics are not suited for the coach to give many cues because there are few breaks in the action. Cues are only effective when they are used between events or when given to players not currently involved in the action.

Cues may also be used to aid the athlete in planning for specific situations that might occur. For example, the football coach teaches defensive backs to use the cue of the offensive end to determine if the play is a run or a pass. If the end blocks down on the defensive tackle, the defensive back comes up to play the run. If the end comes down field, the defensive back covers the end. The shortstop in baseball may use cues such as how many are out, the score, and how hard the ground ball is hit to determine whether or not to try for a double play. These types of cues are situational and should be practiced so the athlete will know what to do when the situation arises in the game.

Veteran youth baseball coaches are notorious for taking advantage of beginning coaches by having all their players bunt during the first game. Beginning coaches are likely to have forgotten to tell their players how to handle bunts. Thus, the cue of "watch for the bunt," given by the beginning coach to an inexperienced team, has little impact if the players have not practiced a response for that cue.

Figure 2.   Cues will only be effective if the athletes can apply them to familiar situations.

*Feedback is the major way young athletes learn
to correct and improve sport skills.*

Feedback

Feedback refers to the information a young athlete receives after attempting a skill. Some feedback information is available to the athlete during the movement and after it is completed. For example, the third baseman can see if the throw to first base was accurate and arrived in time to get the runner out. The tennis player can see if the forehand shot was inbounds and was difficult for the opponent to return. The athlete also receives information from the body's sensory system concerning how the movement felt. This information can be compared with what the athlete intended (i.e., the movement plan), what discrepancies were noted, and what adjustments are planned for the next attempt. (For more information on feedback, see Chapter 3.)

The athlete may also receive information from other people. For example, the coach may tell the quarterback that the ball is being released too early, resulting in the throw being too high for the receiver. The quarterback's task is to use this feedback (called knowledge of performance or KP) to adjust the throwing pattern and release the ball at a later point in the movement. Other players may also provide KP by telling the quarterback how to adjust the pattern on the next attempt.

Knowledge of performance is very important because the athlete often cannot see the movement and may not know the reason for the performance errors. Other people may also supply feedback about the outcome of the movement (called knowledge of results or KR). A good example of someone who provides KR is the home plate umpire in baseball. This official calls balls and strikes which is a source of KR to the pitcher. Coaches and other players may also provide KR such as calling serves in tennis out or in, or telling the young swimmer his or her time in the 100-meter freestyle. The intent of KR is the same as that of KP; the athlete should compare the KR with the intended outcome, note the discrepancy, and decide what adjustments are needed in the next attempt at the skill. The difference between KP and KR is that KP focuses on the movement, while KR provides information about the outcome of the movement.

Knowledge of performance (KP) and knowledge of results (KR) should be used in specific ways by the coach. First, KP and KR should be used in a positive way. For example, when a ground ball goes between the legs of the second baseman, the coach could give KP in either a positive ("Good try, Tommy. Next time put the fingers of the glove down and you will catch the ball") or negative ("That's dumb, Tommy. How many times have I told you to put the fingers of the glove down?") way. In both instances the coach has provided the athlete with knowledge of performance so that the error may be corrected on future attempts, but Tommy will feel much better about himself and future skill attempts if positive reinforcement is provided with the KP.

Smoll and Smith (1984) suggest a sandwich approach to correcting errors: start with a compliment ("That was a good try for the ball"), then give the corrective instruction ("Put the fingers of the glove down"), and end with another positive statement ("You will catch it next time"). Remember that corrective instruction is not always necessary. Frequently, young athletes know what was wrong about their performance. In these cases, the coach should just offer encouragement.

A second important feature of KP and KR is the frequency with which they are provided. The temptation is to provide this source of feedback information after every attempt. However, research (Salmoni, Schmidt, & Walter, 1984) has indicated that providing KP and KR after every skill attempt results in the child relying on this source of information, rather than on internal feedback about the feel of the movement. Because coaches want their young athletes to become self-correcting, KR and KP should be provided on only about 50% of the skill attempts during practice sessions.

Even when KP and KR are provided, the coach should encourage the child to think about how the movement felt in relation to the information the coach provided. Unless the child thinks about the information provided and attempts to change a feature of the movement plan, the next attempt will not be any more skillful.

Sometimes, however, the coach can provide too much information to the young athlete. If a child is given more information about the skill and the sport situation than can be used effectively, performance may deteriorate. Thus, the coach must select a few important aspects of the movement and then have the athlete concentrate on correcting them. This is especially important for younger children and less skillful players.

Sport Knowledge and Sport Performance

Being able to perform sport skills successfully is not sufficient for success in sport. The young basketball player who can dribble the ball effectively yet often dribbles it out of bounds is not having success. The centerfielder in baseball who can catch all the fly and ground balls but never throws to the correct base is not successful. To be a successful player, the young athlete must not only be able to perform the skill, but must also have the knowledge of how and when to use the skills that have been mastered. Thus, the successful player has mastered the sport skills, has acquired knowledge about the sport situations to be encountered, and has practiced the skills using the sport knowledge so that he or she is prepared for all situations which may arise during the contest.

Sport-specific knowledge is as important to success as being able to perform the specific sport skills.

Figure 3.   Coaches should provide only one or two important cues at a time to young athletes.

Sport Specific Knowledge

Sport-specific knowledge encompasses the rules and strategies of the game or contest. This section deals specifically with the knowledge base the athlete needs to use his or her skills during the game or contest. For example, in baseball a situation might arise where the score is tied, runners are on first and third base with one out, and a right-handed batter is at home plate. Consider this situation from the point of view of a 12-year-old shortstop. He knows he is a good fielder and can throw effectively—that takes care of the sport skills part of the situation. The rest of the situation involves planning, decision-making, and execution by the shortstop. How does he decide what to do when the ball is hit to him? There are many choices, depending on how hard and where the ball is hit. Of course, his first choice is to make a double play on a hard hit ground ball. But what if the ball is hit more slowly and either to his right or left? What if the ball is hit to the second baseman, or the centerfielder?

If the coach has not practiced all of the situations, young athletes begin with a real disadvantage. They may not even understand all of the options and possible decisions. But consider the situation in which the athlete is not only skilled, but has practiced all of the options and decisions. How might his or her reasoning processes go? Of course, the knowledgeable and skillful player will have planned as many actions as possible in advance.

Consider the athlete's thinking in the example listed previously as involving a series of if-then statements:

- If the ball if hit hard at me or to my left, then I will try for the double play.
- If the ball is hit hard to my right, then I will check the runner at third and either try for him at home, or bluff him back and take the force play at second.
- If the ball is hit slowly toward me, I will charge it and then either throw to home if the runner on third tries to advance or throw to first if the runner stays at third.
- If the ball is hit to the pitcher, first baseman, or second baseman, then I will cover second base.

This series of if-then statements does not even consider the options the shortstop must consider if the ball is hit to the outfield, or to the third baseman, or if the batter bunts, or if the runner on first attempts to steal, or if the opposing coach puts on a double steal, or if there is an infield fly, or if one of many other options develops. The point is, if the shortstop is to be successful, the sport-specific cognitive knowledge to be used in decision-making is at least as important as the sport skill.

For the young athlete, sport knowledge may increase considerably during the season, while the level of sport skill performance may remain about the same.

However, the change in sport knowledge allows the athlete to make better decisions during the game or contest, resulting in more successful performance (French & Thomas, 1987). This knowledge is acquired in the same way (and mostly at the same time) as the sport skill: by practicing it.

The behavior and activities of the coach should differ from practices to games.

The Coach and the Game

The coach's behavior during the game should differ considerably from that at practice sessions. First, the coach should consider how different athletes will handle both cues and feedback during the game. During games, players are performing in front of family, friends, and peers. Some athletes do not respond well to cues and feedback even when these are presented in a positive way. Often it may be better to wait to provide information until you can talk quietly with the athlete. Other athletes are not bothered at all by the coach shouting cues and feedback to them. The coach should be sensitive to the athlete's feelings regarding when cues and feedback are given.

Coaches should disregard the 50% rule for the rate of feedback during games and contests. Athletes need information about the quality of skill execution in order to perform as effectively as possible. During games, the coach should provide knowledge of performance whenever there are errors in skills, and then aid the athlete with needed corrections. This should be done with sensitivity for the athlete's feelings and need not be done at all if you are certain the athlete knows what the error was and how to correct it.

One final point about feedback is important. Just as young athletes learn skills by observing and modeling the coach, they learn other behaviors the coach may exhibit in the same manner. While appropriate coaching behaviors are discussed elsewhere in the book (Chapter 2, "Your Role as a Youth Sport Coach"; Chapter 9, "Teaching Sportsmanship and Values"), the coach should be sensitive to the fact that children learn a complete set of behaviors, not just sport skill and knowledge.

Summary

If young athletes are to gain in skill and perform skillfully, the coach must understand how children differ from adults in their thinking and performance. Coaches should recognize that skillful performance consists of being able to do the sport skills as well as the knowledge about how to use the skills in game situations. From this knowledge base, coaches can structure practice sessions to promote maximum skill acquisition and maximize performance during games. The appropriate use of cues and feedback are the best tools the coach has to increase children's sport skill performance. In particular, coaches should be concerned about providing opportunities for less skilled players.

References

French, K.E., & Thomas, J.R. (1987). The relation of knowledge development to children's basketball performance. *Journal of Sport Psychology, 9*, 15-32.

Gallagher, J.D., & Thomas, J.R. (1980). Effects of varying post-KR intervals upon children's motor performance. *Journal of Motor Behavior 12*, 42-46.

Lee, T.D., & Magill, R.A. (1983). The locus of contextual interference in motor skill acquisition. *Journal of Experimental Psychology: Learning, Memory and Cognition, 9*, 730-746.

Malina, R.M. (1984). Physical growth and maturation. In J.R. Thomas (Ed.), *Motor development during childhood and adolescence*. Minneapolis: Burgess.

Newell, K., & Kennedy, J. (1978). Knowledge of results and children's motor learning. *Developmental Psychology, 14*, 531-536.

Salmoni, A.W., Schmidt, R.A. & Walter, C.E. (1984). Knowledge of results and motor learning: A review and critical appraisal. *Psychological Bulletin, 95*, 355-385.

Schmidt, R.A. (1985). The search for invariance in skilled motor behavior. *Research Quarterly for Exercise and Sport, 56*, 188-200.

Smoll, F.L., & Smith, R.E. (1984). Improving the quality of coach-player interaction. In J.R. Thomas (Ed.), *Motor development during childhood and adolescence*. Minneapolis: Burgess.

Thomas, J.R. (1984). Children's motor skill development. In J.R. Thomas (Ed.), *Motor development during childhood and adolescence*. Minneapolis: Burgess.

Thomas, J.R., & French, K.E. (1985). Gender differences across age in motor performance: A meta-analysis. *Psychological Bulletin, 98*, 260-282.

Weiss, M.R. (1983). Modeling and motor performance: A developmental perspective. *Research Quarterly for Exercise and Sport, 54*, 190-197.

Suggested Readings

Martens, R., Christina, R.W., Harvey, J.S., & Sharkey, B.J. (1981). *Coaching young athletes*. Champaign, IL: Human Kinetics (Part 3. Sport Pedagogy).

Thomas, J.R. (Ed.). *Motor development during childhood and adolescence*. Minneapolis: Burgess (Chapters 3, 4, and 5).

chapter six

Preventing Common Athletic Injuries

Holly Wilson Greene
San Leandro, California

Questions to consider . . .

☐ *How can you, as a coach, prevent injuries?*

☐ *What is physical fitness and how can you help your athletes achieve it?*

☐ *How can you, as a coach, make the practice environment safer for your atheletes?*

☐ *If prevention fails, how are you prepared to deal with injuries?*

I njuries in sports are "part of the turf," but does recognizing this fact mean that you have to accept it and every injury that occurs? No! You have a major role to play in diminishing the likelihood of injury.

Ask yourself if your athletes are:

- physically fit?
- properly fitted with specified protective equipment which is in good repair?
- well taught in the execution of sports skills?
- participating in a safe environment?

If you can answer "yes" to all of these questions, you are doing a good job of trying to prevent injuries. However, there may be more that you can do to make sports participation even safer, so read on.

> *Injuries are not predictable, but many contributing factors can be eliminated with a little work on the part of the coach, the athlete, and the parents.*

Much of your injury prevention program takes place well before the beginning of the season. Each athlete must undergo a thorough physical examination, including a classification of his or her physical maturity level. If the physical examinations are given "military style", it may be your responsibility to help organize the stations and schedule your team members. Once physically qualified to compete, each athlete should engage in a complete pre-season conditioning program designed by you. Another of your pre-season responsibilities is to inspect the equipment and see that all necessary repairs or replacement orders are made so all will be ready for the first day of practice.

When the first day of practice, arrives and every day thereafter, your responsibilities for injury prevention will include inspection of the playing area for dangerous conditions. Monitoring the environmental conditions for hazardous levels of heat, humidity, and smog is also important. You may need to change your practice plans if the environment is unsafe.

> *Learning proper techniques of conditioning is more important than learning how to apply tape to an athlete.*

Finally, an important fact to recognize is that tape is not a panacea, especially in youth sports. Strong muscles are much more efficient at protecting joints against injuries than a few layers of cotton or tape, even when expertly applied.

Figure 1. Don't conduct your program as though injuries occur by chance.

Figure 2. Teach your athletes how to prevent injuries.

Sport Physical Examinations

Pre-season physical examinations should be scheduled six to eight weeks before the beginning of the first practice session. The time period must be adequate to allow for the remediation of any physical problems uncovered during the exam or, if necessary, for referral of the athlete to a specialist for further examination. The examination should not be so far in advance of the first practice, however, that the athlete could sustain an injury before practice starts.

Who should carry out the examinations—the family physician, a pediatrician, or a sports medicine specialist? The family physician is most familiar with the athlete's individual health history, but may have little or no knowledge of the stresses involved in the particular sport in which the youth wishes to compete. The pediatrician deals with the health problems of this age group every day. The sports medicine specialist knows the stresses involved in each sport, as well as the standard musculoskeletal tests to determine if the joints, ligaments, and muscles are strong enough to withstand those stresses. Neither the sports medicine specialist nor the pediatrician, however, knows much about the athlete's previous health history. Frequently there is no choice; the decision is made according to who is available and willing to help. The ideal situation would be to have a medical team comprised of a sport medicine specialist and a pediatrician, with pertinent past medical information provided by the family physician on a summary card that is either brought to the exam by each athlete or mailed in by the physician.

Baseline data on flexibility and strength should be collected during the pre-season physical.

Regardless of who conducts the examination, to be complete, it must include tests for range of motion, strength, and ligamentous laxity. The maturity level of each athlete should also be established because it is more important for classifying athletes than age, height, or weight. By using maturity level, the league office can ensure that competition is scheduled between athletes of similar size, strength, and skill.

Grouping athletes by maturity allows for safer competition.

The purpose of the sports physical examination is not to prevent children from playing sports, but to ensure that each one is physically, mentally, and emotionally ready to participate. In cases where the athlete's physical stature and/or maturity level is not suited for a particular sport, the individual should be encouraged to try a sport where success will be more probable and the chance of injury less likely. As the coach, you must recognize that the physician has the final say about whether or not the athlete is physically qualified to participate. Once the decision has been made, it is your responsibility to support it.

Figure 3.   The purpose of the physical examination is to ensure that each child is physically, mentally, and emotionally ready to participate.

Conditioning Program

Conditioning may not be fun but it is the *most important* step in preventing injuries. Being physically fit enables the athlete to:
- avoid nagging aches and pains and minor injuries
- execute skills more efficiently
- participate longer at a higher intensity level

You should arrange your time schedule so that the pre-season conditioning program begins four to eight weeks before the season. Only then will your athletes be physically ready for the first day of practice. The emphasis is on building the components of physical fitness, that is, flexibility, strength, and cardiovascular endurance.

Developing flexibility, strength, and cardiovascular endurance protects the athlete against injury.

The physiological basis for developing physical fitness is the S.A.I.D. Principle, an acronym first used by Logan (1965). It stands for Specific Adaptations to Imposed Demands. The S.A.I.D. Principle tells us that the body will adapt to the demands placed upon it, providing the demand is sufficient to bring about an adaptation. The demand is sufficient only when it is greater than that imposed by everyday activity. The demand must be an overload, but the overload must not be beyond the body's ability to adapt. If the demand exceeds adaptability, tissue damage occurs. Finally, the adaptation is specific to the muscle, organ, or system involved in the conditioning. For example, lifting weight builds strength, but not flexibility or cardiovascular endurance. The key to conditioning is to train, not strain. Always keep in mind that the child is not a small adult. You should not use programs designed for adults to condition the musculoskeletally immature body of a child.

Athletes should work out four to five times per week and, if possible, at the same time of day that practice will be scheduled. This will enable them to become accustomed to activity in environmental conditions that are similar to those in which they will compete. Loose fitting clothing that covers as much of the body surface as the uniform should be worn for the workout. If possible, workout clothing should also have the same fabric content as the uniform. All three factors affect maintenance of the proper body temperature and adaptation (acclimatization) to activity in hot, humid environments. Never allow an athlete to work out in a rubber suit because the rubber does not permit evaporation of sweat from the skin which is the most efficient way of cooling the body in a hot environment. Acclimatization takes longer for children than for adults. Children do not tolerate activity in heat as well as adults because they do not dissipate body heat as effectively. They also have a greater surface area (in relation to body mass) for absorption of heat from the environment. It will take a child approximately 10–14 days of activity in the heat to acclimatize to it.

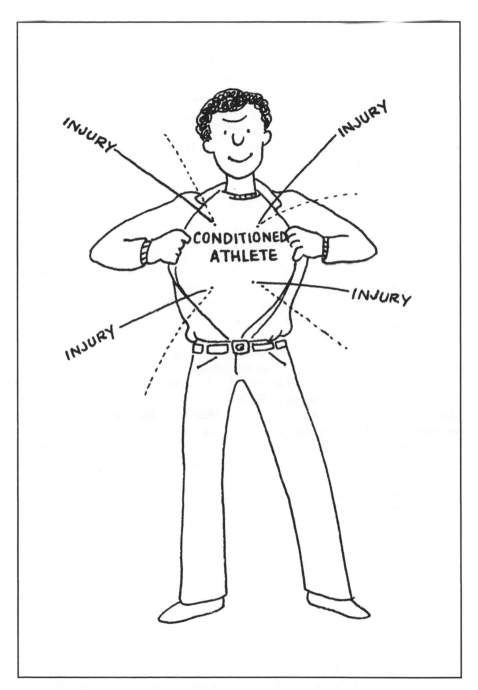

Figure 4.   A conditioned athlete has fewer injuries than one who is untrained.

Children are more susceptible to heat stress than adults.

Once the season begins, conditioning should become part of your practice session schedule. Switch your emphasis to maintaining the level of fitness gained by each athlete during the pre-season program. Practice activities alone are not sufficient to maintain the conditioning that has been attained in the pre-season. In-season conditioning workouts should be scheduled two to three times per week.

Flexibility

Flexibility is the range of motion around a joint. Although you may say an individual is flexible, flexibility is specific to a joint and is dependent on, among other things, the type of joint, the adjacent muscle mass (and fat), and the extensibility of connective tissue (muscles, tendons, and ligaments) surrounding the joint.

In general, females are more flexible than males, but flexibility decreases with age unless maintained through stretching exercises. Touching the palms to the floor without bending the knees and sitting in yoga style with both knees touching the floor are two basic tests for flexibility in the lower body. If both tests can be done without bouncing, the individual is flexible in the low back, hips, and lower extremities. Such flexibility can usually be maintained by a daily stretching routine. Tighter, less flexible teammates will benefit from stretching twice a day. Generally, flexibility should be worked on twice a day during the pre-season and once a day in season.

To increase flexibility, only muscle tissue should be stretched. Stretching ligaments compromises the stability of the joint, thereby increasing its vulnerability to injury. The correct way of stretching a muscle is to apply a slow, sustained stretch. Bouncing and bobbing may stimulate receptors in the muscle, causing them to contract as a protective mechanism, or worse, damaging the muscles, tendons, or ligaments. Points to remember when stretching are:

- A total body warmup should precede the actual stretching. Cold muscles resist stretching and are more prone to injury.
- Stretch the tighter side first.
- Apply a slow sustained stretch that is comfortable. No pain should be experienced. If the muscles shake or quiver, ease up on the stretch.
- Relax and breathe easily. It is impossible to relax if too much stretch is applied. Without complete relaxation the muscles cannot be stretched.
- Hold the stretch for 30–60 seconds.

● Repeat the stretch two to three times.

Your conditioning program should include stretching exercises for the calves, quadriceps, hamstrings, groin, low back, trunk, shoulders, and neck. An excellent resource book is *Stretching* by Anderson (1980).

Strength

Strength is the ability to overcome a resistance. According to the S.A.I.D. Principle, a muscle is strengthened by subjecting it to a workload greater than that to which it is accustomed, but less than that which could cause injury. This workload is thus called an overload. Strengthening a muscle involves an increase in the size of the muscle fibers that make up the muscle, not an increase in their number.

Strength training and exercises are categorized as *isotonic, isometric,* and *isokinetic.* The terms isotonic and isometric refer to the type of muscle contraction that takes place during the exercise. An isotonic exercise is one in which the muscle changes length and movement takes place at the joint. Actually, in isotonic contractions the muscle may either shorten or lengthen; both are isotonic contractions. When the muscle shortens it is a *concentric contraction* and when it lengthens it is an *eccentric contraction.* In a bent knee half sit-up, the abdominal muscles shorten to raise the head and trunk off the floor. Those same muscles lengthen to lower the upper body back to the floor. If the eccentric phase of an exercise is done in a slow, controlled manner, the muscles will also develop strength during this phase of the exercise. They will develop eccentric strength. In athletics, it is important that the muscles be strengthened eccentrically as well as concentrically if they are to function properly and protect against injury.

An isometric exercise is one in which the muscle works maximally against the opposing muscle or an immoveable object. No movement takes place at the joint. Tension is built up within the muscle during the contraction, but the muscle does not change in length. An example of an isometric exercise is to raise your arms to shoulder height, clinch the fingers of both hands together and then attempt to pull them apart. No movement occurs but tension increases in the muscles across the back of the arms, shoulders, and upper back. To build strength using an isometric exercise, the contraction must be near maximum, held for four to six seconds and repeated from one to five times in an exercise period. Allow two to three minutes of rest between each execution. Isometric exercises build strength only at the angle at which the exercise is executed. Therefore, to build strength throughout the range of motion, the exercise must be carried out at a number of different angles.

Isokinetic exercises involve the use of mechanically complicated (and expensive) machines to provide a resistance that remains maximal throughout the range of motion prescribed by the exercise. In comparison, in isotonic exercises the maximum overload that can be safely handled is actually the heaviest weight that can be moved through the weakest part of the range of movement.

Strengthening exercises have physiological benefits other than just the development of muscular strength. Tendons and ligaments become thicker and hence stronger. Bones also thicken and thus become sturdier. By being stronger, they are more resilient to the stresses imposed during conditioning and actual sports participation.

Other components of physical fitness such as power, speed, and muscular endurance are also enhanced by the development of strength. Power is a combination of strength and speed. In athletic events it is demonstrated by the ability to project an object or one's body through space. Speed refers to the rapidity of movement and is limited hereditarily by the ratio of fast twitch to slow twitch fibers in the muscle. Speed is also dependent on other factors such as coordination, tissue temperature, flexibility, and muscle efficiency. As strength increases, both power and speed may improve.

Muscular endurance is the ability to continue work over a period of time. It is related to strength. In a strong muscle, more muscle fibers are developed. Thus, the athlete constantly has reserve fibers to take over as working fibers fatigue from prolonged activity. Both isotonic and isokinetic exercises effectively build muscle endurance.

During the pre-season, strength workouts should be scheduled three times per week, but not on consecutive days. They must be scheduled every 48-72 hours to prevent a decrease in muscular fitness. However, at least 48-72 hours is required for muscle tissue to recover from fatigue and muscle fibers to increase in girth. If the recovery period is inadequate, the muscle tissue becomes overstressed and begins to break down. Strength workouts should be continued in-season, but only two times per week.

Strength is developed by lifting a heavy weight a few times. Isotonic exercise is the most practical method of developing strength, time-wise and financially. The overload can be imposed by moving one's own body weight from point A to point B, by using dumbbells and/or barbells, by air or water resistance, or by using weight stacks on cables.

A weight training program that is frequently used to build strength is the DeLorme Progressive Resistance Exercise Program. According to this program, a heavy weight is a weight that can be lifted ten times in succession while performing the prescribed movement properly each time. The weight is too heavy if less than eight lifts can be properly done and too light if more than twelve are possible. The weight that can be lifted 10 times is called the repetitions maximum (RM). Each lift is called a repetition and repetitions are grouped together into sets. A set is a number of repetitions of an exercise that is executed in succession without a rest period. Rest is allowed between sets.

The athlete executes 3 sets of 10 repetitions for each exercise in the program.

The weight (repetitions maximum), which is the overload, is determined for each exercise by using the 10 rep method.

Set #1 - 1 set of 10 repetitions at 50% RM (1 × 10 at 50% RM)
Set #2 - 1 set of 10 repetitions at 75% RM (1 × 10 at 75% RM)
Set #3 - 1 set of 10 repetitions at RM (1 × 10 at RM)

In the first step of the DeLorme program, the athlete completes one group of ten repetitions, each with an overload equivalent to one half the repetitions maximum determined for that exercise. For example, if the repetitions maximum is 10 pounds, the overload for this first set would be 5 pounds. Starting with the light weight serves as a warm up. In the second step, the overload is three fourths of the repetitions maximum. The final step calls for ten repetitions with the repetitions maximum as the overload. The athlete may not be able to complete the prescribed workout.

When the exercise cannot be executed properly, the athlete should stop and record the number of repetitions. Next time the athlete should strive to do at least one additional repetition correctly. When the complete prescription (3 × 10) can be executed correctly, the overload should be increased by a realistic amount of weight. With the addition of weight, the number of repetitions the athlete can correctly execute may decrease. This is to be expected because the workload is harder. Never increase the amount of weight and the number of repetitions at the same time. Only one variable should be increased at a time. Remember, the key is to train (or maintain), not strain.

The DeLorme method meets the criteria for a sound conditioning program. First, it can be individualized because the repetitions maximum is determined for each exercise, for each athlete. Second, the program makes use of a safe overload. The overload, or repetitions maximum, is a weight that is well within the individual's physical capacity. Finally, the program provides for progression. As strength develops, the overload must continually increase or no further development will take place.

When using weights to build strength, lifting technique is more critical than the amount of weight lifted.

The proper use of free weights, dumbbells, and barbells is a skill. How the exercise is executed is more important than how much weight is lifted. Unlike more expensive equipment where weights are secured and guided by cables, free weights must be controlled entirely by the athlete. When lifting, the athlete should concentrate on the movement. The weight should be lifted slowly to avoid introducing momentum, known as "throwing the weight." This common method of "cheating" decreases the workload on the muscles.

The usual cadence in lifting free weights is to lift the weight to a count of 2, hold it steady for a count of 1 and then slowly lower it to a count of 4. The athlete should breathe normally while lifting, inhaling when lifting the weight and exhaling when lowering it. Spotters are required any time weight is lifted over the head or above the chest when the exercise is performed in a reclining position. When lifting free weights, always check to make sure the collars are tight before lifting the weight.

Each athlete should have a card to record the weight training workout accomplished in terms of the number of sets, repetitions, and overload. Record keeping is important because an athlete may not remember the last overload attempted. An incorrect estimate of the previous overload may result in an injury. A record of each athlete's progress also motivates the individual to work harder. As the coach, you should have a thorough understanding of lifting technique before you start a weight training program for your athletes. Your athletes should also understand and practice a lifting technique before attempting it with weights.

There is currently little agreement concerning the age at which an athlete should begin weight training.

Weight training between the ages of 8 and 18 remains a controversial topic among physicians, coaches, and physical educators. The discussion centers around two arguments: first, any jerking motion when lifting weight could damage a growth center; and second, the level of testosterone in the body prior to the adolescent growth spurt may not be sufficient to adequately stimulate muscle development. Many physicians and physical educators recommended that the body weight be used as the overload to develop strength. Examples of such exercises are bent knee half sit-ups, pull-ups, push-ups, step-ups and toe rises.

Cardiovascular Endurance

Cardiovascular endurance is the ability of the heart, lungs, and circulatory system to meet the body's need for oxygen during activity so that activity can continue for an extended period of time. It actually has two components: *anaerobic fitness*

Figure 5. Following the rules of safety will prevent injuries during weight training.

and *aerobic fitness.* Anaerobic activities are highly intense, but of short duration, such as running the 100-yard dash. Anaerobic activities are so intense that the heart, lungs, and circulatory system cannot meet the body's need for oxygen. The term anaerobic means without air. The competitor is essentially performing without oxygen. Building anaerobic fitness requires highly intense activity of a short duration that is repeated again and again. Wind sprints are an example of an anaerobic activity. The successful competitor learns to withstand the fatigue and muscular pain of anaerobic activity by engaging in demanding conditioning sessions.

Aerobic activities are less intense than anaerobic ones; they are submaximal in nature. The cardiovascular system is able to meet the body's need for oxygen during aerobic activity. Consequently, activity can continue for a longer period of time.

Every sport has both anaerobic and aerobic components. The amount of each is determined by the nature of the sport, as well as the philosophy of the coach. For example, a basketball coach who uses a fast-break offense must stress anaerobic conditioning if the team is to be successful with this kind of offensive strategy.

During the pre-season, athletes should work on cardiovascular endurance three to four times weekly. A common method of developing anaerobic fitness is interval training which, as the name implies, involves alternating periods of work and rest. A brief, intense workout depletes some or all of the immediate sources of energy stored in the body and the rest interval gives the body time to replenish the energy that has been used. An athlete can continue to train longer and harder with interval training than continuous training because energy sources are always available. Coaches must motivate their athletes to work hard on interval training. Fox and Mathews (1974) have written an excellent text called *Interval Training* that not only includes a clear explanation of the training technique, but instructions in how to set up a program for a variety of sports.

Running, swimming, and bicycling are the activities most frequently used to develop aerobic fitness. Cooper (1977) has designed some excellent aerobic programs for these sports as well as others for basketball, racquetball, soccer, volleyball, and tennis. The programs are designed for various age groups, including adolescents. Any one of these programs would be appropriate for the development of pre-season aerobic fitness.

Before beginning an aerobic fitness program, it is important to determine each athlete's level of cardiovascular fitness. Each athlete runs for 12 minutes and the distance covered in that time period indicates how aerobically fit the individual is. A table for fitness level classification can be found in Cooper's book.

A simple method of monitoring improvements in cardiovascular fitness is to count the pulse rate per unit of time. By the end of the pre-season, each athlete's resting heart rate should have dropped a few beats if the workouts were sufficiently intense. Check the pulse by using the radial artery in the wrist. It is located on the palm side of the wrist at the base of the thumb. Count the beats with the index finger for ten seconds and then multiply by six. The pulse rate can also be used to monitor the intensity of the workout. Because the heart beats faster in children, the heart rate must increase to at least 160 beats per minute for 15-60 minutes if the heart, lungs, and circulatory system are to show any adaptation to the aerobic workout. A heart rate between 160 to 200 beats per minute, 60-90% of maximum heart rate, is considered safe for this age group.

Protective Equipment

*Protective equipment must be worn and used
properly if it is to serve its intended purpose.*

Equipment protects the athlete from those hazards in a sport that cannot be eliminated by other factors such as rules. Protective equipment does not prevent injuries unless it is:

- of good quality
- properly fitted
- in good repair (replaced when necessary)
- worn and used properly

No athlete should be allowed in the playing area without proper equipment, including the proper type of shoes. Teach your athletes not only how to use the equipment but how to properly care for it.

Daily Responsibilities

During the season, the coach has additional responsibilities. Every day before practice starts you should check the playing area for hazards, and the environmental conditions such as heat, humidity, and smog. If you conduct practices indoors or outdoors, walk back and forth across the playing area looking for conditions that could inflict injury such as loose boards, water, glass, or holes. In a gym, any objects that project from the walls adjacent to the court boundaries should be padded. Equipment should be stored well away from the sidelines. Spend time looking for hazards, eliminate those that you can, and protect the athletes from those you cannot remove.

Environmental conditions can be monitored by calling the weather bureau or a local radio station for information. High humidity is more of a health hazard to an active athlete than a high temperature. Use the following table (Ryan, 1973) to determine whether or not your practice schedule should be changed to avoid heat stress.

A simple guideline is to be extremely cautious and modify your practices when the temperature and humidity add up to 150 or more.

*Replacing body fluids by drinking plain water
protects the athlete against heat stress.*

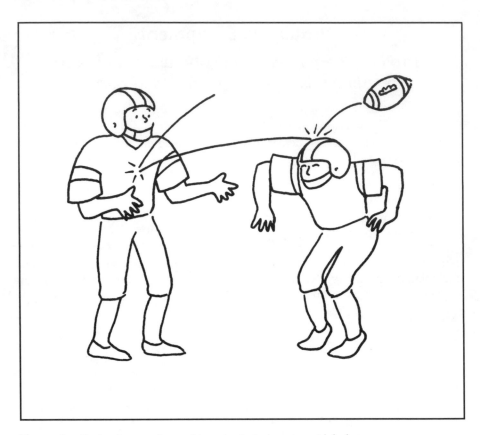

Figure 6.   Protective equipment is worn to help prevent injuries.

Temperature	Humidity	Activity
80-90 F	Under 70%	O.K.
80-90 F	Over 70%	Caution, rest (especially early in the season)
90-100 F	Under 70%	Caution, rest
90-100 F	Over 70%	Shorten practice or change time
Over 100 F		Shorten practice or change time

Replacement of fluids is of utmost importance in preventing heat stress. Water should always be available on the sidelines during each practice or game and athletes should be allowed to drink as much as desired. Athletes should be encouraged to drink water under hot or humid conditions even if they are not thirsty because the feeling of thirst may be delayed until the athlete is dehydrated.

Besides water, you should have ice and a first aid kit at each practice or game. A more complete discussion of this topic is provided in Chapter 16, "Emergency Procedures Every Coach Should Know." Remember: when prevention fails, ice is nice!

Recommendations For Preventing Athletic Injuries

- Include safety awareness as part of your game plan.
- Learn the latest coaching techniques and rules.
- Teach athletes the proper execution of skills and techniques for protecting themselves.
- Broaden your knowledge in principles of conditioning, prevention and care of athletic injuries, and principles and techniques of coaching.
- Use competent officials.
- Schedule contests with opponents of similar size, skill, strength, and maturity level, especially in collision and contact sports.
- Recommend to regulatory agencies that maturity level rather than chronological age be used to classify athletes in collision and contact sports.

References

Anderson, B. (1980). *Stretching.* Palmer Lake, CO: Stretching Inc.

Cooper, K. (1977). *The aerobics way.* New York: Bantam Books.

Fox, E. and Mathews, D. (1974). *Interval training.* Philadelphia, PA: W.B. Saunders Co.

Logan, G. (1965). *Adaptations of muscular activity.* Belmont, CA: Wadsworth Publishing Co.

Ryan, A. (1973). Heat stress and the vulnerable athlete. *The Physician and Sportsmedicine, 1 (1)*, 51 (June).

Suggested Readings

Committee on Sports Medicine, American Academy of Pediatrics. (1983). *Sports medicine: Health care for young athletes.* Evanston, IL: American Academy of Pediatrics.

American Red Cross. (1979). *Advanced first aid and emergency care.* Garden City, NY: Doubleday and Company.

Anderson, B. (1975). *Stretching.* Palmer Lake, CO: Stretching Inc.

Cooper, K. (1977). *The aerobics way.* New York: Bantam Books.

Fox, E. & Mathews, D. (1974). *Interval training.* Philadelphia, PA: W.B. Saunders Co.

Smith, N. (1976). *Food for sport.* Palo Alto, CA: Bull Publishing Co.

Southmayd, W. & Hoffman, M. (1981). *Sportshealth.* NY: Quick Fox.

chapter seven

Goal Setting: Principles for the Coach and Athlete

Martha E. Ewing
Michigan State University

7

Questions to consider . . .

☐ *Why should athletes and coaches set goals?*

☐ *What types of goals should be set to help athletes and the team improve their performance?*

☐ *How do goals influence the performance of athletes?*

☐ *What are the procedures that coaches should follow in order to implement a goal setting program?*

☐ *What problems are associated with implementing a goal setting program?*

Two of the most common problems cited by coaches at all levels of competition is how to get athletes motivated and how to get them to perform consistently. Frequently coaches are faced with athletes who "get up" and perform at or above expectations for the big game, but perform below their abilities against lesser opponents. This "roller coaster" syndrome often results when athletes and coaches focus their attention more on winning than on performance. While winning is one of the goals in sport, performance is the primary ingredient for achieving this goal.

Chapter 8, "Motivating Young Athletes to Optimum Performance," states that one of the reasons young athletes are motivated to perform is because they want to improve their skills. For these athletes, the goal of performing better ranks higher than the goal of winning. From a psychological perspective, athletes' goals allow them to evaluate their performance as being successful even if they don't win the game. This is a healthy environment for athletes. Thus, one of the critical elements of coaching young athletes is to provide a mechanism for helping them to improve their skills and to evaluate their improvement. One effective way to do this is to implement a goal setting program as part of your coaching strategy.

This chapter is presented as a guide for you to follow in establishing a goal setting program. The information is derived from research, discussions with coaches and athletes, and from personal experiences in working with both high school and college athletes. Because situations in youth sport vary considerably, this information should be evaluated and adapted to your specific situation.

A goal is something you are trying to accomplish.

What are Goals?

Most young athletes have dreams of playing at the professional level or of winning an Olympic gold medal. These dreams are goals. For some athletes, these goals will never be more than dreams. For others, these dreams motivate them to practice skills, get into condition, and work harder to learn all they can about their sport. A goal is something you are trying to accomplish, usually within a given time limit. The technique used to set, evaluate, adjust, and reset goals is called goal setting and is the focus of this chapter.

Types of Goals

For goals to be effective as a motivator, it is necessary to set the right type of goals. Although there are many types of goals, the most critical ones are those relating to performance and outcome. Most coaches and athletes believe that outcome goals, like winning, are the most motivational. As long as you win this may be true.

The most common situation in sports is for teams to experience a mixture of wins and losses. Many times a game outcome or season record is determined by factors which are outside of the players' or coaches' control. Consider the following situation. After looking at your roster of players and the schedule of games, you decide that it is very possible that you can win 6 of the first 8 games scheduled. You tell your team that this is the goal. However, because of injuries, key players being on vacation, slow development of the team, or some missed opportunities during the game, you lose the first four games. Even though you may have observed that many players are playing well and, indeed, showing great improvement, the failure to reach your goal is likely to create a negative attitude among the players or the feeling that regardless of what they do they won't be able to win. Thus, athletes learn very early that *Success = Winning* and *Failure = Losing.*

To avoid equating success with winning, you should focus athletes' attention on their performance. In other words, athletes should view their performance in this game relative to their past performance. In this way if athletes play well in a game but lose, they can feel good about their own performance, gain confidence that they are good players, and know that their practice paid off. This will result in a positive attitude and a desire to continue practicing.

Focus athletes attention on improving performance.

The bottom line is that although it is easy and tempting to set outcome goals, this type of goal often results in negative motivation, loss of self-confidence, fear of failure, and false conclusions about the individual's self-worth. If, as was stated earlier, performance is the main ingredient in winning, the obvious conclusion is that coaches should help athletes focus their attention on performance goals rather than on outcome goals.

How Goals Affect Performance

Given the fact that goal setting leads to improved performance, it is important to understand how goals affect sport performance. Fundamentally, goals direct an athlete's attention and action to specific skills. For example, when working with young baseball players on fielding ground balls, you stress to them the importance of getting in front of the ball and getting the glove on the ground. After demonstrating exactly how you want them to perform the skill, you put

Figure 1. Success means improving one's performance.

them into a drill where they are to field balls that are rolled to them on the ground. The key to successful performance of this skill is getting into the proper position, not how many balls they stop or how accurately they throw the ball after fielding it.

Prior to beginning the above drill, you set a goal of getting into position 5 times out of 6. Now the athlete is aware of exactly what behavior is expected and works to meet this goal. Athletes quickly learn that if they meet this goal they will be rewarded with a pat on the back, a "good job" or other positive reinforcement. For those who don't meet the goal, the expectation is that they will receive the reinforcement with more practice. Remember that the reinforcement must be immediate and contingent upon reaching the goal as discussed in Chapter 8.

Reinforce athletes who meet the goal.

Important by-products of directing an athlete's attention to specific aspects of skills are increased effort, persistence, and greater expectancies of success. Athletes who have relevant performance goals are likely to spend more time concentrating on their performance than athletes who have no goals or goals that focus only on outcomes. In addition, athletes with performance goals will persist at learning and perfecting these skills for a longer period of time. Finally, athletes who meet goals expect to reach higher goals in the future.

The relationship between goals and performance is a positive one and should result in players being more motivated to practice and improve their performance. This increased motivation to practice is what coaches are seeking. In addition, there are positive psychological benefits associated with setting goals for performance. Specifically, athletes who have been educated to set goals have a greater enjoyment of the sport and are more satisfied with their improvement than athletes who do not use a goal setting program. In essence, a goal setting program results in athletes feeling good about themselves and their performance regardless of the level of their ability.

Goal Setting Principles

Certain principles should be considered in establishing a goal setting program. Your role as the coach of young athletes and coordinator of the goal setting program is threefold:
1) to help athletes understand how to set appropriate goals for themselves;

2) how to select skills or subskills for which athletes should set goals; and

3) how to interpret the results of performance relative to the goals set. The principles presented in Table 1 should help you in this role.

Specific Goals

The use of *specific* goals produces more desired practice and performance behaviors than do *general* goals. For example, telling an athlete to strive for six rebounds in a game or practice results in behavior closer to the goal than does telling athletes to get as many rebounds as they can or to do their best. The goal set must be based on your perception that they have the ability to reach this goal. Attempts should be made to set *quantifiable* goals rather than *qualitative* goals. In other words, setting the goal in basketball of "outhustling" the opponents (a qualitative goal) would be better stated as "picking up more loose balls" than the opponents. In this way, a look at the stat sheet provides immediate feedback, and focuses their attention on the specific behavior that results in "outhustling" the opponent.

Realistic Goals

Perhaps the most critical element to the success of any goal setting program is the ability to set goals that are realistic for the individual to accomplish. If athletes know that they cannot reach a goal, they will put forth less effort to achieve it. For example, your 200 yard freestyle relay team in swimming has been performing the event in 2 minutes. For the upcoming league championship meet, you set a goal that is 8 seconds faster than they have ever swum the event. The relay team perceives that they are doing their very best already. For each swimmer to take 2 seconds off their performance in *one* week appears to be "mission impossible." Psychologically, the swimmers will feel greater pressure to perform, which results in an increase in muscle tension and a "seed" of doubt about their

1. Be specific, not general.
2. Be realistic, but challenging.
3. Be flexible, adjust goals up *and* down.
4. Set short-term goals, not long-term goals.
5. Support is needed from coaches and parents.
6. Evaluate performance and goals, provide lots of feedback.

Table 1.   Principles for setting effective goals.

1. Determine the areas in which to set goals.
2. Determine the level of goal to be set.
3. Identify specific strategies for achieving goals.

Table 2.   Steps for implementing a goal setting program.

ability to achieve this goal. Under these circumstances, the end result is often a very bad performance. For goals to be motivating, they must be realistic (within the ability of the athlete to perform), but challenging.

Flexible Goals

For goals to be effective over the course of a season, athletes, coaches, and parents must be willing to adjust goals up *and* down. As goals are met, naturally, they should be raised. Of equal importance, however, is the willingness to lower goals when they are obviously out of reach of the athlete or team. This situation is likely to occur after an athlete has been injured or when coaches or parents misjudge the capability of an athlete at a given point in time. Lowering a goal does not mean that the athlete is a bad performer. Indeed, leaving the goal at an unrealistic and unattainable level is sure to result in a loss of motivation and effort. Remember, goal setting is a process and as such should be changing. Being unwilling to lower goals means you would rather see an athlete quit after becoming discouraged from repeated failure than helping the athlete gain confidence in his or her ability to improve in a given area.

Short Term Goals

Short term goals are more effective than long term or no goals. Setting goals for a practice or a game will result in increased effort and focus the attention of your athletes on the specific performances needed in the game. In many sports, as opponents change, so do aspects of the game that you want to emphasize. Setting short term goals prevents athletes from viewing the long term goal as beyond their capabilities to attain or to take seriously. Short term goals serve as a means of attaining long term goals. For example, if a runner's goal is to qualify for a higher level meet in the mile run and the cut-off time required is 5 minutes 15 seconds, that runner, whose best time to date is 5 minutes 30 seconds, could set a goal of improving this time by 1 second for 15 consecutive weeks (or whatever the coach and athlete considers realistic). Using this technique results in each week's goal being challenging and realistic. As the athlete attains the short term goals, greater confidence and feelings of self worth will be generated.

Coach and Parent Support

Children in sport need the support of parents and coaches during the goal setting process. This is critical when young athletes are being asked to focus their attention on their performance weaknesses. An athlete who has achieved success and been rewarded by parents and coaches for performance as an offensive player in basketball can become frustrated when the coach asks him or her to concentrate on defensive positioning and rebounding (areas where little success has been experienced). To maintain motivation, athletes must be aware that

Figure 2.   Unrealistic goals can lead to self-doubt and a poorer performance.

parents and coaches believe that defensive performance is important. This aware-ness is generated through a direct reward system or through the questions and comments made to an athlete. For example, if the question to an athlete following a game is "How many points did you score?", the athlete will perceive that offensive performance is most important. Likewise, congratulating a player first on a strong defensive performance leaves the athlete with a mind set that people care about his or her defensive performance. In other words, it will be worth the effort to concentrate and practice positioning and rebounding because it is important to others that the athlete do well in these areas.

When goals are seen as important to others by athletes, an increase in com-mitment is likely to result. Athletes vary greatly in their commitment to achieve certain goals. The level of commitment may be increased when coaches and parents care enough about athletes' goals to reward them for trying to achieve these goals.

Evaluate Goals

Feedback about one's performance is critical to an athlete's persistence in im-proving performance. The feedback provided by coaches or parents is critical to young athletes' understanding of how they are progressing towards the goals that have been set. If the feedback shows that an athlete's performance is at or above the goal set, the athlete evaluates performance positively, is confident that he or she can perform at that level again, and is motivated to maintain the effort to reach the goal. However, further improvement in performance will require that the goal be raised to provide a new challenge. When feedback shows that performance is below the goal, the athlete feels dissatisfied and is motivated to improve future performance. This assumes that the athlete believes he or she can improve and wants to avoid failure in the future.

Too often, goals are set at the beginning of the season and are not discussed again until the end of the season when coaches are looking for explanations for the team's performance. For feedback to be effective in improving performance, the athlete should see that applying the feedback results in meeting goals in subsequent performances.

Implementing a Goal Setting Program

While it is clear that there is a lot to be gained from setting goals, the "how-to" or mechanism for incorporating this program into your practices and games is less clear. The steps listed in Table 2 should facilitate the inclusion of a goal setting program into your planning for the season.

STEP 1: Determine the areas in which to set goals

Goals should be set to focus a young athlete's attention on:
1) specific skills that need to be improved (both strengths and weaknesses);
2) the development of fitness, including strength, stamina, and other phys
    iological components;
3) the improvement of interactions among teammates; and
4) for team sports, the cooperation and coordination of specific activities.

Table 3 provides examples of goals for different sports and the four areas mentioned above.

The first four examples provided in Table 3 are goals that could be set for 9 to 11 year old athletes. The examples for football are more appropriate for high school athletes. It is extremely important to understand that these are only examples of possible goals. Coaches and athletes must decide if a particular example is appropriate for a given individual or situation. Also, it is important to realize that goals could be set for each position on a team and each sub-skill. Finally, these goals should be viewed as one point in time. Although the goals

---

Skills
  1. Softball
       —Field 4 of 5 grounders hit to glove side
       —Hit 5 of 7 pitched balls out of infield.

  2. Tennis
       —Hit 4 of 6 backhands down the line
       —10 volleys in a row to deep corners of the court
       —75% of first serves in service court

Fitness
  3. Basketball
       —Run length of court in 10 seconds
       —Jump rope (continuous without misses) 2 minutes
       —Defensive shuffle 1 length in 25 seconds

Improve Interactions
  4. Soccer
       —Sincerely compliment a teammate 5 times during a practice
       —Encourage teammates every day during conditioning drills
       —Acknowledge the teammate who assisted you on a play

Team Coordination
  5. Football
       —Hold opponent to under 100 yards rushing
       —No quarterback sacks during a game
       —Average 4 yards a carry on the ground

Table 3.   Examples of goals for different areas and skills.

shown are static, goals must be flexible, and adjusted as athletes reach the goal or as it becomes obvious that the goal is too difficult.

In order for goals to serve as a motivator for athletes, it must be determined what skills each athlete wants to work on. Take a few minutes before and after practice and ask each athlete, individually, three questions: What skills do you do well in this sport? What skills do you need to work on? What skills do you want to improve the most this season? These three questions will provide you with a player's perceived strengths and weaknesses and what they are motivated to work at right now. For some athletes, these questions will be difficult to answer and they will want you to tell them. However, you should avoid this temptation. Rather, ask the athlete to think about how well he or she performs certain skills. This line of questioning can be very revealing. Be prepared for those athletes who have either no weaknesses, no strengths, or who know only what their parents have told them. These young athletes need your help to gain a realistic understanding of their abilities. Your support and patience in working with athletes who have false perceptions about their ability can make the difference between their staying in the sport and dropping out.

STEP 2: Determine the level of goal to be set

Many coaches get discouraged with goal setting programs because they don't know the appropriate level to set as the goal. There is no magic formula. However, there are a number of factors to consider in determining the initial level at which to set a goal.

When working with individual athletes, it is important to consider their previous performances, their personal best, and their last performance. These pieces of information provide a starting point. You and the athlete must then determine whether the goals are reasonable, yet challenging. If the athlete is performing very well, it may be necessary to set the goal slightly higher. If the athlete has been injured, the goal may be set lower to provide the necessary challenge. This information, used with your best judgment, is the general approach used in setting goals.

There are additional factors that can be considered in determining the level of goal to be set. An athlete or team's potential should be considered. When working with young athletes who suddenly find that their effort is not producing the desired improvement in performance, it is necessary to consider their potential to improve. Lower goals may be set to allow the athletes to perceive that progress is being made even though the steps are very small. Athletes going through a growth spurt may experience temporary setbacks in skill improvement, but their potential may be enhanced considerably following the growth spurt.

An athlete's commitment to achieving a goal is an important factor to consider. Most athletes are willing to work on those skills that they do well already. It is difficult to get some athletes to spend their time practicing skills that they do *not* do well. The level of commitment is often low in the area of fitness goals. When athletes can be successful without getting in shape, it is difficult to convince them that they should work hard on fitness goals.

Finally, the opportunity to practice must be considered before a goal is set. When working with children, the amount of practice is directly related to the amount of improvement shown. If your team is limited to a one hour practice plus a game per week, goals must be lowered. Slightly higher goals may be set for children who can benefit from practice with their friends. Children who are just learning the skills will require more practice than those who are familiar with the skills.

STEP 3: Identify specific strategies for achieving goals

It is not sufficient to discuss and set goals with your athletes. You must help the athletes understand how to achieve a goal. When working with goals involving skills or fitness, you can develop a series of drills or workouts for athletes to do on their own. These drills and workouts may involve a parent or friend's assistance. Drills and workouts must be spelled out specifically. For example, you may ask an athlete to shoot 15–25 uncontested left-handed lay-ups (depending on athlete's age) every day at home and record the number made. Because this athlete is taking off on the wrong foot, you encourage him or her to have a friend or parent watch just the take-off to provide feedback to the athlete. For each *incorrect* attempt (not missed attempt) the athlete must repeat the lay-up. This strategy insures that the athlete is getting more practice using the correct technique. Once the athlete is consistently demonstrating the correct technique, you should focus the athlete's attention on making 8 of 15 or 20 of 25 attempts, whatever is reasonable and challenging. As coaches we *must* be more concerned with correct technique rather than outcome.

Common Problems with Goal Setting

The advantages of a goal setting program are obvious. However, many youth sport coaches are reluctant to work with their athletes in setting goals and evaluating goal attainment in a systematic way. Indeed, coaches have identified several problems associated with goal setting. The most common problems are listed in Table 4. These problems result from a lack of experience in using a goal setting program, not because goal setting is a bad coaching technique.

Goal setting requires time and commitment from the coach.

Goal Setting is Time Consuming

One of the first questions asked by volunteer coaches concerns the amount of time needed to work with athletes to identify, set, and evaluate goals. While there is a time commitment involved, goal setting is a skill that is used by most

1. Goal setting is time consuming.
2. Setting performance goals is too difficult.
3. Setting realistic goals.
4. Recognizing individual differences.
5. Overloading athlete with too many goals.
6. Coaches must evaluate goals and be committed to the program.

Table 4. Problems with a goal setting program.

successful athletes. Like any skill, learning it will require a certain amount of time. The benefits derived from setting goals and attaining them makes the time element more than worthwhile.

Setting Performance Goals is Too Difficult

There is no doubt that considerable experience is beneficial in setting performance goals. It is more difficult than looking at the schedule of games for the season and deciding which ones you can win and which ones you will most likely lose. In this technique, the number of wins, plus a couple more for those you perceive to be a toss-up, becomes your goal. However, as discussed earlier, there are few, if any, benefits to be gained from setting outcome goals. If you want your athletes to hit the ball better and field balls with fewer errors, athletes must focus their attention on these skills, not on winning or losing. This is particularly true for young athletes who are learning the skills as they are playing the game. A fear of failure can be developed in many potentially good athletes by discounting their improved performance when it did not result in a win. Successful athletes set performance goals and let winning and losing take care of itself.

Setting Realistic Goals

Many coaches and athletes argue that they do not set goals because it is too difficult to set realistic goals. This problem may result from a lack of sport experience by coaches. High school and college coaches have indicated that over the years they have found that when athletes perform at a certain level, the individual's chance of victory increases. Inexperienced coaches cannot be expected to know what level of goal is realistic. On the other hand, not knowing the appropriate level should not be an excuse for not trying to set goals which can be adjusted as coaches gain a greater understanding of what level of performance is needed at a given age. There is nothing wrong with trial-and-error as a technique to determine realistic goals.

Recognizing Individual Differences

For goals to be effective in motivating athletes, coaches must recognize that one goal or level of goal is not appropriate for every individual on the team. Most coaches have no difficulty picking out the fastest runners, the best passers or throwers, or the best hitters on their team. Often we set goals on the performance of these better performers, forgetting that their goals are too difficult for less skilled athletes. When the less skillful performers begin to lose confidence or are less enthusiastic about practicing, coaches become frustrated. Coaches must set goals relative to the athlete's level of ability if they are to be effective in increasing self-confidence or motivation.

Goal Overload

One of the most common errors made by coaches who employ a goal setting program is focusing the attention of athletes on all the goals set. For example, let's assume that you have set 20 goals for an athlete or team that encompass offensive and defensive skills, plus special situations. Before the game you go over the goals with the team, stressing the importance of these goals to the outcome of the game. This approach, common as it may be, results in each athlete trying to focus attention on 10–20 goals, depending on whether they play both offense and defense. It would not be possible even for adults to focus their attention on 10 goals during a game. To avoid "goal overload" in young athletes, limit their attention to 3 or 4 goals. These goals should coincide with the skills and strategies that were taught or worked on during practice. For example, if you had emphasized fielding during practice, you should stress those goals that relate to fielding during the game. This does not mean that you ignore all other goals. Rather, you select different goals to focus on for different games. Experienced coaches will evaluate the strengths and weaknesses of both their team and the opponent's team and select goals that will allow them to take advantage of their strengths and the opponent's weakness. The key for all coaches is to limit the number of goals to 3 or 4 per game. As athletes get older, the number can increase slightly, but should never exceed 7 or 8.

Coach Evaluation and Commitment

The last problem to be discussed is the key to the success of a goal setting program. Specifically, if coaches are not committed to spending the time and effort to conduct a goal setting program that follows the principles discussed in this chapter, then setting goals will not result in any significant changes in an athlete's performance. Because goal setting is a skill that must be learned, coaches and athletes must be willing to spend the time to learn to set goals and adjust them appropriately.

A major part of the success of a goal setting program is evaluation of the performance relative to the attainment of the goal. Coaches must evaluate athlete's performance, and provide feedback and rewards for attaining goals. If coaches do not provide the evaluation of an athlete's performance, these athletes are likely to evaluate their own performance in terms of winning and losing. Young athletes want to know what the coach thinks about their performance.

If you tell them in all honesty that you saw improvement in their skills, they will experience an increase in self-worth, self-confidence, and motivation to show you that they can perform even better.

Conclusion

Setting goals in sport is a critical skill that must be learned by athletes and coaches of young athletes. It is a skill that is used by most of today's successful athletes. To be effective, performance goals, not outcome goals (i.e., winning and losing) must be set. Coaches must provide feedback to young athletes so that their practice and effort will result in achieving their goal. The benefits to be derived from achieving a goal include increased self-worth, self-confidence, and motivation to continue practicing. In essence, athletes will have a reason to work hard. Goal setting is a powerful tool that produces confident, hard working athletes when used correctly. As youth sport coaches we must not lose sight of our goal, which is to teach sport skills to young athletes. Goal setting is one tool that can help all of your athletes, regardless of their ability level.

References

Gould, D. (1980). *Motivating young athletes.* East Lansing, MI: Institute for the Study of Youth Sports, Michigan State University.

Locke, E.A. and Latham, G.P. (1985). The application of goal setting to sports. *Journal of Sport Psychology, 7* (3), 205–222.

Locke, E.A., Shaw, K.N., Saari, L.M., & Latham, G.P. (1981). Goal setting and task performance: 1969–1980. *Psychological Bulletin, 90,* 125–152.

Martens, R., Christina, R., Harvey, J. Jr., & Sharkey, B. (1981). *Coaching young athletes.* Champaign, IL: Human Kinetics Publishers.

Author's note: I wish to express my thanks and appreciation to Dr. Deborah Feltz and Mr. Gary Williamson for their suggestions on an earlier draft of this chapter.

8

chapter eight

Motivating Young Athletes for Optimum Performance

Deborah L. Feltz
Michigan State University

Questions to consider . . .

- [ ] *Why do children participate in youth sports?*

- [ ] *Why do children drop out of youth sports?*

- [ ] *How can you make practices and games more enjoyable?*

- [ ] *How can you help your players keep winning in perspective?*

- [ ] *How can you prevent your players from becoming psyched-out?*

O ne of the benefits of youth sports is that they can help children develop a positive motivation toward achievement. As a coach, you play a significant role in developing a positive motivation of striving to achieve success and preventing a motivation based upon a fear of failure. Previous research has suggested that the motivation of young athletes will be positive and strong and they will persist in a sport if their needs are met by that sport. In order to help your athletes develop or maintain a positive motivation toward achievement in sport, you must understand why they participate and why some drop out.

Why do children participate in sports?

By interviewing more than 100,000 young athletes between the ages of 6 and 18 years in the state of Michigan, researchers at the Institute for the Study of Youth Sports found that young athletes most often participated in organized sports for the following reasons (State of Michigan, 1978):

- to have fun
- to improve their skills and learn new ones
- to be with friends or make new friends
- to succeed or win

To have fun. Young athletes receive great satisfaction from the challenge provided by youth sports, especially in testing their skills in practices and games. However, in order to have fun, they need to participate.

To improve their skills and learn new ones. Personal skill improvement is a universal objective of young athletes. Athletes want to be able to see their improvement in comparison to themselves and to others.

To be with friends or make new friends. Many young athletes view their sports participation as a chance to be with their friends while doing something they all enjoy. Friendship motives may be the most important reason for initial participation in youth sports for some athletes. However, these athletes usually develop their other achievement motives as their skills improve and they experience success.

To succeed or win. Young athletes like to win and they like to feel successful. It is important, however, to help them realize that they can still feel successful even though they may not win. It is also important to realize that striving to win is not the only objective of young athletes. In one study, more than 90% of the young athletes reported that they would rather play on a losing team than sit the bench on a winning team (Orlick & Botterill, 1975). Young athletes have multiple reasons for participating, and fun and skill improvement may be just as important to them as winning.

Figure 1. Children and adults may have different reasons for their sports participation.

Why do children drop out of sports?

Knowing why some children stop participating in a youth sport can help you find ways to encourage them to continue playing. In a survey of 1773 young athletes who had dropped out of different sports, researchers found that these children dropped out because they did not achieve the goals they set when they initially decided to play (State of Michigan, 1978). This is not surprising if you consider that their reasons for getting involved in sports represent goals that can only be achieved through participation. When these goals are not being met, drop out occurs. Some of the reasons most often cited for dropping out of sports are:

- became involved in other activities
- was no longer interested
- did not play enough
- did not like the coach
- skills were not improving

Because of other activities. Children are often very good at assessing their relative ability in various activities. They may 'shop around' and participate in several sports and other activities before deciding which one provides them the greatest chance of success. Dropping one sport to achieve in another sport or in other activities, such as music, dance, and scouting, is acceptable. When children tell you or their parents that they want to pursue other activities, they should be encouraged in their new pursuits, but welcomed to return to the sport at a later time if they wish.

Because they were no longer interested. For many children, participating in sports is a prestigious achievement. However, once they get involved, some may determine that it is not as glamorous as it first appeared. Although these children may have enjoyed their sport experience, they may decide that other interests are more important and/or enjoyable. Children with interests in other areas should not be forced by parents or pressured by coaches to continue their participation in sport or any other program. Doing so often transforms a normally well-behaved child into one who becomes a discipline problem.

Because they did not play enough. Children sign up for sports because they anticipate the enjoyment and skill development that will result from their involvement. Many young athletes who cite 'not playing enough' as a reason for dropping out were telling coaches that they needed more playing time in order to achieve their goal. These children are not asking to be starters or even to play the majority of the time. However, to be told indirectly that they aren't even good enough to get on the playing field during a game is devasting to a child's feelings of self-worth.

Young athletes need to see improvement in their skills.

Because their skills were not improving. Young athletes want to learn skills and see themselves improving in those skills. Coaches need to recognize that

Figure 2.   A competent coach keeps all of the children involved during practices and games.

each athlete is different in his or her skill level. Instruction should be designed to help each athlete on the team improve in performance abilities.

Because they did not like the coach. This reason for dropping out may be another way for athletes to tell coaches that they were not playing enough and their skills were not improving enough. Athletes who quit because they do not like the coach usually explain that the coach yells at them, the coach plays only his or her favorite players, and that the coach is unfair. To be effective, coaches must treat young athletes with the same respect that coaches expect from the athletes.

How can you help motivate your players?

Athletes are motivated most highly when they obtain what they seek from their participation in sport. Therefore, you should select motivational techniques that are based upon the reasons athletes have for joining the team, provided that their motives are healthy for the individual and the team. The following strategies may help you improve your players' motivation.

Know your athletes—why are they participating? Young athletes differ in their personalities, needs, and objectives for playing sports. You must, therefore, get to know your athletes as individuals in order to determine why they participate. One way to accomplish this is through a team meeting at the start of the season. Ask your players why they are participating and what their personal objectives are for the season. Continue these conversations before, during, and after practices and special events or whenever you have a chance to talk one-on-one with players.

Help athletes improve their skills and learn new skills. Skill improvement is one of the most important reasons for joining a sports team. Therefore, practice sessions should focus on skill development, with regular opportunities for players to measure their progress. In addition, you can help athletes set performance goals that are appropriate for them. For example, as young players are first learning to field a ball in baseball or softball, tell them that if they can stop or block a ball hit to them, they have been successful. As players improve, they should be encouraged to increase the number of times they can field the ball successfully. Chapter 1, "Goal Setting: Principles For the Coach and Athlete," provides additional information about this topic.

Practices and games should be enjoyable. As indicated by various studies, young athletes want to have fun. This means they want to play, not sit on the bench or stand in long lines waiting their turn at a drill. One of the best ways to ensure that practices are enjoyable is to use short, snappy drills that keep all the athletes involved as much as possible. You can also keep your players' interest by incorporating new drills. Your players may even be able to invent useful drills of their own. Chapter 12, "How to Conduct Effective Practices," contains additional information about this topic.

Having a chance to display their skills during a contest is an excellent motivator.

In games, too, all players can be involved even if they're sitting on the bench. Team members can be encouraged to watch the individuals who are playing similar positions in order to learn from their good techniques or their mistakes. They can also watch for strategies used by the other team. Most importantly, however, they should all have a chance to play in every game. The knowledge that they will have a chance to display their skills during the contest is a primary source of motivation prior to and after the experience. Players who sit on the bench, knowing they will be unable to test their skills in a game, are not having fun.

Allow players to be with their friends and to make new friends. Allowing your athletes to have fun with their friends does not mean that their socializing has to disrupt your practices. You can encourage opportunities for them to develop their friendships by initiating activities such as a mid-season pizza party which would take place outside of practice. This will require more time on your part, but you will also get to know your players better and may find these activities very rewarding.

Help players understand the meaning of success. Children learn at an early age to equate winning with success and losing with failure. If athletes win a game, they feel good or worthy. If they lose, they feel imcompetent or unworthy. This attitude toward winning can be very discouraging to players, unless they are always winning (an impossibility for at least 50% of the participants). One of your most important roles, therefore, is to help your players keep winning in perspective. One way to accomplish this is to help your players understand that winning a game is not always under their control. For example, after losing a game, you may tell your team, "We ran the offense well today, but their defense played very well, so we didn't get as many baskets as we expected."

Your players also need to know that, although striving to win is an important objective in sports, being successful in their sport also means making personal improvements and striving to do one's best. This attitude can be developed by:

- encouraging maximum effort during practice and games
- rewarding that effort
- helping your players set important but realistic goals that they can attain and thus feel successful

In helping your players understand the meaning of success, it is important not to punish them when they fail, particularly if they gave a maximum effort.

Your coaching approach is the most important factor that influences player motivation.

Use the positive approach to coaching. Probably the most important factor that influences your players' motivation is the approach you take in coaching. There are many different styles or approaches used by coaches, but most fall into two categories: the negative approach and the positive approach. The negative approach is one where the coach focuses on performance errors and uses fear, hate, and/or anger to motivate players. The positive approach, in contrast, is one where the coach focuses on the correct aspects of performance and has plenty of encouragement and praise for players when they perform correctly. The principles behind these approaches are discussed in greater depth in Chapter 14, "Principles of Effective Coach-Athlete Interaction."

The negative approach doesn't work very well with young athletes. Constant criticism, sarcasm, and yelling often frustrate young athletes, deteriorate their self-confidence, and decrease their motivation because they are just developing their skills and have fragile self-concepts. A positive, supportive approach is essential when coaching young athletes if high levels of motivation are to be maintained.

> ## The negative approach doesn't work very well with young athletes.

Help players set goals. Athletes need a way to compare their current and past performances to determine whether they are successful. This can be accomplished through goal setting. By using an individualized goal setting strategy, each athlete can regain control over his/her own success or failure, rather than depending upon game outcome. Players should be reminded when setting goals that there are some factors which can determine the outcome of a game that are out of a player's control. For example, the person your athlete is defending may be playing the best game of his or her career. Although your athlete is playing very well, there is just no stopping the opposing player. Or, due to injuries, a player is forced to play goalie even though he or she seldom practices in that position. These examples highlight the need for you to have your athletes establish personal improvement goals that are consistent with the objective of winning, but not entirely dependent on its achievement. Several guidelines for goal setting that can markedly help performance are described in Chapter 7.

What about psyching-up your players?

Some coaches believe the best way to motivate a team for competition is to get them "psyched-up" before the game. With young athletes, however, getting 'psyched-up' is not usually the problem; rather, the problem for them is getting 'psyched-out.'

> ## Young athletes worry most about performance failure.

Sources or causes of competitive stress. Young athletes have had little experience in practicing control over their emotional arousal and in dealing with the pressures that lead to competitive stress. Competitive stress in young athletes

Figure 3.   Young children need positive, supportive adults as coaches and officials.

can originate from many sources—the player, the teammates, the coach, and/or the parents. When young athletes are asked what might cause them to worry, the most frequent answers given are anxiety over improving their performance, participating in championship games, falling for a 'sucker move,' performing up to their level of ability, and what their coach would think or say (Feltz & Albrecht, 1986; Gould, Horn, & Spreemann, 1983). Thus, young athletes are most likely to be worried about performance failure. Young athletes also seem to worry about other uncertainties such as their personal worth to the coach, teammates, and parents. Many players worry about whether their coach, teammates, or parents will still like them if they lose or make a mistake. This worry about failure and personal worth may increase players' anxieties which, in turn, may cause poor performance and eventually decrease motivation.

Preventing competitive stress. A good way to help your players avoid the effects of competitive stress is to reduce their fear of failure. This can be achieved by encouraging them to enjoy the game and to do their best. When your players lose or make a mistake, don't express displeasure; rather, correct their mistakes in a positive way by using the following steps:

1. Start with a compliment. Find some aspect of the performance that was correct.
2. Then tell the player what was wrong and how to correct it.
3. End with another positive statement such as "Keep working at it. You'll get it."

This approach allows players to keep practicing their skills without the fear of making a mistake. The following guidelines may be helpful in preventing competitive stress:

- Don't set unrealistic goals.
- Use the positive approach when correcting mistakes.
- Eliminate the type of 'pep talks' that communicate overemphasis on the game and the outcome.

Summary

Children play sports because they want to improve their skills, have fun, be with friends, and be successful. Children who drop out of sports typically do so because one or more of their goals were not met. You can maximize your players' desire to participate, and help prevent them from dropping out, by getting to know them as individuals. Learn why they are participating; focus on skill development in practice sessions, and make sure the practices are enjoyable. Allow time for friendships to develop by creating a cordial environment both on and off the playing field. Help players understand the meaning of success and have them set realistic goals.

Figure 4. Adults should reduce, not contribute to, the competitive stress of young athletes.

Using a positive approach to coaching is the most effective way to improve players' performance. Positive coaching will also make playing and coaching more enjoyable.

Having realistic expectations of players' performance will provide more opportunities to give rewards. However, where players make mistakes, use the positive approach to correcting errors. The positive approach involves issuing a compliment, correcting the error, and then finishing with another positive statement. Using a positive approach and helping players reach their goals are effective ways to motivate your players toward maximum performance.

References

Feltz, D.L. & Albrecht, R.R. (1986). Psychological implications of competitive running. In M.R. Weiss & D. Gould (Eds.), *Sport for children and youths* (pp. 225-230). Champaign, IL: Human Kinetics.

Gould, D., Horn, T., & Spreemann, J. (1983). Sources of stress in junior elite wrestlers. *Journal of Sport Psychology, 5,* 159-171.

Orlick, T., & Botterill, C. (1975). *Every kid can win.* Chicago: Nelson-Hall.

State of Michigan. (1978). *Joint legislative study on youth sports programs: Phase II, agency sponsored sports.* East Lansing, MI: Author.

Suggested Readings

Gould, D. (1980). *Motivating young athletes.* E. Lansing, MI: Institute for the Study of Youth Sports.

Orlick, T. (1980). *In pursuit of excellence.* Ottawa, Ontario: Coaching Association of Canada.

Smoll, F.L., & Smith, R.E. (1979). *Improving relationship skills in youth sport coaches.* East Lansing, MI: Institute for the Study of Youth Sports.

Singer, R.N. (1984). *Sustaining motivation in sport.* Tallahassee, FL: Sport Consultants International, Inc.

chapter nine

Teaching Sportsmanship and Values

Maureen R. Weiss
University of Oregon

Questions to Consider . . .

☐ *Can sport build character?*

☐ *What is sportsmanship, anyway?*

☐ *How is sportsmanship developed?*

☐ *What are the levels of moral reasoning?*

☐ *How can coaches teach sportsmanship to their athletes?*

O ne of the major arguments that coaches and parents use to emphasize the importance of sport participation in the lives of children is that "sport builds character." The basis for this statement is that the sport setting offers unique teaching situations in which children can learn to distinguish between 'right' and 'wrong' behaviors. Advocates of sport have claimed that among the lessons learned in gymnasiums and on fields all over the world are desirable behaviors toward teammates, opponents, officials, and coaches, fair and honest play, and equal opportunity for all to play and enjoy sport.

Despite the claim that sport builds character, opponents of youth sport are quick to suggest that, instead, sport builds 'characters.' Unfortunately, reports in newspapers and on television frequently point out that in many instances participation in sport has done more to teach children inappropriate behaviors and attitudes than to develop desirable habits.

The question of whether sport does build character or characters may, however, be a moot point. The important issue is that sport *can* build character when conducted by informed and sensitive coaches who understand how moral growth is developed and how they can facilitate this process. Developing sportsmanship is not an automatic process, however. Coaches must take the opportunity to turn sport dilemmas into teachable moments if moral development is to occur. Youth sport represents a unique setting for the teaching of values because sport situations present opportunities to experience a number of moral dilemmas. The values learned in sport can, in turn, generalize to situations that occur in everyday life.

Developing sportsmanlike behaviors and attitudes is not an automatic consequence of participating in sport.

This chapter provides information on how sportsmanship or moral development is fostered and how, as a coach, you can contribute to this development as you plan practices and facilitate team discussions. An understanding of this process will increase the probability that you will build character in your athletes and not 'characters.'

What is Sportsmanship, Anyway?

A basic understanding of what constitutes sportsmanlike attitudes and behaviors is necessary because sportsmanship can be defined in many different ways. For example, some coaches emphasize the "golden rule," while others might encourage specific behaviors such as shaking hands after a competition or not questioning an official's decision. These various definitions often confuse children as they encounter different moral dilemmas in sport.

When Martens (1978) asked children to define sportsmanship, they responded with the following descriptions:

- playing by the rules
- being even-tempered
- respecting the decisions and requests of coaches and officials
- taking turns
- letting others play

While most would agree that these are sportsmanlike behaviors, one also recognizes that the items on this list conform to social norms or conventions that are necessary to maintain the "spirit of the game" and to ensure the orderly occurrence of game events. Other such conventional behaviors might include shaking an opponent's hand before or after a match, helping an opponent up from a position on the ground, and avoiding unnecessary roughness.

The definition of sportsmanship and the promotion of moral growth, however, goes beyond the identification of conventional game behaviors. It must also include the reasoning behind the decisions that were made about whether actions are right or wrong. That is, proper development of sportsmanship must include both the display of appropriate sport attitudes and behaviors and the *rationales* children use to judge the rightness or wrongness of such behaviors. For example, children may "act" in a desirable manner but their thoughts about *why* they should or should not act in a particular way are just as important as the observable behaviors.

There are many reasons why children decide to act or not act in a particular way. These reasons behind the judgments of the rightness or wrongness of a behavior indicate the child's level of moral development or sportsmanship. As an example, John, Sally, and George are three young athletes who all said that "In the game of basketball it is not right to foul a person from behind on a breakaway layin." All three children, however, expressed different reasons *why* such a behavior is not desirable:

John: "If you make that kind of foul, you will probably *get thrown out of the game* by the referee."

Sally: "It's *against the rules* to foul like that. Besides, I wouldn't want someone to do that to me."

George: "It's not *fair* to treat people in that way—they might get hurt."

The definition of sportsmanship must include the reasoning behind decisions of what is correct and incorrect behavior, and not only the observable expression of desirable behavior.

John based his decision on what the consequences of the action would be while Sally argued that breaking the rules of the game is wrong. George's decision was based on considering the rights and responsibilities of all the individuals involved. Thus, the moral level of young athletes cannot be safely determined by the observable expression of what is considered 'sportsmanlike behaviors.' It is also necessary to ensure that young athletes make decisions based on the most mature reasoning processes of which they are capable. This requires the use of certain instructional techniques, as well as providing opportunities to fully discuss the moral dilemmas which are directly or indirectly experienced in sport.

How are Sportsmanlike Behaviors and Attitudes Developed?

Sportsmanship must be learned; it is not an automatic result of having to make judgments on how to act in certain sport situations or dilemmas. Taking into consideration the two major schools of thought on how sportsmanship can be developed, several general ways of promoting moral growth can be offered. The "social learning approach" focuses on the ability of young athletes to adhere to social conventions and norms that are considered acceptable in the sport setting. Learning these behaviors is the result of:

- having appropriate models who display sportsmanlike behaviors
- being rewarded for desirable sport behaviors such as shaking hands or refraining from a verbal argument with an official
- being penalized for undesirable sport behaviors such as illegal actions (cheap shots) and uncooperative attitudes toward teammates

Sportsmanlike behaviors can be learned through positive role modeling and consistent, clear reinforcement for desirable and undesirable actions.

The other school of thought on how sportsmanship is developed is called the "structural developmental approach" (Haan, Aerts & Cooper, 1985; Kohlberg, 1984). This approach focuses on the organization and structure of individuals' thoughts as they attempt to explain the rightness or wrongness of a given action. Sportsmanship thus refers to the tendency to behave in accordance with one's most mature moral reasoning patterns, which changes as children grow and develop. According to Haan et al., sportsmanship is learned and enhanced by:

- being involved in sport moral dilemmas and having opportunities to resolve the conflicts which arise
- discussing the experience with all involved parties
- coming to a mutual agreement about the resolution of the dilemma (called moral balances)

Sportsmanship also means the development of mature moral reasoning patterns, which are fostered through experiencing moral dilemmas, discussing these dilemmas, and creating moral balances.

From the "structural developmental" perspective, reasoning and behaviors are linked in such a way that the young athlete's ability to decide or judge whether actions are right or wrong is based on considering the physical or psychological consequences of particular actions. Thus, consolidating the best of both approaches, it is clear that the following conditions are critical for the development of sportsmanship:

- appropriate modeling behaviors by the coach
- reinforcement (rewards and penalties) for players' desirable and undesirable behaviors
- instructional techniques that provide opportunities for moral dilemmas to arise
- opportunities for discussions about how moral dilemmas might be resolved
- opportunities for negotiating and reaching consensus about what actions are to occur if the dilemma is to be resolved

What Levels of Moral Reasoning Do Individuals Express?

According to "structural developmental" approaches, morality or sportsmanship is determined by the reasoning principles used in making moral judgments and guiding behaviors. Thus, in a previous section, we saw that the same behavior (not fouling an opponent on a breakaway layin) was explained by different ways of thinking about the action. As children grow and develop, the process by which they organize information changes and the reasoning behind their moral behaviors has the potential to mature. An understanding of the levels of moral reasoning through which children progress is critical for recognizing how and when to enhance sportsmanship.

As children grow and develop, their ability to reason about moral action matures.

According to Haan (1977), individuals can develop through five levels of morality. The first two levels are characterized by *self-interest*. The first level of morality involves the use of power over others, complying with others when forced to do so, and compelling others when possible. At this level, an action is judged as right or wrong depending on the outcome of the action. In judging whether sliding into second base with spikes up is sportsmanlike, a person at this level might say, "It's fair because I didn't get caught."

At the second level of moral reasoning, an "eye for an eye" view is adopted in which one seeks an advantage with the recognition of the necessity of trade-offs or compromises. A child at this level would say, "It's fair because she ran over me at first base earlier in the game."

Self-interest is the guiding principle for the first two levels of moral reasoning.

In contrast to the self-centered focus of the first two levels, the third level of moral reasoning is characterized by an *altruistic viewpoint*, seeking to make harmonious exchanges for the good of others. The reasoning at this level might be: "I'm a good person who does not try to hurt my opponent and I would expect to receive the same treatment from others."

The third level of moral reasoning is characterized by treating others as we would like to be treated.

A person at the fourth level of moral reasoning uses objective and *impartial external rules* as a basis of moral judgment. This focus on the "common interest" of all involved parties results from experiences of bad faith in trusting the altruistic notions of all people. Following rules and regulations protects one from needing to trust in another person's good intentions. The reasoning at this level might be: "Win or lose, you play by the rules. The rules say "no sliding with spikes up" so you must play by these rules.

The fourth level of moral reasoning is characterized by adherence to external rules and regulations.

Finally, level five of moral reasoning is based on the *mutual interest* and well-being of all concerned parties. Individuals at this level seek mutual agreements or moral balances within specific situations, which attempt to optimize the interests of all. An example would be, "It's not right or fair to slide with spikes up . . . it violates the rights of individuals in sport to be protected from physical (or psychological) harm."

The most mature level of moral reasoning is guided by considering the mutual interest of all concerned individuals.

These five levels describe the developmental nature of moral growth, from interactions that are self-centered through those which involve a mutual interest. The structural-developmental view, which emphasizes the maturation of thought processes and the feelings that come into play as individuals engage in moral exchanges, complements the social learning approach and enhances the opportunities and strategies for coaches to influence the sportsmanship of young athletes.

So, what is the importance of knowing these levels of moral reasoning? An understanding of these levels is important in your goal of enhancing the level of *reasoning* about moral dilemmas in sport rather than just being concerned about the behaviors exhibited by athletes.

How To Teach For Sportsmanship

Although the social learning approach has been the traditional prescription used by most coaches to develop sportsmanship, recent evidence strongly suggests that a structural developmental approach can also enhance moral growth in

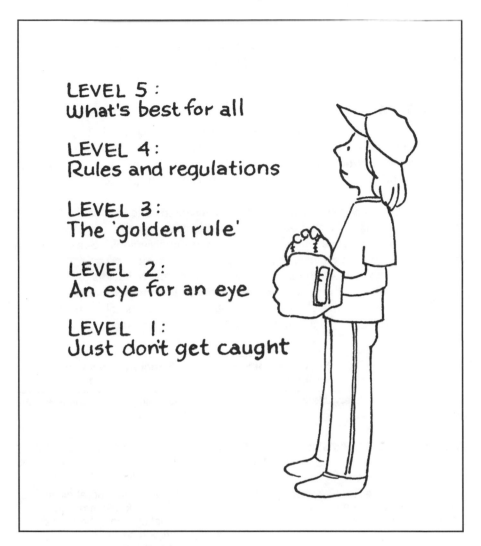

Figure 1.   An understanding of the levels of moral reasoning through which children progress is critical for recognizing how and when to enhance sportsmanship.

sports (Bredemeier, Weiss, Shields & Shewchuk, 1986; Romance, Weiss & Bockoven, 1986). The prescription for coaching techniques targeted at developing sportsmanship is to employ the "best of both worlds" in terms of the two approaches. The purpose of this section is to provide you with these specific strategies. Remember that employing such techniques will not interfere with, but rather, enhance your primary coaching role: the development of physical skills.

Table 1 provides a summary of the two approaches to developing sportsmanship, including primary focus, definition of sportsmanship, means by which sportsmanship is developed, and coaching prescriptions.

Preseason Planning

Teaching sportsmanship requires that you plan how you will do it, just as you would plan for the teaching of various sport skills, strategies, and rules. The key here, however, is how to incorporate sportsmanship content into your team meetings and practice sessions without distracting from physical skill development.

1. Develop a written sportsmanship code. A written code (see Table 2) should identify specifically what behaviors are considered acceptable for your team in practice and competitive settings, and which are unacceptable. Seek to obtain consensus from your athletes in adopting a code of ethics.

2. Prepare alternative rationales for identifying certain behaviors as acceptable or unacceptable. For the various behaviors identified in the sportsmanship code, provide reasons for what is "right" on the basis of self-interest, altruism, objective and impartial rules, and agreements based on the mutual interests of all involved

	Social Learning Approach	**Structural Developmental Approach**
Focus of developing sportsmanship	Observable behaviors	Reasoning behind observed behaviors
Definition of sportsmanship	Actions which conform to social norms (e.g., shaking hands, not swearing)	Actions based on the most mature moral reasoning level of an individual
How sportsmanship is developed	• Reinforcement (rewards and penalties) • Modeling	• Experiencing moral dilemmas • Discussing dilemmas • Creating "moral balances" through consensual agreement
Specific coaching strategies	• Written sportsmanship code— specific behaviors identified as desirable or undesirable • Rewarding demonstrated appropriate behavior • Punishing unacceptable behaviors • Evaluation of self as a proper role model	• Built-in sport dilemmas during practice • Team discussions about actual dilemmas experienced in sport • Encouraging negotiations and agreement about subsequent consequences or actions • Inductive discipline (provide rationales)

Table 1. Two approaches in developing sportsmanship.

Areas of Concern	Sportsmanlike Behaviors	Unsportsmanlike Behaviors
Behavior toward officials	• when questioning officials, do so in the appropriate manner (e.g., lodge an official protest, have only designated individuals, such as a captain, address officials)	• arguing with officials • swearing at officials
Behavior toward opponents	• treat all opponents with respect and dignity at all times	• arguing with opponents • making sarcastic remarks about opponents • making aggressive actions toward opponents
Behavior toward teammates	• give only constructive criticism and positive encouragement	• making negative comments or sarcastic remarks • swearing or arguing with teammates
Behavior toward spectators	• make only positive comments to spectators	• arguing with spectators • making negative remarks/swearing at spectators
Rule acceptance and infractions	• obey all league rules	• taking advantage of loopholes in rules (e.g., every child must play, so coach tells unskilled players to be sick on day of important game)

Table 2.   Youth sports sportsmanship code. From Gould (1981).

parties. The list of behaviors and alternative reasons listed could become the target of early team discussions of rules and regulations.

3. Prepare scripts of sportsmanship dilemmas to be used in team discussions. There are many "gray" areas of right and wrong behaviors in various sport situations. An attempt to enhance moral growth can be made by writing out possible scripts and plausible responses to each situation. Then athletes should be engaged in discussion and negotiation of these scripts and encouraged to come up with the most feasible solutions. Parsons (1984) provided examples of ten situations and possible solutions. One example is: "In a regional tournament in high school baseball, the center fielder rushes in to catch a sinking line drive. He traps it between the ground and his glove in what appears to be a spectacular catch. The center fielder is unsure if the umpire saw the play." Possible responses include:

- the player should immediately confess he trapped the ball
- the player should wait for the umpire's decision and abide by it
- if the umpire rules "no catch," the player should disagree on the grounds the umpire could not see the play

- if the umpire asks whether he trapped the ball, the player should say he did (did not) (did not know)

While this strategy is consistent with a structural developmental view, being involved in *actual* dilemmas, as opposed to hypothetical dilemmas, is more conducive to the development of more mature levels of moral reasoning and sportsmanlike behaviors. Thus, the following suggestions for implementation *during practice* are given.

Planning Practices

1. Build moral dilemmas into your practices. Typically, coaches have planned practice to minimize the occurrence of moral dilemmas by selecting fair teams and distributing equipment equally. However, unless young athletes are exposed to opportunities for experiencing dilemmas and discussing them, sportsmanship and moral development are not likely to occur. Some possible dilemmas might include:

- not putting out enough equipment or enough of the 'best' equipment for all athletes
- devising a drill in which there are unequal opportunities for practice, for example, one person is always on offense
- devising a drill so that players might be tempted to "hurt with words" (laughing, yelling), such as having to demonstrate weak skills, having unfair relay teams
- devising a drill that provides possible opportunities for "rough play," for example, "hamburger rebound drill" in which two individuals block out one person simultaneously and go for the ball

After these dilemmas are presented, follow up with opportunities for discussing them.

2. Provide opportunities to discuss moral dilemmas and to create moral balances. The moral dilemmas described above cannot exist on their own. After experiencing unfair play or verbal aggressiveness, for example, players should be brought together (all parties involved, which could be two persons or the whole team) and encouraged to discuss the dilemma in relation to individual needs and interests. For example, in his program of moral development in a physical education class, Romance (1984) implemented a game dilemma in the form of a "score ten" basketball shooting game. Students, in pairs, were asked to make the baskets as a two-person team. The first team to make ten baskets was the winner. After the activity, adequate time for dialogue was allowed, in which discussion focused on how each team decided what was fair in who attempted how many shots.

The creation of moral balances or reaching consensus based on mutual interests and needs is the essential conclusion to experiencing and discussing dilemmas. As players interact about their thoughts and feelings about rights and responsibilities implied within the dilemmas, they should be encouraged to come to an agreement on subsequent action to be taken.

3. *Allow your athletes to design their own drills or activities.* When athletes are involved in the design of their experiences, it offers excellent opportunities for them to experience dilemmas, take the role of others, engage in dialogue and negotiations, and ultimately, to reach a group consensus. A specific example offered by Romance (1984) is the game of "pickle in the middle" (basketball passing). Students (in threes) were instructed to play the game, given the following parameters: "try to pass the basketball back and forth between two players while a third player (in the middle) tries to touch it. Passers must stand on the red lines and if the middle person touches a pass, that person changes places with the passer. If, during the drill, your group feels that the game would be improved by adding to or changing the rules, then do so immediately." Post-game discussions centered on rule changes which the groups made and how these changes related to individual needs and interests.

4. *Reward individuals who display desirable behaviors.* Following a social learning prescription, individuals should be rewarded for behaviors demonstrated which conform to the sportsmanship code. Be specific with the positive reinforcement—"Way to give Greg a chance to play that position, Joe;"—and try to refrain from tangible rewards such as candy or money. Instead, verbal or non-verbal ("High five," thumbs up) praise or tallies on a sportsmanship progress chart are more effective indicators of approval and feedback. An "unsung hero" or "sportsperson of the week" award is also a powerful means of rewarding moral behaviors.

5. *Use inductive discipline to penalize individuals who display undesirable behaviors.* The process for distributing penalties will need to be thought out in terms of warnings and kinds of consequences. Regardless of the number of warnings or number of minutes deprived from playing, however, make sure that the player who committed the infraction not only knows what behavior he or she violated but *why* it was an unacceptable behavior. This is what inductive discipline is: providing the underlying rationale for punishment. The reasoning given for why the behavior was inappropriate should be at a level just above the child's curent level of moral reasoning, if possible. Another strategy to deal with discipline, which is grounded in moral development, is to have two players who have engaged in verbal or physical aggression go off to a designated area to work out a solution after hearing each others's feelings about the moral conflict.

6. *Display sportsmanlike behaviors as a role model to your players.* Because your players will generally believe what they see over what they hear, it is imperative to practice what you preach. If respect for one another's teammates is encouraged, you, too, must treat players with respect. If respect and compliance to officials' decisions are encouraged, either you must serve as a model for these behaviors or define conditions under which "discussing" a play with the official is acceptable. Because coaches are often unaware of their own behaviors dem-

onstrated during practices and games, it may be a good idea to have a trusted friend observe you every so often with a copy of the sportsmanship code in hand. After practice, discussion can focus on which behaviors were violated and why, and solutions for emitting alternative responses to similar dilemmas of sport morality.

Summary

The kinds of situations that emerge in sport settings offer unique opportunities for enhancing moral growth. This is because coach-athlete interactions are required for interpreting dilemmas which occur on a daily basis. The development of sportsmanlike attitudes and behaviors, however, is not automatic but must be carefully planned and carried out by the coach. By using a combination of

Figure 2.   Display sportsmanlike behaviors as a role model to your players.

instructional strategies based on both social learning and structural developmental theories, coaches can maximize the development of more mature levels of moral reasoning among their athletes, as well as their sportsmanlike behaviors.

The question of whether sport "can" build character was positively demonstrated through examples in this chapter. Coaches can teach sportsmanship and values through their programs by reinforcing desirable behaviors, displaying appropriate role modeling behavior, building sport moral dilemmas into their practices, encouraging dialogue and negotiation about dilemmas, and facilitating discussions toward the creation of moral balances. Further, these strategies can be incorporated within the context of normal physical skill development, thus achieving the psychomotor, cognitive, and affective goals that are claimed to be available through sport participation.

References

Bredemeier, B.J., Weiss, M.R., Shields, D.L. & Shewchuk, R.M. (1986). Promoting moral growth in a summer sport camp: The implementation of theoretically grounded instructional strategies. *Journal of Moral Education, 15*(3), 212-220.

Gould, D. (1981). Sportsmanship: Building character or characters? In Youth Sports Institute (Ed.), *A winning philosophy for youth sports programs.* East Lansing, MI: Institute for the Study of Youth Sports.

Haan, N., Aerts, E. & Cooper, B. (1985) *On moral grounds.* New York: New York University Press.

Kohlberg, L. (1984). *Essays of moral development: Vol 2. The psychology of moral development.* San Francisco: Harper & Row.

Martens, R. (1978). *Joy and sadness in children's sports.* Champaign, IL: Human Kinetics.

Parsons, T.W. (1984, July/August). Gamesmanship and sport ethics. *Coaching Review, 71,* 28-30.

Romance, T.J. (1984). *A program to promote moral development through elementary school physical education.* Unpublished doctoral dissertation, University of Oregon.

Romance, T.J., Weiss, M.R. & Bockoven, J. (1986). A program to promote moral development through elementary school physical education. *Journal of Teaching in Physical Education, 5*(3), 126-136.

Suggested Readings

Bredemeier, B.J. & Shields, D.L. (1985). Values and violence in sports. *Psychology Today, 19*(10), 22-32.

Gould, D. (1984). Psychosocial development and children's sport. In J.R. Thomas (Ed.), *Motor development during childhood and adolescence.* Minneapolis, MN: Burgess.

Romance, T.J., Weiss, M.R. & Bockoven, J. (1986). A program to promote moral development through elementary school physical education. *Journal of Teaching in Physical Education, 5*(3), 126-136.

Weiss, M.R. & Bredemeier, B.J. (1986). Moral development. In V. Seefeldt (Ed.), *Physical activity and well-being* (pp. 373-390). Reston, VA: AAHPERD.

chapter ten

Observing and Analyzing Sport Skills

Eugene W. Brown
Michigan State University

Questions to consider . . .

☐ *What approach should you use to teach sport skills to young athletes?*

☐ *What knowledge and ability must you have in order to teach sport skills?*

☐ *What are **product** and **process** evaluation of sport skills? How can they be used in coaching?*

☐ *What are the five categories of visual evaluation techniques?*

☐ *Why is it important for a coach to develop an evaluation scheme?*

O ne of your many responsibilities as a youth sport coach is to teach sport skills. In fact, many parents and young athletes perceive this to be your primary responsibility. Therefore, your success as a coach, at least in part, depends upon your ability to teach sport skills.

A simplified model of the interaction between the coach and athlete in teaching and learning sport skills is presented in Figure 1. This process begins by determining the abilities of your athletes through an evaluation of their performances of sport skills. Strategies for improving their performance can then be formulated and put into practice through appropriate teaching and coaching methods. This cycle of events is repeated several times throughout a season with the goal of improving the skill level of the young athletes.

The scheme presented in Figure 1 requires that you have the following prerequisite knowledge and ability:

1) knowledge about how the sport skills are correctly performed;
2) understanding of the level of mental and physical development of the young athletes;
3) ability to employ appropriate teaching and coaching methods; and
4) ability to correctly evaluate performance of sport skills.

Basically, you must know the sport skills before attempting to coach young athletes. If you do not know how the skills of the sport should be performed, you can obtain this information from sport skill books, video tapes, and coaching clinics. An understanding of the level of mental and physical development of young athletes, as well as insights into the methods of good teaching and coaching, can be obtained from reading other chapters of this handbook.

COACH'S ACTIVITY	ATHLETE'S ACTIVITY
Evaluate performance (qualitative and/ or quantitative)	Perform sport skills
Formulate teaching strategy	
Teach sport skills (instruction and/or demonstration)	Listen and observe
Evaluate performance	Perform sport skills
Continue	

Figure 1.   Interaction between coach and athlete in teaching and learning sport skills.

The ability to evaluate the performance of sport skills is essential for coaching.

The purpose of this chapter is to assist you in developing an approach to evaluate the sport skills of your athletes. From Figure 1, it is evident that evaluation of sports skills is an integral part of coaching.

There are two general approaches which you can use to evaluate the sport skills of your athletes. The first and easiest involves a *product* (results) evaluation. Product measurement focuses on the results of performance. For example, a coach who wants to determine the sprinting ability of a group of athletes can measure their time to complete a 30 yard dash. The basketball skill of foul shooting can be measured by determining a percentage of shots made in a given number of attempts. Scores obtained from the place where a ball strikes a target is an example of product measurement for the skill of pitching a baseball. In most sports, the products (results) of performance can be measured in order to assess the ability level of individual athletes on the skills of the sport. However, setting up tests and measuring the performance levels of each athlete on each of the skills in the sport is usually too time consuming and provides no understanding of how the athletes actually performed the skills.

Measuring the outcome of a sport skill does not provide you with an understanding of how the skill was performed.

The second method of assessing the ability of your athletes to perform sport skills is *process* (form) evaluation. Process evaluation focuses on the quality of movement and must be applied during the performance of sport skills. This is difficult, especially when a sport skill occurs very rapidly or when several body parts move simultaneously in different directions. Instead of taking time to set up individual tests to measure the results of sport skills, process evaluation takes place while the athletes are involved in drills and scrimmages. It does not necessarily require you to set aside a certain amount of practice time to conduct this type of evaluation. However, it does require you to know what constitutes "good form" in each of the sport skills and how these skills should be observed.

In order to evaluate the performance of sport skills, you must know what to look for and how to look for it.

Figure 2. The ability to evaluate the performance of sport skills is essential for coaching.

Visual Evaluation Techniques

Specific techniques for observing sport skills will facilitate your use of process evaluation. These techniques can be applied to all sport skills. The techniques are grouped into five categories:

1) vantage point;
2) movement simplification;

3) balance and stability;

4) movement relationships; and

5) range of movement.

The techniques in each of these categories are accompanied by an explanation and at least one applied example. These explanations are stated in general terms. However, each example is applied to a specific sport skill. Through experience, you will be able to make additional applications of the visual evaluation techniques to the sport skills which you are teaching. Additional application of the techniques will help you develop a keener ability to evaluate skills, as well as develop a greater insight and understanding of the form that is required to perform sport skills correctly.

If young athletes practice sport skills with improper form, it may be a limiting factor in their future performance.

Vantage Point

Whenever the form of performance of sport skills is being evaluated, the vantage point of observation should always be carefully considered. The position of both the performer and observer determines what can and cannot be seen. If vantage point techniques are not applied, other visual evaluation techniques may be useless. The following techniques should always be used.

1. *Technique:* **Select the proper observational distance.**

   Explanation: When observing total body movements, the vantage point should be at a distance where the entire sequence of movement can be seen. When looking at smaller components of body movement, observation should take place closer to the performer.

   Example: The body movements in the entire tennis serve should be observed from relatively far away from the performer, as compared to an evaluation of the foot work during the serve.

2. *Technique:* **Observe the performance from different angles.**

   Explanation: This is especially important when all body parts are not easily seen because their view is obstructed by equipment, clothing, or other body parts.

   Example: During a wrestling take down, the body parts of one wrestler may obstruct the coach's view of the other wrestler.

3. *Technique:* **Observe the performance from a carefully selected angle.**

   Explanation: This technique is important when observing the performance of any physical skill. However, it is extremely important when form evaluation is made of activities which are not readily repeated. An activity which requires

Footwork in tennis serve

Form of tennis serve

Figure 3.   The vantage point of observation should be at a distance where the entire sequence of movement can be seen.

the athlete to expend a great amount of strength and energy is one example. The occurrence of a rare event during competition is another example. In both of these situations, select the most appropriate vantage point because a second observation within a short period of time may not be possible.

Example. The movement patterns of a soccer goalkeeper about to receive a penalty kick during a game should be viewed, if possible, from a pre-determined vantage point.

4. *Technique:* **Observe activities in a setting which is not distractive.**

Explanation: Noise and/or visual distractions can interfere with skill evaluation. Excessive noise may prevent the hearing of a sound pattern of movement. Other performers and objects close to the performer may visually interfere with skill evaluation.

Example: The back handspring in gymnastics has a distinct sound pattern

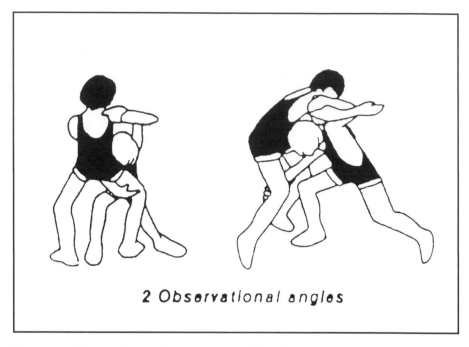

Figure 4. Observe the performance from different angles.

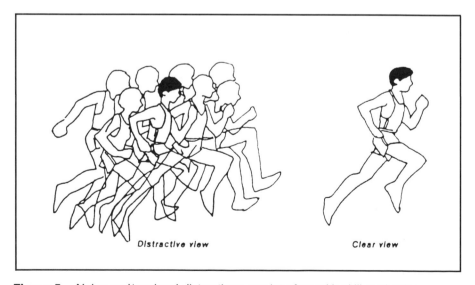

Figure 5. Noise and/or visual distractions can interfere with skill evaluation.

which is caused by the placement of the hands, then feet, on the mat. This "flip-flop" sound pattern provides important information about the timing of the performance.

5. *Technique:* **Observe the performance in a setting with a vertical and/or horizontal reference line.**

Explanation: If the orientation (slope or lean) of body parts or implements is important to a successful performance, the skill should be performed in an uncluttered area in which an object in view with the performer provides a vertical or horizontal reference. The line of the object will assist the observer in determining the orientation of the body parts and/or implement.

Example: The angle of swing of the bat by a softball player can be more easily evaluated if performed in a backstop where the poles provide vertical and horizontal reference lines.

6. *Technique:* **Observe a skilled reference model.**

Explanation: When experiencing difficulty in analyzing the performance of an athlete, the observation of a skilled performer may help. This technique should be used cautiously because of possible size, strength, and maturational differences between the two performers.

Example: The starting position in the blocks of one track sprinter could be compared to that of a more skilled sprinter in the same race.

Always consider your observational vantage point and the setting for performance when attempting to evaluate sport skills.

Movement Simplification

In addition to applying vantage point techniques when attempting to more fully understand the form of performance, the initial observations should simplify the movement. An understanding of the simplified form of performance will be helpful in subsequent observations of skill components which are more difficult to observe.

During initial observations of a sport skill, you should attempt to understand a simplified form of performance.

7. *Technique:* **Observe slower moving body parts.**

Explanation: In certain activities, it is difficult to see extremities or striking implements that move very fast. Therefore, look first at the slower moving body parts (usually the hip area) to gain some initial understanding of the movement. There is often an increase in the speed of movement from the center of the body out to the extremities. This principle is very similar to the action of a whip in which the handle moves the slowest and the end of the whip the fastest. It should be noted, however, that in some skills the extremities may move slowly.

Example: The coach should initially look at the position and motion of the hips in a gymnast attempting a cartwheel before evaluating the position and motion of the arms and legs.

Example: The planted non-kicking foot in the soccer instep kick can provide insight into the direction and distance of the kick.

8. *Technique:* **Observe separate components of a complicated skill.**

   Explanation: When looking at complex physical skills, it is often appropriate to break down the entire skill into phases (or components) of movement. Most activities are easily divided into three phases: *preparatory phase* (action or positioning of body parts prior to the execution of the skill), *movement phase* (the execution of the skill), and *follow-through* (the continuation of the motion

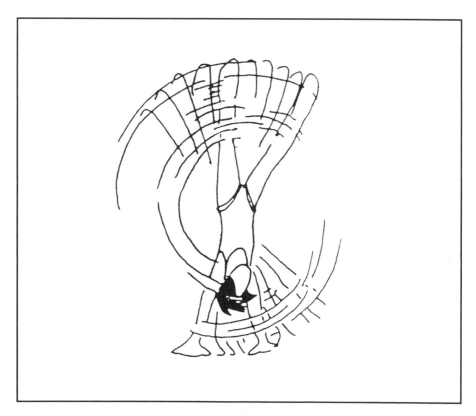

Figure 6. In certain activities, it is difficult to see extremities that move very fast.

of the body and body parts). Some complicated skills may be even further subdivided. Once the component parts of a skill have been determined, you should concentrate on only one part of the entire performance at a time. When the performance of one component is fully understood, subsequent parts should be analyzed. Dividing the activity into component parts can simplify the analysis of complex movement patterns.

Example: A basketball lay-up could be divided into the approach and take off (preparatory phase), the shot (activity phase), and continuation of the in-flight phase of the jump to regain a position for landing, followed by a successful landing (follow-through).

9. *Technique:* **Observe the timing of performance components.**

   Explanation: Separate component parts of a skill may be performed correctly without the successful execution of a skill. This may be due to the inability of the performer to properly time the execution of the component parts.

   Example: A baseball batter who pauses between the stride toward the ball and the movement of the bat backward in preparation for the swing is not timing the body movement correctly.

> *Understanding the simplified form of performance is a basis for subsequent evaluation of the specific elements of a sport skill.*

Balance and Stability

The following two visual evaluation techniques should be considered when balance and stability are important components of a skill. They should also be considered in activities which precede either from a balanced position to motion or from motion to balance.

> *Balance and stability are specific elements which are important to the performance of many sport skills.*

10. *Technique:* **Look at the supporting parts of the body.**

    Explanation: The supporting parts of the body are called the base of support. For example, in standing, the base of support is provided by the feet. By increasing the area between the supporting body parts, the stability is increased. Conversely, decreasing the area of the base of support decreases stability and allows the body to become more mobile.

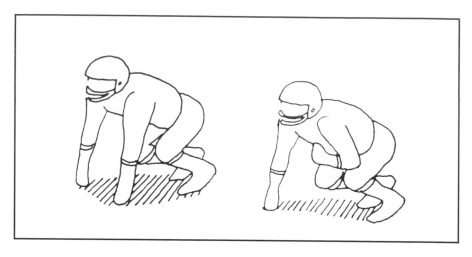

Figure 7.   Look at the supporting parts of the body, and the height of the body above the base of support.

Example: A football lineman can increase stability by going from a 3 to a 4 point stance. An end can increase mobility by going from a 3 to a 2 point stance.

11. *Technique:* **Look at the height of the body and body parts.**
Explanation: If the body and body parts are high above the base of support, the performer is relatively unstable. Lowering the body and body parts increases balance.
Example: Stability of offensive guards on a football team is more easily upset when they are standing upright than when in a 3-point stance.

Movement Relationships

The motion of one or more body parts may influence the motion of other body parts. These relationships may cause either desired or undesired performance of a skill. Therefore, visual evaluation should not always concentrate on the body parts which are of primary importance to performance, but may also be directed to others which can influence the form of performance.

> *Because the parts of the body are linked*
> *together, movement of each part has an*
> *influence on the others.*

12. *Technique:* **Look for unnecessary movements.**
Explanation: Any movement or muscle tension which does not positively contribute to the desired performance is a waste of physical effort. This often

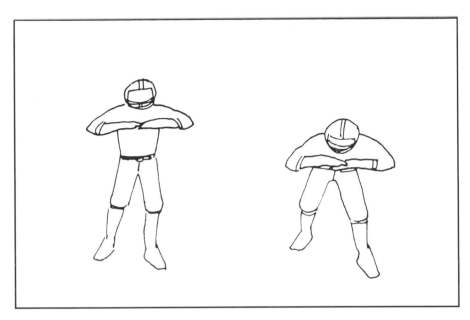

Figure 8. Stability of offensive guards on a football team is more easily upset when they are standing upright.

leads to an earlier onset of fatigue. Also, undesired movements may have to be compensated for by the motion of other body parts which may increase performance problems.

Example: Excessive lateral (side to side) movement of an athlete's legs and feet during running is countered by opposing lateral movements of the arms and hands. Both of these actions detracts from forward progress.

13. *Technique:* **Look for movement opposition (counter-balancing).**

Explanation: The movement of the leg on one side of the body is often countered by the motion of the arm on the opposite side in an attempt to maintain balance of the body. Thus, the movement pattern of the arms can sometimes provide insight into leg movements and vice versa.

Example: The forceful swing of the hurdler's leg over the hurdle is opposed by a lateral and forward swing of the opposite arm.

14. *Technique:* **Observe the motion and direction of swinging body parts.**

Explanation: Swinging body parts (momentum of the parts) can transfer their momentum to the whole body (momentum of the whole). In jumping activities, the upward swinging motion of the arms has a lifting effect to the entire body. It is important for the momentum of the swinging parts to be developed prior to leaving the ground and in the direction of the intended jump.

Example: A basketball player, attempting to jump high in order to block an opponent's jump shot, forcefully swings the arms and trunk upward prior to take off to add to the lifting effect of the push off by the legs and feet.

Figure 9. The movement of the leg on one side of the body is often countered by the motion of the arm on the opposite side in an attempt to maintain balance of the body.

Example: A high jumper forcefully swings the arms and leading leg upward to transfer the lifting effect to the entire body.

15. *Technique:* **Look at the motion of the head.**

Explanation: Because of the head's attachment to the spine, its motion is often an indication of the trunk motion to follow. A turn of the head to the side is followed by a turning of the shoulders and trunk to the same side. Forward motion of the head (flexion of the neck) precedes a tucking of the trunk. Backward motion of the head (extension of the neck) is followed by an arching of the back.

Example: A diver attempting to perform a twisting dive forcefully turns the head in the direction of the intended motion.

16. *Technique:* **Observe the location and direction of applied force.**

Explanation: The application of force to an object or person has different effects. This depends upon where the force is applied. If the force is applied to the center of the object, it will tend to move in the direction of the force. If applied off center, it will tend to spin or turn the object.

Example: A wrestler attempting to turn an opponent over from the stomach onto the back can apply an off center lifting and turning force to the opponent's arms and legs.

Range of Movement

Sometimes the form of the movement pattern may appear to be correct, but the performance of a skill may lack the desired speed or force. The following visual evaluation techniques will be helpful in assessing skills in which speed and force of movement are important.

Speed and force of movement are important elements of many sport skills.

17. *Technique:* Observe the range of motion of body parts.

Explanation: If the range of motion of body parts is relatively large, this provides an opportunity for the muscles to speed up the motion of the body parts over a longer period of time. In activities where maximum speed or force of movement is desired, it is important to have a large range of motion. However, if controlled movement is desired, the range of movement should be decreased.

Figure 10.   Observe the location and direction of applied force.

Example: A batter attempting to hit a home run should move the body parts and bat through a large range of motion. However, if a batter is trying to hit the ball to a certain place on the field ("place the ball"), the range of motion should be reduced in order to have better control of the bat.

18. *Technique:* Look for a stretching of the muscles.

Explanation: Motion of body parts in a direction opposite to the intended direction of movement places the muscles "under stretch." This is often accomplished by an extended backswing. In activities where maximum speed or force of movement is desired, stretching the muscles is important. Stretching the muscles increases the range of motion of the body parts. When muscles are stretched, they act like a spring. This also aids in the subsequent contraction of the muscles which are "under stretch."

Example: An ice hockey player attempting to impart maximum velocity to the puck in a slap shot should swing the arms and stick and twist the trunk back in order to stretch the muscles of the trunk and shoulders prior to the uncoiling on the forward swing.

19. *Technique:* Look for a continuous flow of motion.

Explanation: In striking and throwing skills, a continuous chain of events should occur. The chain of events should begin away from and proceed toward the hand or foot which is to move fast. Each link in the system should add speed to the preceding event until the maximum speed is attained. The addition of more links to the chain of events increases the potential for speed of movement. However, additional skill is usually required to control the faster movement.

Example: When striking a baseball, the continuous flow of motion should progress in sequence through the following links: legs, trunk, upper arms, lower arms, hands, and bat.

Example: The flow of motion in the soccer kick progresses in sequence through the following body parts: trunk, hip, upper leg, lower leg, and foot.

Application of Visual Evaluation Techniques

All coaches use observation of performance as a basis for evaluation and subsequent instruction. However, some coaches are more effective than others in observing athletic skills, learning from their observations, and utilizing what they have learned to instruct their athletes.

Effective evaluation of sport skills requires a planned approach.

Several visual evaluation techniques were presented in this chapter. To use them effectively, the following scheme should be considered:

1. *Always consider vantage point techniques.* Before you attempt to analyze

Figure 11. Stretching the muscles increases the range of motion of the body parts.

the sport skill of any athlete, you should properly position yourself. This position will determine what you will see.

2. *Simplify the movement.* Your initial observations should be directed at gaining an understanding of the movement in its simplified form. You should get a general understanding of how the skill is being performed before attempting to look at the specifics of a sport skill.

3. *Focus on the specifics.* Once you have a general understanding of how a sport skill is being performed, you can then direct your attention to specific

components of the skill. This should involve the consideration of balance and stability, movement relationships and/or range of movement in your visual evaluation techniques.

The techniques of process evaluation presented in this chapter were generally stated and can be applied to all sport skills. As you become familiar with each technique, it will be easier to develop an evaluation strategy which applies appropriate techniques to specific sport skills. A considerable amount of practice is required to reach this level of familiarity. However, your efforts will be appreciated when the added insight and understanding of sport skills is applied to helping young athletes.

References

Brown, E.W. (1983). *Evaluating skills of young athletes.* East Lansing, MI: Michigan Institute for the Study of Youth Sports.

Suggested Reading

Greenlee, G., Heitmann, H., Cothren, B., & Hellweg, D. (1981). *Kinesiology.* From Basic Stuff Series I, vol. 2. Reston, VA: American Alliance for Health, Physical Education, Recreation, and Dance.

Hay, J.G. & Reid, J.G. (1982). *The anatomical and mechanical bases of human motion* (pp. 261–281). Englewood Cliffs, NJ: Prentice-Hall, Inc.

SECTION III:
FUNDAMENTAL SKILLS
OF COACHING

■ **Planning for the Season**

■ **How to Conduct Effective Practices**

■ **Equating Children for Sports Competition**

■ **Principles of Effective Coach-Athlete Interactions**

■ **Conducting a Sport Orientation Meeting for Parents**

chapter eleven

Planning for the Season

Jeanne Foley
Michigan State University

Questions to consider . . .

☐ *What coaching benefits can you gain by advanced planning and organization?*

☐ *How long will it take you to adequately prepare for the start of the season?*

☐ *When should you start planning for the up-coming season?*

☐ *What items should you consider in constructing a season plan?*

☐ *How can you make the best use of your plan?*

A well-considered overall season plan provides many advantages to you as a coach of youth sports. Being organized will also help you avoid many of the difficult situations that can confront a coach. The primary benefit of planning in advance is that the young athletes in your charge will be assured of learning as much as possible in the limited time available for practices and games. With proper organization, you will be ready to teach sport skills in a reasonable order and have your players adequately prepared for competition.

Time spent in planning before the season starts will save you time later on. You can refer to your season plan and to last week's notes to plan this week's practices, instead of starting all over for each practice. Being ready ahead of time will also reduce the stress on you and your players that might be caused by last-minute attempts at preparation for practice sessions or games.

An organized coach is respected by players and trusted by parents.

The effects of advanced planning and organization will be apparent to your players and their parents. The organized coach is generally more respected by players and inspires more confidence from their parents. An effective plan makes for efficient and well-paced practices and adequate preparation for games. This maintains the interest and enthusiasm of participants in your program and increases the chances of achieving individual and team goals for the season.

When to Start Planning

You should begin thinking about your overall season plan at least three to four weeks before the first practice. If this is your first coaching experience, you may want to spend some time talking with veteran coaches, attending coaching clinics or workshops, and reading background material in your sport. If you are new to this particular team or league, find out about the age and skill level of the athletes you'll be coaching. Some persons to contact for this kind of information include the program director, other coaches in the program, and parents of previous or current participants.

Start your planning at least three to four weeks before the first practice.

After checking out the program and spending some time thinking about how to approach the season, spend a couple of one to two hour sessions putting your plans down on paper. If you will have any assistants or co-coaches, involve them in the planning process. Have your basic outline ready a week to ten days

Figure 1. Organized practices are an essential part of a successful season.

before the first practice. This will allow you to go into your parent orientation meeting (discussed in Chapter 15) ready to field specific questions about your coaching plans and expectations for progress during the season.

Content of the Season Plan

The first step in constructing your season outline is to put together a master calendar for the whole season. Events to include on this schedule are:

- all practices - date, time, place
- all games - date, time, place
- parent orientation meeting
- coaches meetings or league information sessions
- preseason organizational meeting for your team (hand out equipment, go over rules, set goals)
- postseason get-together

Partitioning the Season Calendar

The completed season calendar will give you a framework for your overall season plan. You'll be able to see at a glance how much time is available for teaching and when you'll need to be ready for games and other events. You may want to divide your season into sections as follows.

1. *Preseason*—the time between the first practice and the first game, usually spent on teaching basic individual skills and those team skills necessary for the first game.

2. *Early season*—the first third of the competitive season, when the emphasis will still be on teaching and reviewing individual fundamentals and introducing basic team concepts.

3. *Midseason*—the middle portion of the competitive season, during which the focus shifts toward improving team play while still reviewing and building individual skills.

4. *Late season*—the final third of the competitive season, when practices are used for correcting mistakes and weaknesses shown in previous games and for introducing more advanced team strategies.

Outlining Objectives for the Season

A detailed discussion of goal setting is provided in Chapter 7. In preparing for the season, you will find that setting goals for yourself and your team will help you identify specific objectives for your season. General categories of objectives

Season Calendar

MONTH _____ MAY _____

Sunday	Monday	Tuesday	Wednesday	Thursday	Friday	Saturday
1 PARENT ORIENTATION MEETING 4 PM, RM. 8 COMMUNITY CENTER	**2**	**3**	**4**	**5** TEAM ORGANIZA- TIONAL MEETING 4:30 PM PARK SHELTER	**6**	**7** PRACTICE 1:30-3 PM OAK PARK FIELD #3
8	**9**	**10**	**11** PRACTICE 4:30-6:00 CITY PARK FIELD #2	**12**	**13**	**14** PRACTICE 10-11:30 AM CITY PARK FIELD #5
15 COACHES MEETING 2 PM COMMUNITY CENTER, ROOM 10	**16**	**17** GAME 1 5 PM CITY PARK FIELD #2	**18**	**19**	**20**	**21** PRACTICE 10-11:30 AM CITY PARK FIELD #1
22	**23**	**24** GAME 2 4 PM OAK PARK FIELD #3	**25**	**26**	**27** (Need cones for baserunning drill) →	**28** PRACTICE 2:30-4 PM OAK PARK FIELD #1
29	**30**	**31** GAME 3 5 PM CITY PARK FIELD #4				

NOTES AND COMMENTS: _____

_____

_____

_____

Season Calendar

MONTH _____

Sunday	Monday	Tuesday	Wednesday	Thursday	Friday	Saturday

NOTES AND COMMENTS: _____

_____

_____

_____

Example of Typical Game and Practice Notes:
(from week #4 of sample season calendar)

SUNDAY	MONDAY	TUESDAY	WEDNESDAY	THURSDAY	FRIDAY	SATURDAY
	GAME 2 4PM, Oak Park Field #3 Baserunning needs work! Relays from outfield look good. Need to work Ricky in at catcher next game May need to introduce bunting sooner than planned — could have used it today....			Remember to call league office re: new home plate #3 needed at Oak Park at Field		PRACTICE 2:30 – 4:00 PM OAK PARK, FIELD #1 Practice dragged today. Spent too long on throws to home plate. New baserunning drill is great. Tom, Bobby and Janet need extra work on catching pop flies.

Steps in Making an Outline of Basketball Skills

Breakdown a skill by outlining its subskills. Start with the major categories, then successively break each category down into smaller components until you arrive at single skills which can be taught one at a time in practice.

First Division:	I. Individual Skills II. Team Skills

Next step—
Breakdown each of
the main
categories:

I. Individual Skills
   A. Offensive
   B. Defensive

Continue breaking
down each category

A. Offensive
   1. Dribbling
   2. Passing/Receiving
   3. Shooting
   4. Cutting (Moving without the ball to get free for a pass)
   5. Driving (Moving with the ball—to the basket)
   6. Screening and using screens
   7. Offensive Rebounding

Continue until you
reach single skills
that can be taught
one at a time in
practice

1. Dribbling
   a. Mechanics
      1) Stance
      2) Fingertip/wrist ball control
      3) Off arm as guard arm
      4) Eyes up
      5) Using either hand—dribble on side away from defense
   b. Types
      1) Control
      2) Speed
      3) Hesitation
      4) Crossover
      5) Reverse

to consider are skills, knowledge, physical fitness, and attitudes. Each of these is discussed in the following sections.

Skills. Outline the major individual and team skills that are appropriate to the ability and experience level of the group you'll be coaching. Limit the skills to be taught to those that are essential to the game at the level of competition anticipated in your program. Break the major skills down in to subskills. Determine the order in which to teach the skills; note on your calendar when to introduce each one. Guidelines for selecting appropriate skills are provided in Chapter 5.

Teach the basic, necessary skills well instead of trying to cover all levels of skills in one season.

Knowledge. Sessions on rules, fundamentals and strategy of the game, training principles, and other mental aspects of the sport should be included in your overall plan. Some of these areas can be discussed at the preseason organizational meeting. Others can be handled during brief "chalk talks" at practice. List the important topics to be discussed and note on your calendar when each one will be considered.

Physical fitness. Conditioning should be a secondary objective to skill development in youth sports programs, especially for children below the age of 14. Conditioning of young athletes should be accomplished via continuous skill-development drills and play in games and scrimmages rather than by using drills in which the sole purpose is conditioning. Further information on conditioning can be found in Chapter 6.

Attitudes. A major positive outcome of sports participation should be development of healthy attitudes towards sports, competition, fitness, winning and losing, teamwork, self worth, and respect for others' abilities and inabilities. Fostering the development of such healthy attitudes is part of your role as a coach. Although a specific day can't be assigned for each of the areas, listing them in your coaching objectives will ensure your attention to them throughout the season.

Preparing a File of Drills

The bulk of your practice time will probably be spent on drills, particularly in the early part of the season. A sensible choice of drills is therefore very important in determining how much your players will learn. Drawing up a list of drills during your preseason planning will allow you to have both variety and consistency in your practices. Having a few good drills at hand for each basic skill will prevent the overuse of any one drill. You'll also be able to avoid wasting time continuously teaching new drills if you use your drill file and previous practice outlines to plan each practice.

*Plan to have a few good drills ready for each
basic skill on your preseason outline.*

There are many sources of tried and tested drills that you can use to help you put together your drill file. You may be able to recall some favorite drills from your own playing or coaching experience. Talking to other coaches and attending coaching clinics can also provide many good ideas for drills. If your skill outline still has gaps not covered by drills from these sources, there are many books available on drills for any sport. The public library, local bookstores, your sport program's headquarters, and other coaches are all good places to obtain information about drills.

Each time you locate a good drill, write it on a 3 × 5 index card. Include in your description of the drill:

- diagram
- written explanation
- equipment needed
- number of players needed or size of groups to use
- time required for the drill

The card can then be filed in a box which you've divided into categories matching your outline of skills and subskills.

Example of a Card in a Drill File

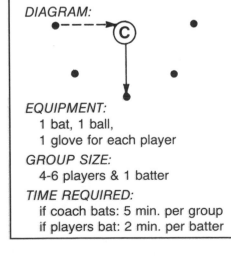

DRILL NAME: <u>PEPPER</u>

DIAGRAM:

EQUIPMENT:
  1 bat, 1 ball,
  1 glove for each player

GROUP SIZE:
  4-6 players & 1 batter

TIME REQUIRED:
  if coach bats: 5 min. per group
  if players bat: 2 min. per batter

EXPLANATION: Coach or player with bat stands in middle of a semicircle of players who are about 5 ft. apart and 10 ft. from the batter. One player has a ball. Drill starts when player tosses ball underhand to batter, who hits it to a player in the semicircle. This player immediately tosses it back to batter, who hits it to another player (continues nonstop.) Drills quick fielding reflexes, also drills eye/hand coordination if players are used as batters.

Figure 2.   Good drills are available from many sources.

Your drill file may not be complete when the season starts, but you'll at least have enough drills on hand to get started and you'll have identified the areas for which you need more drills. As you get into your season, you may learn new drills from other coaches or your players. You may also find yourself able to make up a drill for a specific situation. Update your file by adding cards on these new drills, weeding out or modifying drills that didn't work, and by making notes about drills that worked particularly well. Once started, your drill file will help you stay organized for the current season and will give you a head start on seasons to come.

Equipment Inventory

Before the first practice session, you'll need to determine what equipment is needed and what is available. Find out what is provided by the program, what the participants are expected to provide, and what you must provide. If any skills or drills require special equipment, make a note of this on your master calendar for that day.

Communication System

Plan ahead for a chain of communication to notify players and parents of schedule changes and cancellations. You may want to set up a telephone network or "calling tree" by which you call a few designated team members and each of them passes the message on to a portion of the rest of the team. It is also a good idea to establish a place where you can post written notices of such messages in the event of missed telephone calls or late changes. A bulletin board or sign post may be available for this purpose at or near your practice site.

A calling tree and a place to post messages are good methods of getting information to your team.

The telephone network and/or bulletin board location should be announced at the parent orientation meeting and at the preseason organizational meeting with your players. Distributing a list of telephone numbers and addresses of coaches and players will also aid communication.

Using the Season Plan

The area in which your season plan will provide the most help and save you the most time is in your weekly practice planning. At the beginning of each week, you can take the week's basic outline from your calendar and use it to construct a detailed outline of each practice for that week. The outline for each practice session should include:

- warmup
- new skills to teach (from this week's calendar notes)
- skills to review and drill (from previous weeks' calendar notes)
- scrimmage or game-type situations
- cooldown

Figure 3. Enlist the aid of your team members and parents when messages have to be sent in a hurry.

PRACTICE OUTLINE   DATE: _Mon., Jan. 21_   TIME: _1-2:30 P.M._   PLACE: _North Gym_

		TIME
WARMUP	1. 5 min. stretching 2. 5 min. light calisthenics and easy jogging	10 min.
NEW SKILLS TO TEACH	1. Fast break defense – 2 on 1, 3 on 2 2. Crossover dribble	20 min.
SKILLS TO REVIEW AND DRILL	1. Layups – right- and left-handed 2. Defensive stance and footwork 3. Rebounding: Blocking out the shooter 4. Shell drill for zone defense shifts 5. Shooting off the pass	30 min.
SCRIMMAGE OR GAME SITUATIONS	2 × 10 min. scrimmages: 1. 2-3 zone defense, no press, stress quick passing 2. Player-to-player defense, full court press on made basket	20 min.
COOLDOWN	1. 5 sets of 2 free throws, jog 1 lap around court between sets 2. stretching	10 min.
OTHER	Chalk talk – discuss upcoming game; remind players of equal playing time policy – support each other when you're on bench & others are playing	10 min. (off court)

PRACTICE OUTLINE

DATE: _____   TIME: _____   PLACE: _____

	TIME
WARMUP	
NEW SKILLS TO TEACH	
SKILLS TO REVIEW AND DRILL	
SCRIMAGE OR GAME SITUATIONS	
COOLDOWN	
OTHER	

Components of the Season Plan

- Calendar

- Objectives
  1. Skills
  2. Knowledge
  3. Physical Fitness
  4. Attitudes

- Drills

- Equipment

- Communication System

Drills to practice new skills and review old skills can be taken right from your drill file. In the preseason and early season when fundamentals are being taught, simple drills concentrating on a single skill should be used. Later in the season or when reviewing previously taught skills, you will want to use more complex drills involving a combination of related skills. More information on planning effective practices will be provided in Chapter 12.

Adjustments to the Overall Plan

After each practice or game, jot down a few notes on your calendar about drills that were good or bad, skills that need more work, items needing to be covered in a chalk talk, and so on. These notes and the outlines you've saved from each practice will help you make any necessary adjustments to your overall plan.

Figure 4. Good planning and organization by you, the coach, will make the season more enjoyable for everyone.

Postseason Evaluation

Your initial season plan, practice outlines, notes, and adjustments will help you evaluate your accomplishments at the end of the season. You'll be able to see if preseason team, individual, and coaching goals have been met. Your notes should show what worked and what didn't and how your plan might have been improved. Chapter 20 provides further information and forms for the postseason evaluation.

Conclusion

With your master plan for the season in hand, you are ready to make the best possible use of your opportunity to work with young athletes. Organized and efficient practice plans, constant updating of practice formats based on previous practices and games, and effective evaluation are all benefits of taking the time to build a plan for the season.

The effort you have put into planning and organization will be rewarded by seeing your players progress in skills, fitness, knowledge, and attitudes during the season. The time and energy spent on your first attempt at an organized approach to coaching will also pay off when you go into the next season with a solid base of plans, notes, and drills upon which to build.

References

Blase, K., & Vogel, P., (Eds.). (1985). *AHAUS associate coaches manual*. Denver, CO: Amateur Hockey Association of the United States.

chapter twelve

How to Conduct Effective Practices

12

Thelma Sternberg Horn
Miami University

Questions to consider . . .

☐ *What type of preparation should you do before practices?*

☐ *What is "active time" and how can it be increased?*

☐ *How can you avoid practices that don't seem to accomplish anything?*

☐ *How much time in a practice should be spent scrimmaging?*

I n the past several years, researchers studying children in sport have found that one of the primary reasons children join youth sport programs is because they want to learn new skills or improve existing skills. These researchers have also found that children show the greatest motivation and practice effort when they really believe that they are or will be "getting better" at an activity. As coaches, we must remember, however, that all children do not learn sports skills "automatically" just by participating in a competitive sports program. Rather, skill learning or improvement occurs most efficiently under controlled conditions. It is not necessarily that practice makes perfect, but rather that planned and guided practice leads to improved skill performance.

Practice does not always make perfect. Planned and guided practice leads to improved skill performance.

The coach's responsibility is to design instructional activities and conduct practice sessions in such a manner that each young athlete can show some improvement in skills. Unfortunately, the conditions under which many coaches work—without assistant coaches, with large teams, minimal practice time, poor or inadequate equipment, and athletes at varying levels of skill—pose a real challenge to the coach who wants to see each child achieve a certain level of sport competence. Although these problems sometimes seem overwhelming, the solution lies in carefully planned and highly organized practice sessions. Coaches who effectively use each minute of practice time and who design instructional activities that match their athletes' present capabilities are most likely to reach their goal of helping each child learn something at each practice.

The purpose of this chapter is to provide youth sport coaches with some guidelines which will help them to design and conduct effective practice sessions. We will begin by examining how coaches can organize sport skills so that they can be taught in the most efficient manner. Next, we will discuss both the importance of "active time" and the means by which the amount of "active time" in practice sessions can be increased. Finally, we will identify the basic components which should be included in an individual practice plan.

Organizing Skills for Effective Teaching

Many of the fundamental sport skills such as the volleyball serve, basketball lay-up, tennis forehand, and the back handspring are actually quite complex motor skills which require coordination and timing to execute correctly. For children,

Figure 1.   One outcome of effective practices is happy participants.

and even for adults, these skills are usually most efficiently learned by breaking them down into sequential parts and having the performer master each part. When teaching a basketball lay-up to a group of 11- and 12-year-old children, for example, it would be bad teaching for you to simply explain the technique, demonstrate the skill, and then expect the young athletes to learn such a complex skill just by practicing it a number of times. In order for them to learn to do a lay-up in the most efficient way, you should break the skill down into parts. You might begin by teaching the children the basic shot mechanics regarding the target area, initial hand/ball position, body position relative to basket and court, ball release motion and the follow through. Then the other skill components such as the dribbling approach and the take-off can be added in a sequential order.

By using a sequence of steps such as that just described, the young athletes learn a complex skill like the basketball lay-up by mastering parts of it at a time. Not only is this approach a more effective way to teach motor skills to children, but it also helps each child gain a feeling of success right from the beginning.

> *Complex skills are most efficiently*
> *learned in steps.*

When preparing to teach a particular sport skill to your athletes, you will need to set up a sequential instruction plan. This instructional plan will require you to organize the skill into a series of learning steps, and then identify appropriate instructional activities for each step.

Organizing the Skill into Learning Steps

You should begin your practice preparation by organizing the skill that you want to teach into learning steps. These steps will actually represent the breakdown of that skill into component parts. Imagine a staircase, with the easiest or most basic component placed on the bottom step, and each succeeding stairstep representing the addition of a new and more complex skill component. Figure 2 illustrates this sequence of learning steps by showing how a softball coach prepares to teach the team to field ground balls. Based on the age and skill level of her athletes, the coach decides to organize this skill into a series of six learning steps. The first and most basic step is for each young athlete to learn and practice the basic fielding technique. At this stage, the coach plans to teach them the proper stance, glove position, and fielding motion. Once the players can demonstrate that they know the proper technique, the coach will then progress to learning step #2, which is fielding ground balls hit or thrown directly at them. When the players can consistently and correctly field easy balls hit at them, the coach will then move on to learning step #3, which is fielding balls hit to the glove side, and then to step #4, which is fielding balls hit to a non-glove side. After her players have mastered these movement skills, they can then progress to the fifth step, which is to develop their ability to field all types of ground balls including bunts and bouncers. As a final step, the coach would have each athlete learn the fielding skills which are specific to the various infield positions.

An experienced coach will realize that all of the young athletes may not be able to progress through all of these learning steps. In fact, depending on the age and previous experience of her players, most of them may not be able to go farther in one season than step #3 or #4. However, over the three or four

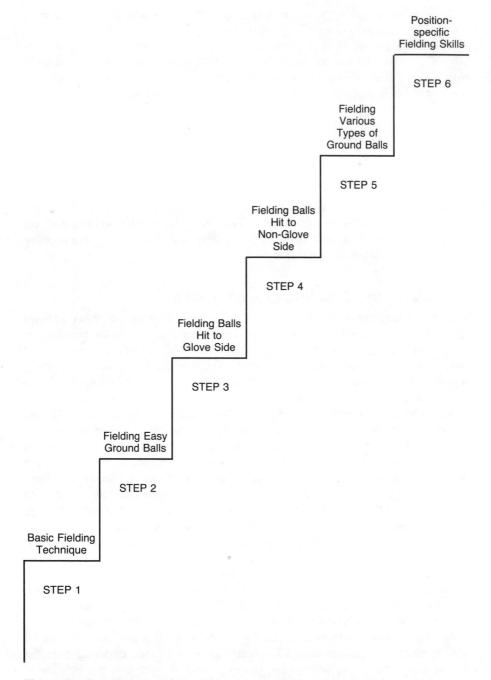

Figure 2.   Learning steps for teaching young athletes to field ground balls.

years in which these players participate in this age-group softball league, each should be able to progress to the top of the staircase. Thus, the set of learning steps outlined for each relevant sport skill can serve as a series of both long and short term goals for each athlete and the coach. Chapter 5 contains additional information about matching objectives to the skill level of your athletes.

Selecting or Designing Appropriate Instructional Activities

After you have outlined the learning steps for the skill you want to teach, the next task is to design or select instructional activities or drills which will help the athletes learn the parts of the skill that are listed at each step. These learning activities may consist of skill demonstrations, chalkboard talks, lectures, or skill drills. A combination of these activities will usually be most effective. Using Figure 2 as an example, each learning step would begin with a demonstration and brief explanation by you to provide the players with information about the particular skill movement. This type of mental activity would then be followed by a skill drill or drills to allow players to practice that movement pattern. Skill drills can either be specifically designed by you or can be selected from any available sport book. Regardless of the source, it is important that you keep the following three points in mind when selecting or designing skill drills.

The instructional activity selected for each learning step should focus primarily on the skill component to be learned. Because practice and repetition are important when children are learning a new skill movement, the instructional activity selected for each learning step should allow the athlete to concentrate only on that skill component. When working on step #4 from the outline provided in Figure 2, an appropriate drill would be to have the athletes form three vertical lines on the infield. You and two assistant coaches (or players) would throw or hit ground balls to the glove side of the first player in each line. The player would field the ball, using the appropriate technique, throw the fielded ball back to the coach, and then go to the end of the line. This type of drill is appropriate in this instance because it focuses the players' attention almost solely on the mastery of a particular skill component, in this situation the movement pattern required to field ground balls hit to the glove side, and provides them the opportunity to practice that technique a number of times.

Young athletes need to learn and practice sport skills under controlled conditions before they can be expected to do them correctly in game or scrimmage situations. Many coaches make the mistake of using scrimmages as their primary type of practice drill. These coaches typically tend to take 10 or 15 minutes at the beginning of a practice to explain and demonstrate to their athletes how to do a particular skill, but then spend the remaining practice time for a scrimmage. The players are expected to execute the demonstrated skill in the scrimmage even though they were not given an opportunity to actually practice it. Because repetition is a very important aspect of the learning process, it is essential for children to practice a new skill a number of times under controlled conditions before it can become an automatic movement. It is only after they have learned the skill through practice drills that they can be expected to use it correctly in an actual game.

Coaches must plan to provide individual players with feedback during drill activities. Learning occurs most efficiently when players receive feedback telling them not only whether or not they are doing the skill right, for example "O.K. Joan, that was a good shot", but also giving them corrective or technical information concerning their skill performance; for example, "No, Sally, that time you didn't push off with your left foot." or "Much better, Tom, your toss was higher that time." For additional information about feedback, see Chapter 3, "The Coach As A Teacher."

Young athletes need feedback about their performance from their coaches.

Feedback from coaches during drills should focus primarily on the skill component which is being emphasized in that drill. For example, when players are working on the softball fielding drill described in one of the previous sections, the coach's feedback to players should provide them with an assessment or corrective information concerning their movement to the glove side to field a ground ball. Such skill-specific feedback focuses the athletes' attention on the skill movement that the coach wants them to learn in that particular drill.

In summary, you should prepare a *sequential instructional plan* before you begin to teach your young athletes a new sport skill. Even better, however, would be for you to take some time at the beginning of the season to outline a sequence of learning steps for each of the fundamental sport skills that your athletes will need to learn over the season. Although this type of pre-season preparation would require a considerable amount of your time, the advantages for both you and your athletes are numerous: (a) the sequence of learning steps outlined for each skill would provide you with a guideline for the things you would like to accomplish over the season; (b) the set of learning steps can serve as a convenient group of short term goals which can help you provide each of your athletes with a sense of achievement or accomplishment (see Figure 3); and (c) you can use this sequential outline as an effective means of evaluating the status and progress of individual athletes on the team.

At the beginning of the season, the set of learning steps can be used to identify where each of the athletes is on each of the fundamental sport skills. This assessment may help you determine the strengths and weaknesses of the athletes and to design appropriate practice activities for each player. Then, at the end of the season, this outline can help you evaluate the progress that the team and/ or individual athletes have made. The advantages, then, of having a series of learning steps prepared for each skill far outweighs the time and effort it may take to prepare them at the beginning of the season.

Increasing the Amount of Active Time During Practices

Research has shown that one of the characteristics which distinguishes effective from ineffective teachers and coaches is how efficiently they use their instructional or practice time. To illustrate this difference between coaches, let's review the practice activities of two individuals who coach in the same coeducational youth soccer league. Coach A is scheduled to practice with his team from 9:00 to 10:30 A.M. on a Saturday morning, and Coach B takes over the same field for practice with his team from 10:30 to 12:00. As objective observers of both practices, we are going to examine how these coaches use their allocated 90 minutes of practice time. We'll use stopwatches and an observation chart to record the type and duration of each practice activity. One of our purposes in doing this is to calculate for each coach an "active time" score which will represent the total amount of the 90-minute practice period in which his players were actively engaged in skill learning activities. These activities could include practice drills, scrimmages, skill demonstrations, or even lectures by the coach about soccer skills and strategies. In contrast, "non-active" or non-learning time occurs when players have to stand in line for long periods of time during drills or sit out of scrimmages or drills, or when the coach uses the time to organize an activity such as giving non-skill related directions, organizing players into groups, disciplining individuals, or getting equipment set up.

*Effective practices are those which contain a
high percentage of active time.*

After observing each of our coaches for a 90-minute practice, we find that Coach A's team spent a total of 38 minutes of practice time in active learning situations while Coach B's athletes had 72 minutes of active time. A more detailed analysis of a ball trapping drill conducted by the two coaches showed that each athlete on Coach B's team actually practiced the skill a total of 20 times while each athlete on Coach A's team only practiced that skill five times during the same 12 minutes of drill time. Assuming that this particular practice is typical of those conducted over the season, we conclude that Coach B appears to be a

Figure 3.   Good coaches teach complex skills in progressions.

more effective manager of his practice time than does Coach A. Continued observation of these two coaches would probably show that Coach B manages to get more active time into each of his practices because he spends less time in organizational activity, and designs drills so that all players can be actively involved for the greatest amount of time.

Reducing Organizational Time

The first major difference between Coach A and Coach B is that Coach B devoted considerably less practice time to organizational activities. Although the two coaches run the same number of drills, Coach A spends an average of 10 minutes for each drill getting his players organized by assigning them to groups, telling each group where to practice, and giving them detailed instructions. In contrast, Coach B's players are able to begin their drill activities with an average of only two or three minutes of instruction and organization per drill. Similarly, when it comes to demonstrations or chalkboard talks, Coach A spends a lot of time getting his players organized and quiet while Coach B's players automatically get into a set postion and are quickly ready to pay attention.

The reason Coach B is able to devote less time to organization is because he, like most effective coaches and teachers, spends some time at the beginning of each athletic season teaching his athletes certain practice procedures which will ultimately reduce organizational time during subsequent practice periods. Examples of these standard procedures include the following:

- establishing a standard set of conditioning or warm-up activities which players are expected to begin as soon as they arrive at practice or which can be done on the sidelines before the practice field or court becomes available.
- identifying a standard formation that players are to assume for skill demonstrations, coach lectures, and team talks such as forming a semi-circle on the 50-yard line or sitting around the perimeter of the volleyball court.
- labeling or naming commonly used drills/practice activities so that the coach does not need to describe them each time they are used
- identifying standard rotation patterns to use when using skill drills. For example, in basketball, soccer, or volleyball, rotate in the direction of the ball or pass.
- setting up pre-assigned groups for 2, 3, 4-player drills so that players do not waste time finding partners. These groups should be changed periodically so that the same individuals do not practice together for the entire year.
- establishing and enforcing a standard code of conduct. For example, when the coach is talking, players listen; when the coach blows a whistle, all activity ceases; players are expected to run off and into the infield between innings; athletes take turns setting up and taking down equipment.
- establishing a standard formation or field placement for certain commonly

used drills. For example, for all 2-person/1-ball drills, the players form two horizontal lines about 15 feet apart with partners facing each other.

The above suggestions, which represent some general organizational ideas, could easily be adapted by you to develop relevant standard practice procedures specific to your sport. The guiding principle, however, is that you should try to decrease the amount of time that you spend in practices on organizational activities and thus increase the amount of time available for "active" learning activities. This principle is especially important when you only have a limited number of practices or a minimum amount of on-field or on-court practice time.

Maximizing "Active Time" for All Players

The second difference between Coaches A and B is evident in the way they set up and conduct their practice drills. For example, let's assume that both coaches spend a total of 20 minutes of their Saturday practice on a "throwing-in" drill. Because both coaches have already taught their players the proper technique for throwing in the ball from the sidelines, they are now using an on-field skill drill to have players practice that technique. For his practice drill, Coach A uses the format and procedures illustrated in Figure 4. In this set-up, Player X_1 "throws in" from behind the sideline to the coach, who is positioned on-field and represents a teammate. The coach traps the throw-in ball and then passes it back to Player X_2 who is now at the end of the players' line. The coach watches each performer and gives appropriate feedback.

Coach B, on the other hand, has elected to use the drill format illustrated in Figure 5. In this set-up, the first player in each of the three player lines "throws in" to his or her on-field teammate (Players X_6, X_{12}, X_{18}) who traps the ball and dribbles back to the respective sideline area, passing off to the next player in line, Players X_2, X_8, and X_{14}. The first player to throw in rotates to the on-field position, and the second player in line proceeds to throw in. The coach moves between the lines giving appropriate feedback as needed.

Although the two coaches are both practicing the same skill, they are using different drill formats. The result is that each player on Coach B's team practices the throw-in skill a minimum of 15 times while each player on Coach A's team is lucky to practice it five times. In addition, although the emphasis in Coach B's drill is on the correct execution of the throw-in, his players are also getting an opportunity to perfect and practice their trapping and dribbling skills. In contrast, Coach A's athletes are basically non-active during the time when they are not practicing the throw-in. If we were to record the amount of active time for an individual athlete on each of these teams, it is apparent that the athletes from Team B might have gotten about 12 to 14 minutes of active time during this drill while the athletes on Team A probably got no more than four to six minutes of active time. Such differences between coaches in time allocation may very well affect how well their athletes will learn this skill.

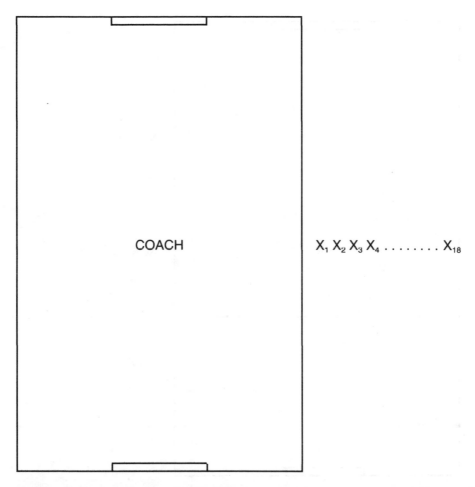

COACH $X_1 X_2 X_3 X_4 \ldots \ldots X_{18}$

Figure 4.   An example of an ineffective drill format, in terms of the "active time" involvement of the athletes. Drill format used by Coach A to practice the soccer throw-in.

Design drills so that each player can be actively involved.

Increasing the amount of active time in practices will most likely have an additional benefit in that children are less apt to cause disciplinary problems when they are active. Requiring young children to wait in a long line for their turn to perform, as illustrated in Figure 4, encourages them to engage in pushing,

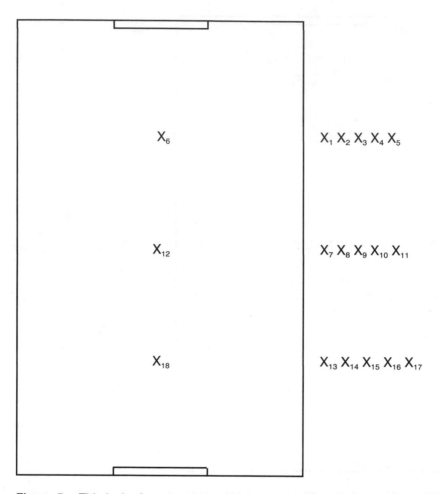

Figure 5.   This is the format used by Coach B to practice the soccer throw-in. The number of athletes who are active is considerably greater than in the format of Figure 4.

shoving, arguing, and other disruptive behaviors. Keeping them actively engaged in a skill drill reduces their boredom and increases their interest in and enjoyment of practice session.

Designing an Effective Practice Plan

In the previous two sections of this chapter, we have discussed the guidelines you should use in designing effective learning activities for your practices. In this section, we will focus more generally on the organization and chronological sequence of events of a typical practice session.

Although there may be considerable variability from one practice to the next in terms of available time and your primary practice objectives, most of your practices should follow the same basic format. The recommended format, which is outlined in Figure 6, suggests that athletes begin each practice with some general and sport-specific *warmup activities*. The coach should plan and organize these warmup activities carefully so that they can be accomplished quickly.

Following this conditioning period, coaches should plan to have players *review skills* that they have previously learned. In most sports, this portion of the practice session will usually consist of fast-paced skill drills which emphasize repetition, smooth execution, and refinement of fundamental skills. These drills typically will serve as an adequate warmup or prelude for the third portion of the practice which will focus on *teaching of new skills*. Activities during this time period should be based on your previously developed outline of the learning steps. Teaching of new skills should consume a large share of your practice time, particularly during the first half of the season. Guidelines for the preparation of these practice activities have been discussed in detail in the previous sections.

Although the instructional portion of a practice is very important, it is also necessary that players have an opportunity to practice skills under game-like conditions. Therefore, you should reserve some practice time for a *scrimmage* or *game-type drill*. Your objective during this activity should be: (a) to make

ACTIVITIES	ALLOCATED TIME
Warm-up/Conditioning	15 minutes
Review of Skills	25 minutes
Work on New Skills	40 minutes
Game-type Scrimmage	25 minutes
Cool-down	5 minutes
Team Meeting	10 minutes
Coaches' Evaluation	Post-practice

Figure 6. Outline of a sample practice plan which is based on a two hour time period. (The two-hour drill is suggested for mature players. Practice sessions for children less than 14 years of age should be shorter, based on age, skill level, temperature, intensity of the practice, etc.)

sure players are able to use skills they have learned in previous instructional activities in a game situation; and (b) to help players understand the rules and strategies, thus preparing them for up-coming competitive events.

Following an intensive or fast-paced scrimmage or game-type drill, players should engage in some type of cool-down activity (see Chapter 6 for more information on conditioning). Finally, practice for the athletes should conclude with a brief *team meeting* which usually would include an evaluation or discussion of the day's activities and organizational information provided by you regarding future practices or games.

You should take some time following each practice session to *evaluate the practice* in terms of the players' performance and their progress. It would be most helpful for you to jot down some quick notes concerning both the effectiveness of the practice activities and some recommendations for future practices. For example, "Tomorrow in practice, we must work on baserunning strategies" or "Sue is still having problems with her backhand. She should work with the ball machine on Tuesday." These notes can then be used to design effective plans for subsequent practice sessions.

Summary

The purpose of this chapter is to provide guidelines for the effective organization of practice activities. Initially, the use of these guidelines will place greater demands on your time. Organizing skills by outlining a sequence of learning steps and corresponding instructional activities will require a considerable investment of time. Time will also be required for you to seek assistance from books, coaching clinics, or fellow coaches. Similarly, to achieve the maximum possible amount of active time in each practice will require creativity and careful pre-practice organization.

Coaches who truly want to make sport participation an enjoyable and beneficial experience for their young athletes must be willing to make such a time commitment. As we noted earlier in this chapter, children are most highly motivated and exhibit the greatest enjoyment when they really believe that they are "getting better" at a sport or physical activity.

Your goal as a youth sport coach is to help each child, no matter what her or his initial physical capabilities are, to learn something at each practice. The rewards for the time and effort you put into the planning of practices will come when a child achieves a level of skill he or she has not reached before. Perhaps, with some luck, you may even someday overhear a parent of one of your athletes say to another, "Even though our team went zero and eight for the season, my little Freddie really learned a lot from his coach."

References and Suggested Readings

Gould, D. & Weiss, M. (1980). *Teaching sports skills to young athletes.* East Lansing, MI: Institute for the Study of Youth Sports.

Martens, M., Christina, R.W., Harvey, J.S. & Sharkey, B. (1981). *Coaching young athletes.* Champaign, IL: Human Kinetics Publishers, Inc.

Siedentop, D. (1983). *Developing teaching skills in physical education.* Palo Alto, CA: Mayfield Publishing Company.

Singer, R.N. (1982). *The learning of motor skills.* New York: Macmillan Publishing Company.

chapter thirteen

Equating Children for Sports Competition

Vern Seefeldt
Michigan State University

13

Questions to consider . . .

☐ *How do children define "What's fair?" in sports competition?*

☐ *What are the common ways of selecting children for athletic teams?*

☐ *What characteristics of children should adults consider when grouping them for sports competition?*

☐ *Who is most likely to be eliminated under the commonly used methods of selecting children's teams for athletic competition?*

C hildren at play spend much of their time discussing the concept of *fairness.* As they grow up they also develop a keen sense of "what's fair." Teams chosen by children for purposes of competition are carefully equated according to the impressions that children have about the role that each team member will play in the contest. Children have distinct impressions about the abilities of their playmates in relation to the goals of the contest, even to the point of refusing to play with someone who may be highly skilled, but "cheats."

Children engage in many admirable processes in an attempt to achieve fairness. Unfortunately, these procedures are seldom permitted in situations where adults organize the competition for children. In children's play, if one team has an obvious advantage, the teams may exchange players. They may also change the rules so that the team with an apparent advantage is handicapped in some way. We are all familiar with the situation in which a right handed baseball player who has already hit several home runs over the left field boundary is restricted henceforth by being required to hit the ball to right field or suffer the consequences of being called *out* for any ball that is hit fairly to left field.

Children will frequently halt a game in which the score is too uneven for it to be considered a contest. The "mercy rules" evoked by adults are far too permissive in the eyes of the children because for them the impression of "what's fair" has long been exceeded when adults are finally willing to "call the game." They have little tolerance for the large differences in scores that are sometimes permitted when adults supervise the games of children.

Adults who supervise youth sports may also be depriving children of an important ingredient in a democratic society; that is, the ability to settle disputes through discussions, arguments, and negotiations. The rules imposed on children's play by adults seldom have a place for interaction between two individuals and when such discussions occur they are usually between a coach and an official. Children are taught to stand by and watch while adults arbitrate the disagreements. While it is impractical to suggest that the adult control of children's sports should incorporate more elements of democracy and resort less to dictatorial methods, we, as coaches, are obligated to study the problems of inequality that are introduced when we do not consider the needs of children in sports experiences.

What's Fair in Children's Sports?

Defining *fairness* in children's sports is easy if we state our interpretation in philosophical terms, but translating *fair play* into solutions of practical problems is difficult. For example, few adults would disagree with the following definition: fairness in children's sports means that all children have the right to learn sports skills in a non-threatening environment; one that is free of bias regarding social

Figure 1. An important ingredient in sports competition for children is *fairness*, or an equal opportunity for each team to win.

standing, race or gender. However, when this definition is applied to everyday playing conditions, the following questions emerge:

- Should every child, regardless of ability level, be a member of a team?
- Should the chronological age ranges that are so strictly enforced by some leagues and associations apply to all children?
- Should children with physical and emotional handicaps be permitted to play? If not, what criteria should be employed to restrict their participation?

- Should boys and girls of all ages compete against one another? If not, at what age should the restrictions begin?

The previous questions underscore some longstanding dilemmas in children's sports. In situations where the traditional model of sports experiences is in force, we see little application of the philosophical definition of *fair play*. However, modest gains in equating teams for competition and providing opportunities for children of varying abilities have been made. These departures from tradition will be discussed, with the view that an interpretation of *fairness* from a child's perspective will lead to a greater emphasis on equality in children's sports that are supervised by adults.

Methods of Equating Teams

The processes whereby children are placed on teams for athletic competition have evolved over a 40-year period. The overriding motive for the various methods of selecting teams appears to be *convenience*, with a secondary factor being *to win*. Neither of these motives is related to fairness; in fact, some would argue that selecting a team for the primary purpose of *winning* evokes actions that are contrary to the principles of *fairness*. As discussed in the following descriptions for equating teams, even some of the methods used to promote equity are demoralizing to the children who must participate in the process in order to play.

Choosing Sides

The technique of having the two most respected (and generally the most skillful) persons act as captains who then choose teams has a long tradition in the free-play activities of children. The devastating result of such a selection process is that it ranks publicly each individual within a peer group. There is also a high probability that the rankings will remain stable from day to day, resulting in the same individuals being chosen last on each occasion.

A more desirable method for equating participants for small group play is to select the entire team at once. This eliminates the process of alternate choices and the determination of who will be chosen last. One individual may say, "We'll take Jim, Mary, Bob, Marty and Phil" with the assumption that the persons not named will constitute the opposing side.

The Player Auction

A common but highly undesirable method of selecting participants for sports teams involves an *auction* during which coaches bid for players who have been placed on a master roster. Coaches are usually awarded a quota of points, which they may distribute in any way, provided they have acquired a specified number of players by the time the bidding ends. This process is unfair for several reasons: a) coaches who are unfamiliar with the players are at a disadvantage; b) coaches may expend all of their *points* on a few highly skilled players with the hope that these talented individuals will carry the team; c) the remaining players, who by virtue of the point allocation system were selected with the expenditure of a few points, are likely to be disregarded in the practices and games because they are viewed as not being as worthy as the players for whom the bidding reached higher levels; and d) highly skilled players are likely to consume most of the available points, leaving the coaches with no recourse but to underrate the remaining participants. In addition, information about the points that were bid for specific individuals is likely to reach the players, who must then suffer the consequences of an inherently unfair system.

Distribution of Talent by Rating of Competencies

One method to ensure that all teams have a certain number of players at each ability level within a restricted age range is for coaches or administrators to rate the participants during each year. If ratings of competence are available and the number of teams is known, then the distribution of talent according to the previous year's performance is possible. Several problems are common to this system, too, but the procedures which are so damaging to players' self-concepts, as indicated in some of the previous systems, are reduced or eliminated.

Shortcomings to the selection of talent according to coaches' rating include: a) the ratings may not reflect the individual's true ability; b) abilities may have changed since the ratings were recorded; and c) individuals who did not participate in the program during the previous year will not have a rating. Despite these potential shortcomings, equating teams according to coaches' ratings has much to recommend it.

Team Selection Within Geographical Boundaries

Selecting players from one geographical area to constitute a team is popular because it is convenient. The players are usually acquainted, they can often walk to the practice area because such sites are frequently associated with neighborhood schools, and if practices and games are held in areas that require transportation, it is easier for parents to arrange car pools.

The disadvantages of having all of the players on a team from one geographical area include: a) a reduced possibility that the children will make new friends through their sports experience; b) a tendency to have children play under the direction of one or several coaches during their entire eligibility; c) a tendency toward uneven talent between teams because of cultural and ethnic differences within communities that may emphasize or deemphasize certain sports.

Figure 2.   Equating teams is likely to be traumatic for those who are not skillful unless adults devise alternate methods of selecting competitors.

First Come—First Served

This procedure also falls into the category of a *convenient* distribution of talent. The number of players on a team is predetermined and children are placed on rosters as they register. As soon as the quota for one team is filled, another team is begun. This system of establishing teams on a first come—first served basis has many disadvantages, but unfortunately, it has survived because parents and children have devised strategies to "beat the system." For example, coaches who know the abilities of a group of players could have them sign up at the same time, thus virtually assuring that the entire group would be placed on the same team.

If the system of first come—first served is truly random, then players from many geographical areas may be on the same team, thereby creating some advantages and some disadvantages. As we have already suggested, this system has no built-in procedure to monitor the distribution of talent, thereby lending itself to manipulation by adults.

Unrestricted Recruitment

This method permits coaches to recruit players regardless of where they live and then enter the entire team as a competitive unit. This system of establishing teams encourages the "win-at-all costs" philosophy of youth sports and therefore has little to recommend it. Coaches who are aggressive and knowledgeable about players' talents are likely to have the best teams. Players who are relatively unskilled are not likely to be asked to join a team.

The emphasis on recruitment is contrary to the promotion of a philosophy that youth sports are available for all children. Therefore it should be discouraged except for special circumstances in which every child has been assured of a place on a team and the recruitment of players is designed to promote *elite* teams for players whose abilities are too advanced for their participation in general competition. Only when all children have been assured of a place within the general structure of a sport should we make provisions for special teams whose participation is governed by an exclusive set of rules and conditions.

Characteristics that Influence Performance

Grouping children so that each team has an equal chance of success is an important but difficult task for administrators and coaches. Ideally, each team should be arranged so that every child has an opportunity to improve his/her physical and social skills and be able to display them successfully in games and contests. Translated into wins and losses, this means that each team would win and lose approximately one-half of its contests. Yet, in the American model of sports, a team with a 50-50 record is generally not considered successful. In practical terms, there are many variables that determine the relative success or failure of sports experiences. If these variables and their influence on performance are understood by the adults who organize children's competition, then decisions made on behalf of children are likely to result in good experiences. The following variables should be considered when grouping children for sports competition.

Chronological Age

The universal criterion for grouping children for sports competition, and for many other events, is chronological age. As a measure of achievement, it is readily available because it is so commonly used. Yet, as coaches, we are aware of the

Figure 3. Selecting teams of equal ability means that many criteria must be considered.

differences that exist within children of any one age group. In fact, as the children grow from infancy to adolescence, the differences within one age group in size, maturity, social, and mental achievement all increase with each passing year. Many of the differences in children within one chronological year are due to genetics, but some of the factors such as emotional maturity may be highly influenced by the child's environment. Whatever the causes, the differences generally are beyond the control of the coach. Our responsibility is to understand how they influence sports performance and adjust the conditions so that they maximize the opportunities for children to be successful.

For practical reasons, sports teams are generally divided into two-year age groups. For example, baseball teams may be constituted for children who are 9–10 years, 11–12 years, and so on. Thus, every other year children will either be within the youngest or the oldest age category within their competitive groups.

Ideally, teams should be formed within one-year age categories, with opportunities for the more mature, highly skilled children to move into the next age category and those who are smaller, less mature, and lacking in skill level would be moved to a younger age level. However, practical considerations generally dictate a two-year age span. The principle for consideration when classifying children for sports competition by chronological age is: *whenever possible, age categories should be restricted to two years, with classifications at one-year intervals being ideal.* Even within these limited boundaries, children will experience greater success if exceptions based on extreme proficiency or lack of success are permitted to move children either back or ahead of their chronological age groups.

Skill Level

The overriding determination of success in sports is an ability to perform the physical skills by which the sport is recognized. Although there are many types of sports skills tests, doing well on such tests does not always guarantee that these test scores will transfer to skilled performances in games and contests. However, a coach whose tests are as similar as possible to the events that are likely to occur in games will have a good indication of a child's abilities. This information also may be used to determine what should be taught in practices and to assess the progress that individuals have made during the course of the season.

The determination of skill level and ability in children's sports must always be considered in relation to others with whom the child competes. A ten-year-old baseball pitcher may be highly skilled within his/her age group, but only average when compared to the eleven- and twelve-year-old children in the next level. Other factors, such as body size and social maturity, may be more important than skill level in certain situations. For various reasons, the skill level of a child should not be the only consideration when decisions are made about group placement.

Body Size

The variations in height and weight within and between age groups of boys and girls is shown in Table 1. Note that a difference of nine or ten inches in height between the taller and shorter individuals of the same age is common at age nine and thereafter. In weight the difference between the smallest and largest children is even more dramatic. At age 10 and thereafter the largest boys and girls weigh approximately twice as much as their smallest peers. This difference in size is particularly critical in sports where collision or body contact are expected. For example, the highly skilled but small ice hockey player may not be able to protect him/herself in all situations, despite an advantage in skating ability. As coaches, we must consider the influence of body size on the success and safety

	RANGE IN HEIGHT (INS)			RANGE IN WEIGHT (LBS)	
Chronological Age	BOYS	GIRLS		BOYS	GIRLS
4	37.5 - 43.5	37.5 - 42.7		31 - 46	28 - 45
5	40.0 - 46.0	39.5 - 45.5		33 - 52	33 - 50
6	42.5 - 48.5	42.0 - 48.5		37 - 58	35 - 56
7	44.5 - 51.0	44.0 - 51.7		42 - 66	40 - 66
8	46.5 - 53.5	46.0 - 53.5		45 - 78	44 - 77
9	48.5 - 56.0	47.5 - 56.0		47 - 88	48 - 88
10	50.0 - 58.5	50.0 - 58.7		52 - 98	53 - 103
11	52.0 - 61.0	52.5 - 61.5		58 - 114	60 - 120
12	54.0 - 63.5	55.0 - 64.0		63 - 128	66 - 132
13	56.0 - 66.5	57.0 - 66.0		74 - 143	75 - 147
14	58.5 - 69.5	58.5 - 67.5		83 - 158	83 - 160
15	61.0 - 71.5	59.0 - 68.0		94 - 174	87 - 172
16	63.0 - 73.0	59.5 - 68.0		105 - 187	95 - 178
17	65.0 - 73.5	59.5 - 68.5		115 - 202	96 - 181
18	65.5 - 73.7	60.0 - 68.5		118 - 212	99 - 182

Table 1.   The ranges of body size, as determined by height and weight, are large in middle childhood but they become enormous during adolescence. (Data from the National Center for Health Statistics, © 1976. Ranges include the 95th and 5th percentiles.)

of our players. Any child who does not have the capacity to play safely within a specific group should be moved to a level where the possibility of safe play is more likely.

Experience

Exposure of children to a sport at an early age is likely to result in two advantages over those who have never played the sport: an increased skill level, and an ability to use the skills wisely during contests. The use of mental skills, employed as strategies, is an ability that is related to chronological age. For a more detailed discussion of mental skills as they relate to sports performance, see Chapter 5, "Guidelines For Selecting Skills, Rules and Strategies."

Gender

The question of whether girls and boys are able to compete on an equal basis in children's sports is of universal concern to parents, coaches, administrators, and more recently, our courts of law. Clearly, the dramatic gains that have been

Figure 4. Despite claims that children prior to puberty should be able to compete on an equal basis, the greatest gains in sports for girls have occurred in separate-but-equal programs.

made in sports participation by girls and women have occurred in separate-but-equal programs that were mandated by federal law. What is not so clearly established is whether girls are experiencing these same benefits in the co-educational world of youth sports. Preliminary evidence from tests of skills and physical fitness suggest that although there is a tremendous overlap in the values attained by boys and girls of the same age, in tests of strength, power, and endurance, the higher scores are achieved by the boys. This is particularly true in tests of muscular strength and endurance involving the trunk and upper extremities.

The controversy of whether differences between boys and girls in sports performance is due to genetics or based on social-culture stereotypes is of little consequence to the youth sports coach. The important consideration should be whether or not the individual is in an environment in which his/her abilities can be developed to their maximum capacity. When youth sports coaches and administrators become sufficiently knowledgeable about teaching skills, assessing performance levels, and predicting with accuracy the outcomes of our programs, then the gender of the performer will fade in comparison to the importance of many other variables. For a more detailed discussion concerning the issue of gender in sports performance see Chapter 19, "What about Co-ed Competition?"

Summary

Grouping children for sports competition has been a perplexing problem because in the past we have settled for the simplest of solutions: that of using chronological age as the primary criterion for eligibility to enter or continue in competitive events. If we are to increase the successful experiences of children in sport, we must consider competition from the child's viewpoint of "What's fair?" Children's concept of equality, as reflected in the adjustments they make during free play, is much more sensitive to injustice and is less rigid than the rules which adults impose on the games children play.

Adults have devised numerous methods for placing children into groups for purposes of sports competition. The most successful of these, from the viewpoint of providing maximum opportunities for success, restrict the age range of children within a competitive category to one or two years and avoid the devastating effects of exclusion that occur when recruitment is part of the selection process. Systems in which every child who desires to participate in competitive sports is guaranteed an opportunity to develop the motor, physical, and social skills inherent in that sporting experience are highly recommended in lieu of the professional model where only those already highly skilled are permitted to play.

chapter fourteen

Principles of Effective Coach-Athlete Interactions

Frank L. Smoll and Ronald E. Smith
University of Washington

14

Questions to consider . . .

☐ *What is the psychology of coaching, and how can you best apply it?*

☐ *What is a healthy philosophy of winning, and how can you teach it to young athletes?*

☐ *What is the difference between positive versus negative approaches to influencing athletes' behavior?*

☐ *According to the positive approach to coaching, what should you do in response to (a) desirable performance and effort, (b) mistakes, (c) misbehavior by athletes, and (d) violations of team rules?*

☐ *What kinds of coaching behaviors can you use to get positive things to happen and to create a good learning environment?*

☐ *How can you improve your communication skills and level of self-awareness?*

The essence of human interaction involves attempts to affect the behavior of others. As a coach, you are trying to influence athletes in many important ways. You want to create a good learning situation so youngsters acquire the technical skills of sports. You want to create an enjoyable social environment in which athletes relate well to one another and to you. You also want to provide a setting in which athletes develop desirable personality traits. The decisions you make and things you do are attempts to influence athletes in positive ways. Basically, you are trying to increase certain desired behaviors and decrease undesirable behaviors.

The toughest part of coaching is the psychology of getting what you want to teach across to the kids.

Most of the psychology of coaching is simply a set of strategies designed to increase the ability to influence others in desired ways. This chapter presents some psychological principles that contribute to effective coach-athlete interactions. Many of the principles will be recognized as things you already do. There is nothing mystical about them. In fact, it is often said that psychology is the application of common sense, and these coaching guidelines make good sense. In addition, they are scientifically sound!

The principles in this chapter are based on scientific evidence rather than on athletic folklore. They represent the results of a seven-year, two-phase research project on coaching behaviors and their effects on young athletes. In Phase I, a large scale study was done to determine how specific coaching behaviors were related to young athletes' attitudes toward their coach, teammates, themselves, and other aspects of their sport participation (Smith, Smoll, & Curtis, 1978; Smoll, Smith, Curtis, & Hunt, 1978).

Sport psychology research shows that coaching effectiveness can be improved.

Phase II used the results of Phase I to develop a sport psychology training program called Coach Effectiveness Training (CET) (Smoll & Smith, 1980). The coaching guidelines in this chapter form the heart of CET. To test the program, one group of coaches participated in a CET workshop, serving as an experimental group. They were compared with a group of coaches who did not receive any special training.

The results were very encouraging. Careful observations showed that the behavior of CET coaches was much more in agreement with the guidelines than was the behavior of the untrained coaches. The experimental coaches not only learned the guidelines, they successfully applied them! The average won-lost records of the two groups of coaches were similar, but CET coaches were liked better and were rated better teachers by their athletes. The positive psychological climate created by the CET coaches had other effects as well. The athletes of the CET coaches liked their teammates more, and their self-esteem increased over the course of the season (Smith, Smoll, & Curtis, 1979).

> *When things click on a psychological level, you*
> *will get much more enjoyment out of coaching.*

Just as the CET coaches did, you can use the coaching guidelines to improve the quality of your athletes' sport experience. The challenge is not so much to learn the principles, but to adapt them to your own coaching style. This requires dedication on your part. However, the favorable outcomes will be well worth the extra effort!

GUIDELINES FOR RELATING EFFECTIVELY TO YOUNG ATHLETES

The series of coaching "dos and don'ts" are based primarily on: (a) a view of success, or "winning," as consisting of giving maximum effort in striving to accomplish goals; and (b) a positive approach to social influence that emphasizes the use of reinforcement and encouragement while discouraging the use of punishment and criticism.

> *By creating a psychologically healthy situation,*
> *all children can be winners.*

A Winning Philosophy For Youth Sports

During his years as coach of the Green Bay Packers, Vince Lombardi created a professional football dynasty. His team was the powerhouse of the NFL during the 1960s—a team driven to near perfection by an intensely competitive leader. Lombardi's image was immortalized in the famous statement, "Winning isn't everything, it's the only thing." But did you know that Lombardi never said that? Years after his death, his son revealed that his father had been misquoted. What Lombardi actually said was, "Winning isn't everything, but striving to win is."

The common notion in sports equates success with victory—scoring more points, runs, or goals than the opponent. Yet, we suggest that the measure of a person's or a team's success goes beyond records and standings. Success is a personal thing and is related to one's own standards and abilities.

> *"Success is peace of mind, which is a direct result of self-satisfaction in knowing you did your best to become the best that you are capable of becoming."*
> *—John Wooden, former UCLA basketball coach*

Wooden's perspective on success may be the most important reason why he deserves the title "Wizard of Westwood." He realized that everyone can be a success, because success relates to the effort that one puts into attaining one's potential.

Because of the educational potential of sport, children can learn from both winning and losing. But for this to occur, winning must be placed in a *healthy* perspective. The following four-part philosophy of winning is designed to maximize young athletes' enjoyment of sport and their chances of receiving the positive benefits of participation.

1. Winning isn't everything, nor is it the only thing. Young athletes can't possibly learn from winning and losing if they think the only objective is to beat their opponents. Does this mean that you should not try to build winning teams? Definitely not! As a form of competition, sport involves a contest between opposing individuals or teams. It would be naive and unrealistic to believe that winning is not an important goal in sports, but it should not be the most important objective. Children should leave your program having enjoyed relating to you and their teammates, feeling better about themselves, having improved their skills, and looking forward to future sport participation. When this happens, something far more valuable has been accomplished than a winning record or a league championship.

> *Although happy athletes do not always win, they need never lose.*

2. Failure is not the same thing as losing. Athletes should not view losing as a sign of failure or as a threat to their personal value. They should be taught that losing a game is not a reflection of their own self-worth. In other words, when an individual or team loses a contest, it does not mean that the esteem held for them will be any less than if they had won. In fact, some valuable lessons can be learned from losing. Children can learn to persist in the face of obstacles and to support each other even when they do not achieve victory.

3. *Success is not equivalent to winning.* Neither success nor failure need depend on the outcome of a contest or on a won-lost record. Winning and losing apply to the outcome of a contest, whereas success and failure do not. How, then, can we define success in sports?

4. *Children should be taught that success is found in striving for victory.* The important idea is that *success is related to effort!* The only thing that athletes have complete control over is the amount of effort they give. They have only limited control over the outcome that is achieved. If you can impress on your athletes that they are never "losers" if they give maximum effort, you are giving them a priceless gift that will assist them in many of life's tasks.

A major cause of athletic stress is fear of failure. When young athletes know that making mistakes or losing a contest while giving maximum effort is acceptable to you, this removes a potent source of pressure. Moreover, if you apply this same standard of success to yourself, you will be less likely to define your own adequacy in terms of a won-lost record and will more likely focus on the important children's goals of participation, skill development, and fun. You will also be less likely to experience stress of your own when your teams are not winning. When winning is kept in perspective, the child comes first and winning is second (Martens & Seefeldt, 1979). In this case, the most important coaching product is not a won-lost record; it is the quality of the experience provided for the athletes.

The positive approach is designed to create positive motivation rather than fear of failing.

Behavioral Guidelines

There are two basic approaches to influencing people. The *positive approach* is designed to strengthen desired behaviors by motivating people to perform them and by rewarding or reinforcing them when they occur. The *negative approach* uses various forms of punishment in an attempt to eliminate unwanted behaviors. The motivating factor here is fear. Both of these approaches are used by coaches, but there are two main reasons why the positive approach is preferred. First, it works much better! Second, it creates an enjoyable psychological and social climate. The coaching behaviors and principles contained in the positive approach are discussed in the following.

Figure 1. A healthy philosophy of winning helps to combat fear of failure.

Reacting to Athlete Behaviors and Game Situations

Reactive coaching behaviors occur immediately after individual athlete or team behaviors. They include responses to:

- desirable performance and effort
- mistakes
- misbehavior by athletes
- violations of team rules

The most effective way to build desirable behaviors is to use your "reinforcement power."

Good Plays—Using "Reinforcement Power"

Influencing athletes' behavior in a desirable way involves the process of learning. It is well known that people tend to repeat behaviors that produce pleasant outcomes, and they do not learn behaviors that produce neutral or negative results. In this context, reinforcement refers to any event occurring after a behavior that increases the likelihood that the behavior will occur again in the future. Examples of positive reinforcement that you use include verbal praise as well as nonverbal forms of communication, such as a pat on the back, a smile, applause, and a friendly nod of your head. The cornerstone of the positive approach is the skillful use of reinforcement to increase athletic motivation and to strengthen desired behaviors.

1. Be liberal with reinforcement. In our research, the single most important difference between coaches to whom athletes responded most favorably and those to whom they responded least favorably was the frequency with which coaches reinforced desirable behaviors. You can increase the effectiveness of verbal reinforcement by combining it with a specific description of the desirable behavior that the athlete just performed. For example, you might say, "Way to go, Chris! You kept your head in there on the follow-through." In this way, you combine the power of the reinforcement with an instructional reminder of what the athlete should do. It also tells the athlete to concentrate on a specific event or action.

Reinforcement should not be restricted to learning and performance of sport skills. Rather, it should also be liberally applied to strengthen desirable psychosocial behaviors, such as teamwork, leadership, and sportsmanship. Look for positive things, reinforce them, and you will see them increase. Reinforce the little things that others might not notice. This is not a sickeningly sweet approach with which there is a danger of being phony and losing credibility. When sincerely given, reinforcement does not spoil youngsters; it gives them something to strive for. Remember, whether athletes show it or not, the reinforcement you give them helps to strengthen the good feelings they have about themselves.

Successful coaching requires skillful use of reinforcement.

2. Have realistic expectations and consistently reinforce achievement. Gear your expectations to individual ability levels. For some athletes, merely running up and down the field or court without tripping is a significant accomplishment worthy of praise. For those who are more skilled, set your expectations at appropriately higher levels.

Consistency of reinforcement is particularly important during the early part of the learning process. When new skills are being taught, give continuous reinforcement (i.e., reinforcement after every correct response). More specifically, during the initial stages of learning, reinforcement should be given for any sign of improvement or progress toward the ultimate objective.

Once skills are well learned, gradually shift your reinforcement to a partial schedule in which some correct responses are reinforced and some are not. A partial reinforcement schedule is more effective in maintaining motivation and in preventing the disappearance of a learned behavior that occurs when there is no reinforcement. The effective administration of reinforcement thus requires complete knowledge of teaching-learning progressions, sensitivity to individual differences in athletes' levels of abilities and learning rates, and use of good judgment in applying reinforcement.

3. Give reinforcement for desirable behavior as soon as it occurs. Immediate reinforcement has more potent effects. But even delayed reinforcement is better than none at all!

Don't take athletes' efforts for granted.

4. Reinforce effort as much as results. This guideline has direct relevance to developing a healthy philosophy of winning. To put this philosophy into practice, tell your athletes that their efforts are valued and appreciated, and back up your words with action—reinforcement! Athletes' efforts should not be ignored or taken for granted. As stated earlier, athletes have complete control over how much effort they make, but they have only limited control over the outcome of their efforts. By looking for and reinforcing athletes' efforts, you can encourage them to maintain or increase their output.

If you manage things right, mistakes can be golden opportunities to improve performance.

Reacting to Mistakes

Many athletes are motivated to achieve because of a positive desire to succeed. They appear to welcome and peak under pressure. Unfortunately, many others are motivated primarily by fear of failure. Consequently, they dread critical game situations and the possibility of failure and disapproval. Fear of failure can be an athlete's worst enemy. It can harm performance, and it reduces the enjoyment of competing. The way you react to athletes' mistakes plays a major role in either creating or combating fear of failure.

A typical attitude about mistakes is that they are totally bad and must be avoided at all costs. To avoid this negative view, you should recognize that mistakes are not only unavoidable, but they have a positive side as well. John Wooden referred to mistakes as the "stepping stones to achievement." They provide information that is needed to improve performance. By communicating this concept to athletes in word and action, you can help them accept and learn from their mistakes. In addition, deal honestly and openly with your own mistakes. When you have the confidence and courage to admit to athletes that you made a mistake, this provides a valuable role model. Such a model is important for developing a sense of tolerance for human error and for reducing fear of failure. Remember, the positive approach is designed to create a positive motive to achieve, rather than a fear of failure. The following guidelines provide the key elements in the positive approach to dealing with mistakes.

Whether they show it or not, most athletes feel embarrassed when they make a mistake.

1. Give encouragement immediately after a mistake. Athletes know when they make a poor play and often feel embarrassed about it. This is the time they are in most need of your encouragement and support.

2. If an athlete knows how to correct the mistake, encouragement alone is sufficient. Telling an athlete what he/she already knows may be more irritating than helpful. Do not overload athletes with unnecessary input. If you are not sure if the athlete knows how to correct the mistake, ask the athlete for confirmation.

In giving corrective instruction, don't emphasize the mistake, but instead the good things that will happen if the athlete follows your instruction.

3. When appropriate, give corrective instruction after a mistake, but always do so in an encouraging and positive way. In line with the positive approach, mistakes can be excellent opportunities to provide technical instruction. There are three keys to giving such instruction.

- Know *what* to do—the technical aspects of correcting performance.
- Know *how* to do it—the teaching-learning approach.
- Know *when* to do it—timing.

Most athletes respond best to immediate correction, and instruction is particularly meaningful at that time. However, some athletes respond much better to instruction if you wait for some time after the mistake. Because of individual differences, such athletes are more receptive to your instruction when it is given later.

When correcting mistakes, a three-part teaching approach is recommended.

- Start with a *compliment;* find something the athlete did correctly ("Way to hustle. You really ran a good pattern!"). This is intended to reinforce a desirable behavior and create an open attitude on the part of the athlete.
- Give the *future-oriented instruction* ("If you follow the ball all the way into your hands, you'll catch those just like a pro does."). Emphasize the desired future outcome rather than the negative one that just occurred.
- End with another *positive statement* ("Hang in there. You're going to get even better if you work at it."). This "sandwich" approach (two positive communications wrapped around the instruction) is designed to make the athlete positively self-motivated to perform correctly rather than negatively motivated to avoid failure and disapproval.

Use a positive approach to instruction rather than punishment in any form.

4. *Don't punish when things go wrong.* Punishment is any consequence that decreases the future occurrence of a behavior. Punishment can be administered in either of two forms: (1) by doing something aversive, such as painful physical contact or verbal abuse, and (2) by taking away something that is valued by the athlete, or more technically, by removing positive reinforcers that are usually available to an individual, such as privileges, social interactions, or possessions. With respect to the first form, punishment is not just yelling at athletes. It can be any form of disapproval, tone of voice, or action. Constant use of such punishment leads to resentment of the coach and is probably a factor contributing to athletic drop-out.

5. *Don't give corrective instruction in a hostile or punitive way.* Although a coach may have good intentions in giving instruction, this kind of negative communication is more likely to increase frustration and create resentment than to improve performance.

Does this mean that you should avoid all criticism and punishment? Certainly not! Sometimes these behaviors are necessary for instructional or disciplinary

Figure 2.   Use the "sandwich" approach to correcting mistakes.

Figure 3. Punitive coaching behaviors can seriously harm young athletes.

purposes. But they should be used sparingly. The negative approach should *never* be the primary approach to athletes. Although abusive coaches may enjoy success and may even be admired by some of their athletes, they run the risk of losing other athletes who could contribute to the team's success and who could profit personally from an athletic experience. Coaches who succeed through the use of punishment usually do so because (a) they are also able to communicate caring for their athletes as people, so that the abuse is not "taken personally," (b) they have very talented athletes, and/or (c) they are such skilled teachers and strategists that these abilities override their negative behaviors. In other words, such coaches win in spite of, not because of, the negative approach.

Teaching self-discipline is an important youth sport objective.

Misbehaviors, Lack of Attention —Maintaining Order and Discipline

The issues of misbehavior, discipline, and sportsmanship have also been addressed in Chapter 9, "Teaching Sportsmanship and Values." The overlap between the two presentations serves to emphasize the importance of certain coaching principles.

Problems of athlete misbehavior during games and practices can indeed become serious. In dealing effectively with this, recognize that youngsters want clearly defined limits and structure. They do not like unpredictability and inconsistency, nor do they like it when you play the role of a policeman or enforcer. Thus, the objective is to structure the situation in a way that you can avoid having to constantly read the riot act and work to keep things under control.

1. Maintain order by establishing clear expectations and a "team rule" concept.

2. Involve athletes in forming behavioral guidelines and work to build team unity in achieving them.

3. Strive to achieve a balance between freedom and structure.

These guidelines promote a cooperative approach to leadership in that athletes are given a share of the responsibility for determining their own governance. Research has shown that people are more willing to live by rules (a) when they have a hand in forming them, and (b) when they have made a public commitment to follow them.

Team rules should be developed early in the season. In helping athletes to share responsibility for forming rules, use the following procedures:

- Explain why team rules are necessary (they keep things organized and efficient, thereby increasing the chances of achieving individual and team objectives).
- Explain why the team rules should be something they can agree on as a group (they will be their rules, and it will be their responsibility to follow them).
- Solicit suggestions and ideas, and listen to what athletes say to show that their ideas and feelings are valued.
- Incorporate athletes' input into a reasonable set of rules. Rules should provide structure, and yet not be too rigid.
- Discuss the kinds of penalties that you will use for breaking of team rules.

Figure 4. Involve team members when establishing rules and the consequences of violating them.

Here again, athletes should participate in determining the consequences that will follow rule violations.

The advantage of this approach is that it places the responsibility where it belongs—on the athletes themselves. Thus, when someone breaks a team rule, it is not the individual versus your rules, but the breaking of their own rules.

4. *Emphasize that during a game all members of the team are part of the game, even those on the bench.* This rule can play an important role in building team unity and mutual support among teammates.

5. *Use reinforcement to strengthen team participation and unity.* By strength-

ening desirable behaviors, you can help prevent misbehaviors from occurring. In other words, you can prevent misbehaviors by using the positive approach to strengthen their opposites. Similarly, instances of teamwork and of athletes' support and encouragement of each other should be reinforced whenever possible. This not only strengthens these desirable behaviors, but also creates an atmosphere in which you are serving as a positive model by supporting them.

Forming rules is easier than dealing with violations.

Dealing with Team Rule Violations

When you have team rules, you can expect that they will be broken from time to time. As children establish independence and personal identity, part of the process involves testing the limits imposed by adult authority figures—you, their coach! Because this is a very natural way of learning, you should not feel persecuted or singled out. It happens with all coaches and athletes.

1. Give an athlete one warning before imposing a penalty.

2. Allow the athlete to explain his/her actions. There may be a reasonable cause for what the athlete did or did not do, and lines of communication should be kept open.

3. Be consistent and impartial. In other words, avoid showing favoritism by treating *all* athletes equally and fairly.

4. Don't express anger and a punitive attitude. And, of course, never take action for the purpose of retaliating.

5. Don't lecture or embarrass the athlete. It simply is not necessary or beneficial.

A penalty must be paid for violating a rule which the team, not the coach, has established.

6. Focus on the fact that a team policy has been broken, placing the responsibility on the athlete. This should be done without degrading the individual or making the athlete feel he or she is in your "dog house." Remind the athlete that a rule which he or she agreed to follow was violated, and therefore a penalty must be paid. This focuses the responsibility where it belongs—on the athlete—and helps build a sense of personal accountability.

7. When giving penalties, it is best to deprive children of something they value. For example, participation can be temporarily suspended by having the athlete sit off to the side ("time out" or "penalty box"). Taking away game time or a starting position are also effective penalties.

8. Don't use physical measures to punish team members for rule infractions.

It is not educationally sound to have beneficial physical activities, such as running laps or doing push-ups, become unpleasant because they have been used as punishment.

Spontaneous/Self-Initiated Coaching Behaviors

Spontaneous behaviors are actions initiated by coaches which do not occur in reaction to an immediately preceding event. You can use spontaneous or self-initiated coaching behaviors to (a) get positive things to happen, and (b) create a good learning atmosphere.

Show your athaletes that you can teach them to develop their skills, and that you are willing to make the effort to do so.

Getting Positive Things to Happen

1. Set a good example of behavior. Observational learning (modeling), which is based on watching and imitating others, is an important form of learning for children. Most athletes will have a high regard for you, and consequently they are likely to copy your behaviors and deal with sport situations in similar ways. Athletes probably learn as much from what you do as from what you say! Because of this, it is important that you portray a role model worthy of respect from athletes, officials, parents, and other coaches.

The positive approach to coaching is characterized by liberal use of reinforcement and encouragement.

2. Encourage effort, don't demand results. This is another guideline that applies to the healthy philosophy of winning. Most young athletes are already motivated to develop their skills and play well. By appropriate use of encouragement, you can help to increase their natural enthusiasm. If, however, youngsters are encouraged to strive for unrealistic standards of achievement, they may feel like failures when they do not reach the goals. Therefore, it is important to base your encouragement on reasonable expectations. Again, encouraging effort rather than outcome can help avoid problems. This concept is emphasized in the words of John Wooden:

> You cannot find a player who ever played for me at UCLA that can tell you that he ever heard me mention "winning" a basketball game. He might say I inferred a little here and there, but I never mentioned winning. Yet the last thing that I told my players, just prior to tipoff, before we would go

on the floor was, "When the game is over, I want your head up—and I know of only one way for your head to be up—and that's for you to know that you did your best . . . . This means to do the best you can do. That's the best; no one can do more . . . . You made that effort."

3. *In giving encouragement, be selective so that it is meaningful.* In other words, be supportive without acting like a cheerleader. If you give encouragement in an unrealistic and insincere way, you run the risk of losing credibility.

4. *Never give encouragement or instruction in a sarcastic or degrading manner.* For example, "Come on gang, we're only down 37–1. Let's really come back and make it 37–2." Even if you do not intend the sarcasm to be harmful, youngsters sometimes do not understand the meaning of this type of communication. They may think that you are amusing others at their expense, resulting in irritation, frustration, or both.

5. *Encourage athletes to be supportive of each other, and reinforce them when they do so.* Encouragement can become contagious and contribute to building team cohesion. Communicate the enthusiasm you feel, which then carries over to your athletes. The best way to do this is by presenting an enthusiastic coaching model, and reinforcing athlete behaviors that promote team unity.

> *Sport participation should be viewed as a learning situation where you are going to help kids develop their abilities.*

Creating a Good Learning Atmosphere

Young athletes expect you to help them satisfy their desire to become as skilled as possible. Therefore, you must establish your teaching role as early as possible. In doing this, emphasize the fun and learning part of sport, and let your athletes know that one of your primary coaching goals is to help them develop their athletic potential.

Individual attention is another essential component of a positive learning environment. During each practice or game, be sure that every youngster gets recognized at least once. Athletes who usually get the most recognition are either stars, or those who are causing problems. Average athletes need attention too! A good technique is to occasionally keep a count of how often you talk with each athlete to make sure that your personal contact is being appropriately distributed.

1. *Always give instructions positively.* Emphasize the good things that will happen if athletes do it right, rather than focusing totally on the negative things that will occur if they do not. As stated earlier, this approach motivates athletes to make desirable things happen rather than building fear of making mistakes.

2. *When giving instructions, be clear and concise.* Young athletes have a short

Figure 5. Sarcasm is *not* part of the positive approach to coaching.

attention span. In addition, they may not be able to understand the technical aspects of performance in great detail. Therefore, provide simple yet accurate teaching cues, using as little verbal explanation as possible.

3. *Show athletes the correct technique.* Demonstrate or model skills being taught. If you cannot perform the skill correctly, use accomplished athletes for demonstration purposes. A proper teaching sequence includes the following:

- Introduce a skill with a demonstration.
- Provide an accurate, but brief verbal explanation.
- Have athletes actively practice the skill.

Because of the way in which children respond to teaching efforts, a Chinese proverb applies: "I hear and I forget. I see and I remember. I do and I understand."

4. *Be patient and don't expect or demand more than maximum effort.* Acquisition of sport skills does not occur overnight. The gradual learning process is characterized by periods of improvement alternated with intervals during which no progress occurs regardless of the effort expended. Not only must you be persistent, but athletes must be convinced to stick to it and continue to give their best effort.

When an athlete has had a poor practice or a rough game, he or she should not go home feeling badly. An athlete should get some kind of support from you—a pat on the back, a kind word ("Hey, we're going to work that out. I know what you're going through, but everyone has days like that sometimes."). Athletes should not leave feeling detached from you or feeling like a "loser."

5. *Reinforce effort and progress.* Again, the foundation of the positive approach is the administration of reinforcement for effort as well as good performance and a desirable attitude.

RECOMMENDATIONS FOR IMPROVING APPLICATION OF THE COACHING GUIDELINES

A complete understanding of the coaching guidelines is essential for their effective use. In addition, several issues concerning communication skills and self-awareness are important for successful application of the guidelines.

Constantly ask yourself what has been communicated to athletes and whether the communication is effective.

Communicating Effectively

Everything we do communicates something to others. Because of this, develop the habit of asking yourself (and, at times, your athletes) how your actions are being interpreted, and then evaluate if your intentions are being communicated.

Effective communication is a two-way street. By keeping the lines of interaction open, you can be more aware of opportunities to have a positive impact on athletes. Fostering two-way communication does not mean that athletes are free to be disrespectful toward you. Rather, it is an open invitation for athletes to express their views (both positive and negative), with the assurance that they will be heard by you. Furthermore, by presenting a model of an attentive listener, you may be able to improve the listening skills of your athletes.

Be a fair and considerate leader by showing athletes that you care about them as individuals and that you are glad to be coaching them.

Effective communication also is based on viewing a team as individuals and responding to them accordingly. For example, a child who has low self-confidence may be crushed (or positively affected) by something that has no impact whatever on an athlete with high self-esteem. By improving your sensitivity to the individual needs of athletes, you can be more successful. The ability to "read" athletes and respond to their needs is characteristic of effective coaches at all levels.

As a coach, you occupy an important role, and increased awareness can help to improve your effectiveness.

Increasing Self-Awareness

An important part of self-awareness is insight into how we behave and appear to others—knowing what we do and how others perceive what we do. One of the striking findings from our research was that coaches had very limited awareness of how often they behaved in various ways. Fortunately, awareness is something that can be increased. Two behavioral change techniques are recommended, namely *behavioral feedback* and *self-monitoring*.

To begin, try to develop procedures which will allow you to obtain behavioral feedback from your assistant coaches, athletes' parents, or league administrators. In other words, work with those who assist you as a team and share descriptions of each others' behaviors. You can then discuss alternate ways of dealing with problem situations and athletes and prepare yourselves for handling similar situations in the future. This requires an open relationship between adult leaders, a willingness to exchange feedback that may not always be positive, and a sincere desire to improve the ways in which you relate to athletes. Finally, at various times, you may wish to discuss situations with your athletes to obtain feedback from them. This will show your athletes that you are interested in their reactions and are motivated to provide the best possible experience for them.

Self-monitoring (observing and recording one's own behavior) involves taking some time after practices and/or games to evaluate your behaviors and actions. When going through this self-analysis, ask yourself what you did relative to the suggested behaviors in the coaching guidelines. To assist you in this procedure, a brief form is presented for self-monitoring of desirable coaching behaviors.

If possible, obtain the services of another coach or adult observer to monitor your behavior during practices and games. Then compare their perception with yours. If your self-perception does not agree with that of another observer, you need to concentrate on those areas where you disagree, especially if you are overlooking the undesirable elements of your coaching actions.

Coach Self-Report Form

Complete this form as soon as possible after a practice or game. Not only think about what you did, but also consider the kinds of situations in which the actions occurred and the kinds of athletes who were involved.

1. Approximately what percent of the times they occurred did you respond to good plays with REINFORCEMENT? _____

2. Approximately what percent of the times they occurred did you respond to mistakes with each of the following communications?
   A. ENCOURAGEMENT only _____
   B. CORRECTIVE INSTRUCTION given in an encouraging manner ___

   (sum of A plus B should not exceed 100%)

3. About how many times did you reinforce athletes for effort, complying with team rules, encouraging teammates, showing team spirit, and other behaviors? _____

4. Is there anything you might do differently if you had a chance to coach this practice/game again? If so, briefly explain. _____

SUMMARY

This chapter presents psychological principles that underlie a positive approach to effective coach-athlete interactions. The relationship-oriented approach to coaching is complemented by a healthy philosophy of winning, which stresses giving maximum effort in striving for excellence. If young athletes are well trained, give maximum effort, and have a positive motivation to achieve rather than being motivated by performance-disrupting fears of failure, winning takes care of itself within the limits of their abilities. They also are more likely to develop their athletic potential in an enjoyable, rather than in a stressful, sport environment.

Don't underestimate your importance in the personal and athletic development of your athletes, or the extent to which your efforts are appreciated.

The behavioral guidelines for coaches are placed in a context of increasing positive coach-athlete and athlete-athlete interactions, developing team cohesion, and developing in athletes a positive desire to achieve, rather than a fear of failure. The positive approach to influencing athletes emphasizes (a) the liberal use of reinforcement for effort as well as for performance, (b) giving encouragement after mistakes, and (c) giving technical instruction in an encouraging and supportive fashion. When you give technical instruction after a mistake, the guidelines suggest that you first compliment the athlete for something done correctly, then give the correction instruction, focusing on the positive things that will happen in the future if your instruction is followed. Refrain from emphasizing the negative consequences of the mistake. A decrease in the use of punitive behaviors is encouraged. Recommendations are included on how to avoid having to scold athletes frequently for misbehaviors and breaking team rules. This is partly accomplished by establishing team rules early and, in line with the positive approach, reinforcing compliance with them. Reinforcement is also recommended as a means of establishing and strengthening encouragement and support among teammates.

Your use of the coaching guidelines can be improved by applying some basic principles of effective communication. In addition, you can incorporate behavioral feedback and self-monitoring procedures to become more aware of your coaching actions. These techniques serve to increase your chances of having desirable and productive coach-athlete interactions.

REFERENCES

Martens, R., & Seefeldt, V. (1979). *Guidelines for children's sports.* Washington, DC: AAHPERD Publications.

Smith, R.E., Smoll, F.L., & Curtis, B. (1978). Coaching behaviors in Little League Baseball. In F.L. Smoll & R.E. Smith (Eds.), *Psychological perspectives in youth sports.* Washington, DC: Hemisphere.

Smith, R.E., Smoll, F.L., & Curtis, B. (1979). Coach effectiveness training: A cognitive-behavioral approach to enhancing relationship skills in youth sport coaches. *Journal of Sport Psychology, 1,* 59–75.

Smoll, F.L., & Smith, R.E. (1980). Psychologically-oriented coach training programs: Design, implementation, and assessment. In C.H. Nadeau, W.R. Halliwell, K.M. Newell, & G.C. Rogerts (Eds.), *Psychology of motor behavior and sport—1979.* Champaign, IL: Human Kinetics.

Smoll, F.L., Smith, R.E., Curtis, B., & Hunt, E.B. (1978). Toward a mediational model of coach-player relationships. *Research Quarterly, 49,* 528–541.

SUGGESTED READINGS

Seefeldt, V., Smoll, F.L., Smith, R.E., & Gould, D. (1981). *A winning philosophy for youth sports programs.* East Lansing, MI: Michigan Institute for the Study of Youth Sports.

Smith, N.J., Smith, R.E., & Smoll, F.L. (1983). *Kidsports: A survival guide for parents.* Reading, MA: Addison-Wesley.

Smith, R.E. (1986). Principles of positive reinforcement and performance feedback. In J.M. Williams (Ed.), *Applied sport psychology: Personal growth to peak performance.* Palo Alto, CA: Mayfield.

Tharp, R.G., & Gallimore, R. (1976). What a coach can teach a teacher. *Psychology Today, 9,* 75–78.

Weiss, M. (1980). *How do you rate as a coach?* East Lansing, MI: Michigan Institute for the Study of Youth Sports.

chapter fifteen

Conducting a Sport Orientation Meeting for Parents

Frank L. Smoll
University of Washington

Questions to consider . . .

☐ *Why should you have a sport orientation meeting with parents?*

☐ *What organizational issues should be considered in planning and preparing for a coach-parent meeting?*

☐ *What kind of information should be presented to parents?*

☐ *How can you create a positive environment for communicating with parents?*

C oaches undoubtedly have the most direct contact with young athletes, and they have the most significant influence on their athletic development. But parents also play an important role in youth sports. Many parents productively contribute to the success of the program. Unfortunately, however, the negative impact that parents can have is all too obvious. Some parents, through lack of understanding, can undermine the basic goals of youth sport programs and rob children of the potential benefits of athletics. What can you do to prevent this?

Parents usually receive little information or instruction that might help them promote their children's growth through sport. This is where coaches can serve an important educational function. Coaches traditionally and foremost are teachers of young athletes, but they are also in a position to educate parents. The purpose of this chapter is to offer you assistance in developing and conducting a sport orientation meeting for parents.

Having a sport orientation meeting is a good investment for everyone.

As a coach, you unselfishly devote a tremendous amount of time and effort to providing a worthwhile experience for youngsters. And you are often asked to do "just one more thing." However, successful coaches are aware of the importance of securing the aid and support of well-informed parents. Rather than facing the unpleasant task of dealing with problem parents, a sport orientation meeting is the key to reducing the chances of having undesirable situations occur throughout the season. In other words, holding a meeting with parents is well worth the additional time and effort!

This chapter is presented as a guide for you to follow. The content was developed from materials in the youth sport literature, discussions with coaches, parents, and administrators, and from personal experience in conducting sport orientation meetings. Because each coach is unique, you are encouraged to evaluate the information and make modifications to suit your personal situation. This guide provides the content and format that will help you to plan and conduct effective parent meetings.

Parents can learn a lot by attending a sport orientation meeting.

Purposes of the Meeting

The overall objective of a coach-parent meeting is to improve parents' understanding of youth sports. Their input can then increase the value of sport participation for children's physical, psychological, and social development. Some

Figure 1.   Holding a coach-parent meeting is the key to avoiding unpleasant experiences.

more specific purposes, most of which were included in Martens' (1978) listing, are the following:

- To enable parents to become acquainted with you.
- To educate parents about the objectives of youth sports and clarify the goals of your program.
- To inform parents about the specifics of the program and what is expected of the children and parents relative to these details. This includes obtaining parental assistance for accomplishing various tasks and conducting the season's activities.
- To get parents to understand and reinforce the *positive approach* to coaching that you will be using.
- To inform parents about their youth sport roles and responsibilities.
- To establish clear lines of communication between you and parents.
- To help you understand the concerns of parents.

Parents have a responsibility for acquiring basic knowledge about sports.

A sport orientation meeting might also be used to increase parents' knowledge of the sport. Information about basic rules, skills, and strategies is probably not necessary for the more popular sports, but could be beneficial for the lesser known sports. However, time limitations usually prevent their coverage at a parents' orientation meeting. As an alternative, part of an early season practice could be devoted to a lecture-demonstration of sport fundamentals. Parents having little background in the sport should be encouraged to attend this session.

Planning and Preparation

One reason for being hesitant about conducting a parent sport orientation meeting is that you might feel insecure about leading a group of adults. This is not unusual. People are often unwilling to do things for which they have had little training or previous experience. Coaches who have held parent meetings indicate that it is not overwhelming, and the benefits make the meeting a good investment. The meeting does not have to be elaborate to be successful. However, the importance of being well prepared and organized cannot be overemphasized!

Leading a coach-parent meeting can be enjoyable.

When Should The Meeting Be Held?

Schedule the meeting early in the season, if possible—preferably a week to ten days before the first practice. A weeknight or Saturday morning is probably most convenient. This can be determined by talking with several parents to learn of their preference for the day, time, and place of a meeting.

Where Should The Meeting Be Held?

Ideally, your league or club will have a central facility that could be used. If not, the location you select should be easily accessible and should have a meeting room of adequate size, with appropriate features (seating, lighting, etc.). If necessary, solicit the assistance of parents. For example, a business person might have access to a company conference room; a teacher might be able to secure the use of a school room; or a service club member might have use of the club facility.

How Long Should The Meeting Be?

It will take approximately 75 minutes to cover the necessary topics. It is your responsibility to start the meeting on time, keep it moving along, and finish reasonably close to the specified time.

Should Athletes Attend The Meeting?

Some coaches have no objection to having athletes attend the meeting with their parents. They believe it helps improve communication among all those involved. Other coaches find it more productive to conduct the meeting without the children present. Your personal preference will determine the policy adopted. However, if you elect to exclude the children, make special arrangements for parents who might not be able to attend without their children. For example, an additional room might be sought in which the children could be shown an educational sport film under the supervision of an assistant coach.

A written invitation should be sent to parents well in advance of the meeting.

How Should Parents Be Informed About The Meeting?

Use a personal letter of invitation to notify parents. This letter should be sent three weeks before the meeting date. Include brief statements about the objectives of the meeting, its importance, and the parents' responsibility for attending.

Also include information about the date, time, location and directions, attendance by youngsters, and other specifics that you feel are necessary. Send a team roster, including addresses and telephone numbers, with the letter.

As an additional way of promoting attendance, follow-up telephone calls a week before the meeting are recommended. This could be accomplished by enlisting the aid of parents to set up a chain-calling system.

You should develop your reputation as a well-organized leader.

How Can The Content Be Organized?

Provide parents with a written program outline. A carefully prepared outline improves the organizational quality of the meeting, and it helps parents to understand the content. Following an outline makes it easier for you to keep the meeting moving in a crisp, systematic way. This serves to avoid wasteful time lags.

What Other Preparation Is Necessary?

Part of the meeting will consist of a question-answer session. To prepare yourself for the kinds of questions that might be asked, an excellent source is *Guidelines for Children's Sports* (Martens and Seefeldt, 1979). This booklet was written by two youth sport authorities, and was prepared specifically for youth sport coaches.[1]

As an additional consideration, you might want to provide name tags and a sheet on which parents can write their names, addresses, and telephone numbers. Name tags are a good way to learn identities, and they promote the friendly environment that is necessary for a successful meeting. Finally, having refreshments before and after the meeting (coffee and donuts, juice, etc.) is an effective way to promote interaction among the parents.

Content and Conduct of the Meeting

For any educational program, even the very best content is of doubtful value if a cooperative learning environment is not established by the program leader, or if hostility and resistance are created by the participants. If you conduct your

---

[1]For pricing and order information, contact: American Alliance Publications, 1900 Association Drive, Reston, VA 22091, telephone (703) 476-3481.

meeting as a two-way sharing of information, defensiveness and ill will can be minimized. Some of the parents in attendance will have a considerable amount of knowledge about sports. Therefore, it is best to take advantage of their expertise by encouraging them to share it with the group.

Effective communication involves both speaking and listening skills.

As the leader of the session, you will do most of the talking. However, the meeting will be more effective if you involve the parents in a discussion, instead of lecturing to them. You can do this by (a) encouraging parents to ask questions, and (b) directing questions to them from time to time and relating their answers to the main points you want to make. Also, in creating an open atmosphere for exchange it is very important to show respect for the parents. Make them feel that they are a contributing part of the meeting, rather than a mere audience.

The sport orientation meeting described below contains seven separate components. The following program elements are included:

- opening
- objectives of youth sports
- details of your sport program
- coaching roles and relationships
- parent roles and responsibilities
- coach-parent relations
- closing

Parents deserve praise for attending your meeting.

Opening (5 minutes)

Begin the meeting by introducing yourself and your assistant coach(es). During the welcome, let the parents know that you appreciate their interest and concern. Some parents may not care enough to attend, but those who do attend deserve credit. In praising their dedication, point out that they are taking an important step toward assuring a quality sport experience for their children.

In order to gain the parents' respect, your credibility must be established. You can do this by giving pertinent background information about your experience in the sport, your experience as a coach, and special training that you have had, such as attendance at coaching workshops and clinics. Let them know you are

Figure 2. In working with parents, it is essential to develop and maintain open, healthy communication with them.

a competent coach, and that you will make every effort to provide a positive sport experience by doing the best job you can.

During this introductory period, identify the purposes of the meeting. In addition, you might want to invite parents to attend an early season practice session. This will serve to provide them with information about fundamentals of the sport. It will also familiarize them with your coaching style.

A note of caution is in order. You might be conducting a sport orientation meeting for the first time, or might have little experience in leading adults. Do not begin the meeting by announcing this as a personal shortcoming, or by asking for the parents' tolerance. Such statements may reduce their trust and support in you as their child's coach. Self-degrading remarks may also cause parents to question your ability to conduct the meeting. To gain respect, you must show confidence in leading the session.

Youth sports provide a variety of educational opportunities for young athletes.

Objectives of Youth Sports (10 minutes)

After the opening remarks have been made, initiate a discussion of the objectives of children's athletics. Some of the goals are physical, such as attaining sport skills and increasing physical fitness. Others are psychological, such as developing leadership skills, self-discipline, respect for authority, competitiveness, cooperativeness, sportsmanship, and self-confidence. These are many of the positive traits that fall under the heading of "building character." Athletics are also an important social activity in which youngsters can make new friends and acquaintances. Furthermore, sports can serve to bring families closer together. Finally, of course, youth sports are (or should be) just plain *fun!*

Striving for excellence is essential to a healthy *philosophy of winning.*

What about *winning?* With a "winning is everything" philosophy, young athletes may lose opportunities to develop their skills, to enjoy participation, and to grow socially and emotionally. As emphasized in Chapter 14, "Principles of Effective Coach-Athlete Interactions," well-informed coaches realize that success is not equivalent to winning games, and failure is not the same as losing. Rather, the most important kind of success comes from striving to win and giving maximum effort. The only thing athletes can control is the amount of effort they give. They have incomplete control over the outcome that is achieved. Athletes should be taught that they are never "losers" if they give maximum effort in striving for excellence.

This philosophy of success is relevant to parents as well as coaches. In fact, it may be more important for parents to understand its meaning. They can apply it to many areas of their child's life in addition to athletics.

What about the objectives that young athletes seek to achieve in their sports experience? A sport psychologist, Dr. Daniel Gould (1980), summarized the results of two studies that indicated young athletes most often participate in sports for the following reasons:

- to have fun
- to improve their skills and learn new skills

- to be with their friends or make new friends
- for thrills and excitement
- to succeed or win
- to become physically fit

These goals should be considered when you set priorities for the season. In discussing the objectives with parents, focus on goals that are a major part of your coaching. Also, you might want to ask parents which objectives they would like to have you emphasize. Chapter 7, "Goalsetting: Principles for the Coach and Athlete," contains additional information about this topic.

> *Objectives can only be achieved by the cooperative efforts of coaches, athletes, administrators, and parents.*

Inform parents that no objective can be achieved automatically as a result of participation in sports. Moreover, talking about objectives is no guarantee that each child will receive all of the desired outcomes. Coaches, parents, and sport officials are part of a team trying to achieve common goals. By working to reduce chances of misunderstandings and problems, the objectives can be achieved. Encourage parents to view their involvement in youth sports as an integral part of their child-rearing responsibilities.

Another issue requiring clarification is the difference between youth and professional models of sport. Youth sports are believed to provide an educational medium for the development of desirable physical and psychosocial characteristics. These programs are viewed as miniature life situations in which children can learn to cope with realities they will face in later life. Thus, athletics provide a setting within which an educational process can occur. On the other hand, professional sports are a huge commercial enterprise. Financial success is of primary importance and depends heavily on a product orientation, namely, winning. Because of this, there are very different philosophies about the notion of sport for education versus sport as part of the entertainment industry. Chapter 1, "Benefits of Competitive Sports for Children," provides additional information on this subject.

> *A competent coach attends to details.*

Details of Your Sport Program (10 minutes)

During this part of the meeting, present details about the operation of your sport program. In addition to other items that you might think of, give consideration to the following:

- equipment needed and where it can be purchased
- sites and schedules for practices and contests (games, matches, meets)
- length of practices and contests
- team travel plans
- major team rules and guidelines
- special rule modifications to be used at this level of competition
- medical examinations
- insurance
- fund-raising projects
- communication system for cancellations, etc.
- midseason and postseason events

You should also provide information about what is expected of the athletes and parents relative to the program details. Some coaches find it useful to organize a parent committee, giving this committee the task of coordinating parent involvement in many activities of the season.

The positive approach to coach-athlete interactions involves the use of reinforcement, encouragement, and technical instruction.

Coaching Roles and Relationships (10 minutes)

Parents will benefit from knowing about your coaching style. In addition to describing the *positive approach* that you will be using (see Chapter 14, "Principles of Effective Coach-Athlete Interactions"), encourage parents to use this approach in interactions with their children.

Parents often lack knowledge about their obligations to their child's sports program.

Parents' Roles and Responsibilities (20 minutes)

Informing parents about their roles in youth sports and the responsibilities you expect them to fulfill is the most important part of the meeting. To begin, parents must realize that children have a right to participate in sports. This includes the right to choose *not* to participate (Martens & Seefeldt, 1979). Parents should encourage participation, but children should not be pressured, intimidated, or bribed into playing. If children feel forced or pushed to participate, it decreases their chances of receiving the benefits of sports. Parents should therefore counsel their children about participation goals, which includes consideration of the sports selected and the level of competition. The child's decision to play or not to play should be respected by the parents.

Parents can be a potent source of athletic stress.

At this time in the meeting, it is appropriate to point out how parents might unknowingly become a source of stress to young athletes. All parents identify with their children to some extent and thus want them to do well. Unfortunately, in some cases, the degree of identification becomes excessive. The child becomes an extension of the parents. When this happens, parents begin to define their own self-worth in terms of their son or daughter's successes or failures. The father who is a "frustrated jock" may seek to experience through his child the success he never knew as an athlete. The parent who was a star may be resentful and rejecting if the child does not attain similar achievements. Some parents thus become "winners" or "losers" through their children, and the pressure placed on the children to excel can be extreme. The child must succeed or the parent's self-image is threatened. Much more is at stake than a mere game, and the child of such a parent carries a heavy burden. When parental love and approval are dependent on adequacy of performance, sports are bound to be stressful.

As a coach, you might be able to counteract this tendency by explaining the identification process to parents. Tell them that if they place too much pressure on children, they can decrease the potential that sports can have for enjoyment and personal growth. A key to reducing parent-produced stress is to impress on them that youth sports are for young athletes, and that children are not miniature adults. Parents must acknowledge the right of each child to develop athletic potential in an atmosphere that emphasizes participation, personal growth, and fun.

Parents must make important commitments to their children's welfare if the benefits of sports are to be realized.

To contribute to the success of your sport program, parents must be willing and able to commit themselves in many different ways. Al Rosen (1967), a former major league baseball player, developed some questions that can serve as a thought-provoking tool for discussion. In presenting them to parents, emphasize the importance of being able to honestly answer "yes" to all the questions.

Figure 3.   Youth sport parents have many obligations to fulfill.

Can you give up your child? This requires that parents place their child completely in your charge and trust you to guide his or her sport experience. It involves accepting your authority and the fact that you may gain some of the child's admiration that once was directed solely at the parent.

"Perfect" people simply do not exist.

Can you admit your shortcomings? Parents must be convinced that the proper response to a mistake or not knowing something is an honest disclosure. They must not hesitate to openly discuss personal limitations with their child.

Can you accept your child's triumphs? This sounds easy, but it is not always so. Some parents do not realize it, but fathers in particular may be competitive with their sons. For example, if a boy does well in a contest, his father may point out minor mistakes, describe how others did even better, or bring up something more impressive from memories of his own sport achievements.

Can you accept your child's disappointments? Accepting a child's disappointments may mean watching him or her lose a contest while others triumph, or not being embarrassed into anger when their 10-year-old cries after losing. When a disappointment occurs, parents should be able to help their children to see the positive side of the experience.

Youngsters learn from what they see.

Can you show your child self-control? Remind parents that they are important role models for their children's behavior. Your coaching task becomes immeasurably more difficult if parents lose control of themselves at contests. Teaching sportsmanship and self-control to youngsters whose parents obviously lack these qualities may be a difficult task.

Can you give your child some time? Some parents are too busy to become involved in their child's sports program. Often this neglect becomes a source of frustration, because most parents are interested and want to encourage their children. The best advice you can give them is never to promise more time than they can actually deliver. Recommend that parents ask their children about their sport experiences and make every effort to watch some of their contests.

Can you let your child make his or her own decisions? This is an essential part of growing up and a real challenge to parents. Encourage them to offer suggestions and guidance relative to sports, but ultimately, within reasonable limits, they should let the youngster go his or her own way. All parents have ambitions for their child, but they must accept the fact that they cannot dominate the child's life. Sports can offer parents an introduction to the major process of "letting go."

Some parents may want to participate in teaching their children sport skills. Emphasize to them that the *positive approach* to coaching applies equally to parents. Like you, they should encourage their children to do as well as they are currently able, reinforce effort as well as outcome, and avoid the use of criticism and punishment for mistakes. In this way, parents can foster development of a positive motivation to achieve and prevent development of fear of failure.

Parents must conform to acceptable standards of behavior.

The most noticeable parental problem is misbehavior at contests. As part of their responsibilities, parents should watch their children compete in sports. As spectators, their behavior must meet acceptable standards. In this regard, Martens and Seefeldt (1979) recommend the following rules:

- Parents should remain seated in the spectator area during the contest.
- Parents should not yell instructions or criticism to the children.
- Parents should make no derogatory comments to players or other parents of the opposing team, to officials, or to league administrators.
- Parents should not interfere with their children's coach. They must be willing to relinquish the responsibility for their children to the coach for the duration of all practices and contests.

Rather than dictating regulations to parents, use a team approach to forming rules of conduct. There are several things you can do to involve parents in the process. You can introduce the topic by saying something like:
"I think rules for parents' behavior at contests are important for achieving our goals. This will ensure everyone's enjoyment. Rules for parents ought to be something we can agree on. I have a set of rules that I feel are important. To be effective, you must agree that they are appropriate and then strive to follow them, so you ought to think about what *you* want. They should be your rules, too."
Ask the parents if they have any suggestions and ideas, and listen to what they say. Show that you value their ideas and feelings. There is an advantage to this approach. It places the responsibility where it belongs—on the parents themselves.

The conduct of the fans at your games is not your responsibility.

Clearly establish your roles and expectations: (a) impress on parents that as the coach, you are responsible for the team; and (b) as parents, they are responsible for their own behavior. When parents violate these rules, it is the duty of other parents and league administrators to step in and correct the situation.

To conclude this part of the meeting, make arrangements for contacting parents who are not in attendance. In addition to having a parent duplicate and distribute copies of the rules for parents, assign someone the task of "passing on the word" about parents' roles and responsibilities.

Coach-Parent Relations (5 minutes)

Tell parents of your willingness to discuss any problems that might arise. Let them know that you are open to receiving their input. Remember that effective communication is a two-way street, requiring both speaking and listening skills. Also, productive exchange between coaches and parents cannot occur unless there is an atmosphere of mutual respect and courtesy.

> *Effective communication is the key to friendly, productive relations with parents.*

If you keep the lines of communication open, you will be more likely to have constructive relations with parents. There is, however, a proper time and place for interaction with you. That time is not during practices or a contest, and it is never in the presence of the children. Tell parents what times and places are best suited for discussions with you.

There may be some special traits of particular children that you should know about. For example, they may have medical or psychological problems that could affect their participation. Encourage parents to share this type of information with you on a confidential basis. This will better prepare you for dealing effectively with the young athlete, and perhaps with the parents as well.

> *You have an obligation to listen to the concerns of parents.*

The most common cause of coach-parent conflicts is a difference of opinions about the young athlete's abilities. Sometimes parents will disagree with what you are doing as a coach. This might even happen during the sport orientation meeting. If this occurs, do not become defensive. Listen to what they have to say. Some of their suggestions may be helpful. Even if you do not agree, you should listen and evaluate the message. Realize that you, the coach, must make the final decision. Remember that no coach can please everyone. No one can ask any more than that you perform to the level of your present competence.

In establishing good communication with parents, be aware that most parents are really enthusiastic and have a true concern for their children. Sometimes, however, parents simply do not realize the trouble they are causing. Instead of being angry with them, recognize that they have a problem—one that you can help them solve. Your task is to point out to these people, tactfully and diplomatically, the negative influences of their actions and encourage them to become more constructive and helpful.

You should serve as a valuable source of sport information for parents.

Closing (20-30 minutes)

Conclude the meeting with a question-answer session. For this to be worthwhile, you must be ready to cover a wide range of parents' concerns. As indicated earlier, your preparation is best accomplished by reading *Guidelines for Children's Sports* (Martens & Seefeldt, 1979). One of the chapters provides brief answers to the most frequently asked questions about youth sports.

There is an effective technique for starting a question-answer period. You can take the lead in raising questions. Stimulate parent involvement by asking the first few questions, and then guide the discussion. If you do not know the answer to a question, do not be ashamed to admit it. The parents will appreciate your honesty. Rather than giving a weak or incorrect response, indicate that it is a question to which you can both seek an answer. Perhaps someone in the audience will be able to provide the answer. Do not give the impression that every question must be addressed and answered by you.

At the end of the meeting, you might want to take some time to assess its format and content, and your style of presentation. Evaluative comments might be solicited from parents through informal discussion. Feedback can be valuable for making changes to improve the quality of future meetings. Finally, do not forget to thank the parents again for attending.

When coach-parent communication breaks down, unnecessary problems occur.

Follow-up Meetings

If possible, it is highly desirable to schedule a midseason meeting with parents. This will provide an opportunity to present refresher points, discuss the athletes' progress, and cooperatively seek solutions to existing problems.

Figure 4. Coaches and parents play important roles in young athletes' sport experiences.

A postseason celebration is an excellent way to end the season. This could take the form of a family dinner planned by the parents. In addition to having good fellowship and fun, you could take some time to obtain parents' evaluations of your program and your coaching. In your conversations, ask parents to point out things that went well, and get their suggestions for making improvements.

Summary

The "athletic triangle," consisting of a coach, an athlete, and a parent, is a natural aspect of youth sports. And, because it is an essential part of coaching relationships, your role in dealing with parents is very important to the success of your program. Parents will want to have varying degrees of involvement. As the coach, you must be able to channel their genuine concerns and good intentions in a way that supports what you are trying to accomplish. Conducting a parent sport orientation meeting is a first step toward ensuring the attainment of desirable outcomes for all.

This chapter is a guide for organizing and conducting an effective coach-parent meeting for the purpose of increasing parents' understanding of youth sports. Emphasis is given to the need for careful planning and preparation relative to scheduling and location of the meeting, its length, attendance by athletes, inviting parents and promoting their attendance, developing a program outline, and obtaining information for use in responding to parents' questions. The recommended content of the meeting includes the following program elements:

   a) an opening, in which the coaching staff is introduced and the purposes of the meeting are identified;
   b) a discussion of the objectives of youth sports, including consideration of the participation motives of young athletes, and the distinction between youth and professional models of sport;
   c) a presentation of details about the operation of your sport program;
   d) a description of the *positive approach* to coaching that you use;
   e) a discussion of parents' roles and responsibilities relative to counseling their children about sport participation and goal setting, sources of parent-produced stress, parent commitments to child athletes, and rules for parent behavior at practices and contests;
   f) how to achieve friendly and productive coach-parent relations; and
   g) closing the meeting with a lively question-answer session.

Finally, suggestions are presented concerning midseason and postseason gatherings with parents.

References

Gould, D. (1980). *Motivating young athletes*. East Lansing, MI: Michigan Institute for the Study of Youth Sports.
Martens, R. (1978). *Joy and sadness in children's sports*. Champaign, IL: Human Kinetics.
Martens, R., & Seefeldt, V. (1979). *Guidelines for children's sports*. Washington, DC: American Alliance for Health, Physical Education, Recreation, and Dance.
Rosen, A. (1967). *Baseball and your boy*. New York: Funk & Wagnalls.

Suggested Readings

Ferrell, J., Glashagel, J., & Johnson, M. (1978). *A family approach to youth sports*. LaGrange, IL: Youth Sports Press.
Foley, J. (1980). *Questions parents should ask about youth sports programs*. East Lansing, MI: Michigan Institute for the Study of Youth Sports.
Martens, R., & Seefeldt, V. (1979). *Guidelines for children's sports*. Washington, DC: American Alliance for Health, Physical Education, Recreation, and Dance.
Smith, N.J., Smith, R.E., & Smoll, F.L. (1983). *Kidsports: A survival guide for parents*. Reading, MA: Addison-Wesley.

SECTION IV:
SPECIAL CONSIDERATIONS

- **Emergency Procedures Every Coach Should Know**

- **Legal Liabilities of the Coach**

- **Sports for Disabled Children**

- **What About Co-Ed Competition?**

- **Post-Season Evaluation: What Did We Accomplish?**

chapter sixteen

Emergency Procedures Every Coach Should Know

Marjorie J. Albohm
International Institute of
Sports Science and Medicine

Questions to consider . . .

☐ *What are the points to consider in being well prepared for medical emergencies?*

☐ *What are the key steps to follow in general on-the-field management of injuries?*

☐ *What is the accepted immediate first aid treatment for athletic injuries?*

☐ *What types of first aid equipment should* **always** *be available during any activity session?*

☐ *What are the key factors to remember when managing a suspected head or neck injury?*

S ports have had a tremendous impact on the American family. A recent
report has indicated that three out of every five parents in the United States
say their children participate in organized sports activities (Miller Brewing Company, 1983). In addition, three out of every four American parents say that they
almost always encourage their children to participate in sports. With this emphasis
and the growing number of participants, a concern about injury risk, injury rates,
and the proper management of medical emergencies is of great importance.

Preparing for Medical Emergencies

The severity of many medical emergencies which occur in an athletic environment
can actually be minimized by a thorough system of planning and preparation.
In dealing with medical emergencies, it is better to be *over prepared* than un-
prepared.

Preparticipation Physical Examinations

The first step in injury prevention is to make certain that each participant is well
prepared to engage in physical activity. This is accomplished through a physical
examination and a thorough medical history, obtained by a physician.

The physician should be informed that the individual is active in sports and
in what sports he or she usually participates. The physical requirements in terms
of body build and maturity for contact sports are much different than for non-
contact sports. In the physical examination, special attention should be directed
at evaluating the skeletal and muscular systems. If any limitations are imposed
on the individual or if there is any significant medical history, the parents and
the coach must be informed (see sample of physical exam form).

Information Card

An information card must be kept by the coaching staff for each participant.
This card should provide the following information:

- Participant's name, address, age.
- Parents' or guardians' names, address, home and work telephone numbers
  and times when they are available at each number.
- Family physician's name, address, telephone number.
- Significant medical history—limitations.
- Family insurance (information about).
- Hospital preference in emergencies—telephone number.

These cards should be kept in the first aid kit or in the coach's possession at
all times during activity sessions.

Preparticipation Sports Exam

Date of Exam ____ /____ /____

School _____

NAME _____
     (last)   (first)   (m.i.)

AGE _____   BIRTHDATE ____/____/____

SPORT(S) PARTICIPATING IN _____

ENTERING GRADE _____

PARENTS/GUARDIAN _____
                                      (name)

ADDRESS _____

_____
        (city)   (st)

PHONE (_____) _____

FAMILY DOCTOR _____

ADDRESS _____

_____
        (city)   (st)

PHONE (_____) _____

Instructions: If you are presently under a doctors care for any reason (specialist's care for a specific ailment or for a chronic ailment) you will need to check with that physician and obtain a release from that physician, if needed, to participate in athletics.

On the next few pages will be questions concerning your past medical history. Please sit down with your parents and complete all questions. CIRCLE the appropriate answer. When a reply is YES, please give a complete explanation on the back of that page (list the question number, give date of injury or treatment, indicate as near as possible the anatomical location of the injury—ex. Rt. thigh, and the diagnosis). All YES answers are to be fully explained!

Name _____

MEDICAL HISTORY

Disease & Illness

Yes   No   1. Have you ever experienced an epileptic seizure or been informed that you might have epilepsy?

Yes   No   2. Have you had hepatitis during the past three years?

Yes   No   3. Have you been treated for infectious mononucleosis, virus pneumonia or any other infectious disease during the past twelve months?

Yes   No   4. Have you ever been treated for diabetes?

Yes   No   5. Have you ever been treated or informed by a medical doctor that you have had rheumatic fever or scarlet fever?

Yes   No   6. Have you ever been told that you have a heart murmur or high blood pressure?

Yes   No   7. Have you had any illness requiring bed rest of one week or longer during the past year? If so, give date and nature of illness.

Yes   No   8. Have you ever been told you were anemic?

Yes   No   9. Have you ever been told you had hemophilia or other bleeding disorders or currently have easy bruising or bleeding?

Eyes & Dental

Yes   No   10. Do you wear eye glasses or contact lenses? If so, explain which. If contacts, soft or hard.

Yes   No   11. Do you have poor vision in either eye?

Yes   No   12. If the answer to question 10 is yes, do you wear them during athletic participation?

Yes   No   13. Do you wear any dental appliance? If answer is yes, underscore the appropriate appliance, Permanent bridge / Permanent crown or jacket / Removable partial / Full plate.

General

Yes   No   14. Have you ever been told that you have a hernia? If so, is it repaired?

Yes   No   15. Have you had any other operations not listed in this questionnaire during the past two years? If yes, indicate anatomical site of operation and date.

Yes   No   16. Have you had any additional illnesses or injuries during the past two years? If yes, indicate specific illnesses and dates.

Yes   No   17. Have you ever been advised by a medical doctor not to participate in the sport(s) in which you are now contemplating participation?

Yes   No   18. Are you currently on prescribed medications or drugs on a permanent basis or semi-permanent basis? If so, indicate name of drug and indicate why it was prescribed.

Yes   No   19. Are you allergic to any general medication? (ex. aspirin, sulfa, etc.)

_____ 20. Date of most recent tetanus immunization.

Yes   No   21. Have you completed oral polio immunization?

If unsure of above two answers, please call your family physician for verification.

Yes   No   22. Do you smoke tobacco?

Yes   No   23. Do you use any drugs?

Yes   No   24. Do you use alcoholic beverages?

25. Give the name and appropriate date of physician who gave you your last medical examination.

_____

Head & Neck Injuries

Yes   No   26. Have you ever been 'knocked out' or experienced a concussion during the past three years? If yes, give dates of all and if hospitalized.

Yes   No   27. Have you ever had any injury to the neck involving nerves, vertebrae (bones), or vertebrae discs that incapacitated you for a week or longer? Give dates.

Bone & Joint

Yes   No   28. Have you ever been treated for Osgood-Schlatter disease?

Yes   No   29. Have you ever been treated for osteomyelitis?

Yes   No   30. Have you had a fracture during the past two years? If yes, indicate the site of the fracture and date.

Yes   No   31. Have you had a shoulder dislocation, separation or other shoulder injury during the past two years that incapacitated you for a week or longer?

Yes   No   32. Have you ever been advised to have surgery to correct a shoulder condition? If yes, give date.

Yes   No   33. Have you ever experienced a severe sprain, dislocation or fracture to either elbow during the past two years? If yes, give the dates.

Yes   No   34. Have you ever had an injury to your back?

Yes   No   35. If yes to the above question, did you seek the advice or care of a medical doctor?

Yes   No   36. Do you ever experience pain in your back? If yes, indicate frequency with which you experience pain by underscoring the answer: Very seldom / Occasionally / Frequently / Only on vigorous exercise / Heavy lifting.

Yes   No   37. Do you think your back is weak?

Yes   No   38. Have you experienced a strain to either knee during the past two years with severe swelling accompany the injury?

Yes   No   39. Have you ever been told that you injured the ligaments of either knee joint?

Yes   No   40. Have you ever been told that you injured the cartilage of either knee joint?

Yes   No   41. Have you ever been told that you have a 'trick' knee?

Yes   No   42. Have you ever been advised to have surgery to a knee to correct a condition? If so, give date.

Yes   No   43. Have you ever had any foot problems before?

Yes   No   44. Have you had, or do you have, pain in your feet while walking, running or standing?

Yes   No   45. Do you have cramps in your legs after activities or at night?

Yes   No   46. Do you have weak ankles and have you ever strained your ankles previous to this exam?

Yes   No   47. Have you had any surgery which was performed on your feet or surgery which was recommended?

Parents/Guardian:

Is there any reason you feel your son or daughter should not participate in contact sports?

Parents/Guardian/Student:

All of the above questions have been answered completely and truthfully to the best of our knowledge.

date	student signature

date	parent/guardian signature

Medical Exam

Height _____ Weight _____ Blood Pressure _____/_____ Pulse _____

Gross Vision   R ___/___   L ___/___   Urine _____   Respirations _____

General Exam

	Satis.	Unsatis.
Vision		
Hearing		
Heart		
Lungs/Respiratory Tract		
Skin		
Hernia/Genitalia		
Liver, Spleen, Kidney		

Musculosketal

	Satis.	Unsatis.
Ankles		
Knees		
Hips		
Shoulders		
Hand, Wrist, Elbow		
Neck		
Back		
Neurological		

Flexibility

	Right	Left
Groin		
Quads		
Hamstrings		
Calf		
Shoulders		
Elbows		
Back Flexion		
Back Extension		

N = normal   T = tight   L = loose   AT = atrophy

Physician: Please use this space to make any comments regarding an unsatisfactory mark.

I certify that this student athlete has been examined on this date and is found to be able to participate in all supervised athletics as cleared below:

(Circle one, circle same one on front page)

A   B   C

A—Cleared for   Contact   Noncontact   Sports

B—Cleared, pending re-exam
   of _____   Contact   Noncontact   Sports

C—Denied clearance for any activity

Physician Signature _____ M.D.   Date _____

Injury Report

Name _____ Date of Injury _____ Time _____

Body Part Affected

____Arm	____Hand	____Ankle
____Hip	____Knee	____Teeth
____Head	____Foot	____Fingers
____Neck	____Chest	____Thumb
____Back	____Elbow	____Shoulder
____Wrist	____Thigh	

Other _____

Nature of Injury

____Severe cut   ____Dislocation

____Bruise   ____Re-injury

____Fracture

____Sprain

____Muscle strain

Where Accident Occurred:

Describe how Injury Occurred

First Aid Treatment Rendered

Comments:

Playing Status:

   Full _____

   Limited _____

Signature _____

Emergency Plan

A detailed plan which can be implemented when emergencies occur must be prepared in advance by the coach and discussed with the athletes. In many cases, confusion surrounding an emergency presents more problems than the emergency itself.

In anticipation of injuries, a plan must be formulated to prevent confusion and to maintain a controlled situation. Key points and information from this plan should be posted near playing areas and kept in the first aid kit. This plan must include:

- Location of the nearest telephone or how to obtain emergency assistance. Keep 25 cents for a telephone call taped to the inside of the first aid kit.

Figure 1.   Don't wait for injuries to occur before planning how to deal with them.

- Emergency telephone numbers, consisting of: nearest hospital, nearest emergency ambulance service.
- Procedures relating to accompanying injured athlete to hospital (for example, who goes with athlete, who stays with the rest of the team).
- Notification of the parents.
- Supervision of remainder of team while emergency is being addressed.
- Release by physician and return to activity. (Knowing if and when injured athlete can go back to play.)
- Completion of injury reporting forms—each injury/treatment must be specifically documented and signed by appropriate supervising personnel (see sample form).
- Outline to remind the coach/supervisor of appropriate on-the-field management of injuries.

General Procedures for Managing Injuries

The outline for management of injuries should include the following information:

- Designate who will attend to injuries on the field/floor before they occur.
- When an injury has occurred, make eye or verbal contact with official to make certain that time out has been called.
- Approach injured player quickly.
- Check vital signs immediately (breathing, pulse, bleeding, consciousness). If vital signs are impaired, immediately initiate emergency plan to obtain medical assistance and begin appropriate emergency first aid.
- If vital signs are normal, continue evaluation by determining:
  a. location of injury.
  b. severity of injury (for example, obvious fracture, deformity)
- Determine plan for removal of injured athlete from field.
- Initiate the application of R.I.C.E. on sidelines.

The use of R.I.C.E. treatment (Rest, Ice, Compression, and Elevation), is an accepted form of immediate first aid for the management of many sports injuries. The entire treatment serves to minimize swelling and therefore keeps the injured individual more comfortable. This treatment also results in a return to normal activity more quickly. The treatment should be performed for 20 to 30 minutes at a time over the next 48 to 72 hours following an injury. Ideally, the injured individual should undergo the treatment of ice, compression, and elevation three times a day during this time period.

Figure 2.   When injuries occur, consider R.I.C.E. (rest, ice, compression, elevation).

First Aid Equipment

Specific athletic first aid equipment should be readily available at each practice and competitive site during all activity sessions. Do not just provide these items for a game situation. Much more time is spent in practices than in competitive events; therefore practice sessions present greater opportunities for injuries to occur.

On-Site First Aid

On-site first-aid equipment should include:

1. A stocked first aid kit. Rather than purchasing a costly manufactured training kit, consider using a fishing tackle box which is much less expensive. Do not purchase the first aid kit that comes complete with contents. You will need many more items than are usually included in such ready-made kits.

2. A cooler with wet elastic bandages and ice packs. Purchase a durable cooler, with at least a three gallon capacity. Elastic bandages may be of any brand. The best size for young athletes is four inches in width. The bandage should be wet to conduct the cold faster to the injured area when you use the treatment of rest, ice, compression and elevation. Wetting the wrap can be done by soaking them in cold water before putting them in the cooler. Any form of ice may be used. Small plastic bags can be used to make ice bags.

3. *Water.* Use water bottles or an additional cooler with cups.

4. *Towels/blankets.*

In addition, these items should be located in a central area easily accessible to all coaches:

- splints/slings
- crutches
- stretcher
- backboard

Suggested items to be included in the first aid kit:

Taping/wrapping items
- inch-and-a-half white adhesive tape
- underwrap (protection for skin)
- four-inch elastic bandages
- scissors for cutting bandages and tape
- ankle wrap material (cotton, non-elastic two-inches wide)
- tape adherent (will help tape stick to skin)

Bandages
- sterile gauze pads, 3×3, 4×4
- band-aids, variety of sizes
- butterfly bandages
- cotton (balls and pads)

Padding
- foam ⅛ inch, ¼ inch, ½ inch
- felt ⅛ inch, ¼ inch

Ointments
- first aid cream
- vaseline
- sun block lotion

Solutions
- germicide
- hydrogen peroxide
- eye wash, with cup

Miscellaneous
- baggies for ice bags
- tongue blades
- cotton tip applicators
- pin lights
- tweezers
- small scissors
- callus file
- powder
- antiseptic soap
- needle/thread
- mirror/contact lens solution, contact lens case
- nail clipper
- thermometer

Even with the best preparation, all emergencies cannot be prevented. It is imperative to the health and safety of each participant that when these emergencies occur they be handled properly and efficiently. Coaches who have participated in a first aid course will be much more comfortable when implementing the procedures that have been described previously.

Head/Neck Injuries

The biggest factors in the prevention of head and neck injuries are properly fitted protective equipment and proper execution of skills. The head should always be well protected and should never be used as a weapon when executing skills. Consider all head/neck injuries to be potentially serious. When a suspected head/neck injury occurs, approach the player quickly and determine the level of consciousness. If he/she is unconscious, try to raise the level of consciousness by speaking loudly to the player, calling his/her name. Do not shake the individual. Once consciousness has been established or if the player is already conscious, ask questions to determine his/her level of awareness, such as, "What is your name?" "Where are you?" "What is the score?" Ask the athlete if he/she has specific pain, or any tingling or numbness. Look for any obvious deformity or bleeding, especially fluid coming from the ears and/or nose which may indicate a skull fracture. DO NOT MOVE THE ATHLETE AT ANY TIME AND DO NOT REMOVE ANY HEAD GEAR. Call for medical assistance (emergency squad) immediately and let them manage and supervise the removal of the player from the field, court, or pool.

Any time an athlete loses consciouness, even if only for a few seconds, or is

Figure 3.   Call for medical assistance when head/neck injuries are suspected.

disoriented due to a blow to the head, he or she should not be allowed to return to the activity until thoroughly evaluated by a physician. The parents and the athlete should be informed of key symptoms that may occur after the injury which may indicate that a head injury has occurred.

These symptoms include:

- vomiting
- nausea
- headache
- inability to maintain consciousness

The athlete should be watched closely for 48 hours after the injury to see if any symptoms occur. If they do, medical attention should be sought immediately.

Key Points When Dealing with Head/Neck Injuries

● Do not move athlete—call for an emergency squad.
● Do not remove head gear.
● Do not allow athlete to return to activity without a physician's release.
● Be aware of delayed symptoms.

Heat Illness

Heat illness is a common occurrence in hot and humid climates. There are three conditions related to heat illness: heat cramps, heat exhaustion and heat stroke. Prevention is similar for all of these conditions:

● Beware of situations where high humidity and high temperature coexist. Do not play at the hottest time of the day. Schedule games and practices for morning or evening hours.
● Do not conduct practices that require heavy uniforms or equipment if the humidity and temperature are high.
● Get used to high temperatures/humidity through progressively more intense workouts.
● Replace fluids lost through sweating. Drink plenty of water. Take numerous water breaks.
● Make sure individuals have sufficient salt, potassium, and calcium intake through daily meals. Do not provide salt tablets for your athletes.

Heat Cramps

Heat cramps are characterized by multiple muscle spasms occurring in several muscle groups. The individual should stop participating when this occurs and move to a cool, shaded area. Drinking cool water and cooling the body by the application of cold water is helpful. This condition is usually short in duration and the athlete can usually resume participation the next day.

Heat Exhaustion

Heat exhaustion presents symptoms of:

● cold, clammy skin
● pale skin color
● headache
● nausea
● disorientation

The individual should be removed from activity and placed in a cool, shaded

Figure 4.   Fluids should be replaced at the rate at which they are lost.

area. Water soaked towels should be placed around the head and neck to aid in reducing the body temperature. The individual should drink water to replace fluids. A physician should clear the athlete for participation. Usually the recovery occurs within a day or two.

Heat Stroke

Heat stroke is a *medical emergency* and can cause death.
   The symptoms of heat stroke are:

- hot, dry skin
- no sweating

- extremely high body temperature
- symptoms of shock, for example, disorientation, pale, cold, clammy skin

Obtain emergency medical assistance *immediately*. Cool the individual down by removing playing gear, hosing them down with cold water, and placing ice bags on the neck and the entire body. An individual with heat stroke will most likely require hospitalization and must be cleared by a physician before returning to activity.

Key Points in Dealing with Heat Illness

- Monitor the heat and humidity.
- Gradually condition and acclimatize the athletes.
- Allow the athletes to drink water frequently. Water should be replaced as it is lost.
- Recognize key symptoms of heat illness and take immediate action.

Abdominal Injuries

The organs of the abdomen are well protected from most trauma associated with physical activity. However, some emergency situations may occasionally arise from injuries to this area. The internal abdominal organs most susceptible to injury are the spleen, kidneys, liver, and pancreas. These organs are usually injured from a direct blow or severe compression. If these injuries bleed internally and the result is an internal hemorrhage the condition could cause death. Individuals with abdominal injuries may feel well enough to continue activity, but symptoms may appear in the evening or the following day.

Key symptoms which indicate injury to abdominal organs include:

- abdominal pain
- blood in the urine
- pale, cool skin (shock symptoms)
- muscle spasm—rigidity in abdominal muscles

Refer the individual with an abdominal injury to a physician and observe them closely for several days following the injury. Inform the parents of the injury and have them watch for the key symptoms listed above. Tell them to seek medical help immediately if the symptoms listed above should occur.

Key Points When Dealing With Abdominal Injuries

- Be aware of individuals receiving severe contact to the abdominal or back area.
- Observe the injured athlete daily, watching for significant symptoms.
- Symptoms of serious abdominal injury are blood in the urine, abdominal rigidity, shock.

Dislocations

A dislocation occurs when a bone moves out of its normal anatomical position. Dislocations can occur in any joint of the body and can present a medical emergency. Common sites of dislocations are fingers, elbow, shoulder, and knee cap. When a dislocation occurs, tendons and ligaments are torn, and circulation may be affected because blood vessels, arteries and nerves may be involved. NEVER PUT A DISLOCATED BODY PART BACK INTO PLACE. Further damage may occur if you try to reposition the affected area.

When a dislocation occurs, check the pulse in the limb to make certain that circulation is present. If it is not, call for emergency medical assistance *immediately*. If circulation is present, support and immobilize the injured area in the most comfortable position. Obtain medical attention as soon as possible.

Conclusion

Medical emergencies can be minimized and handled properly. However, this requires good planning and preparation. Remember the key points in managing common medical emergencies. Make the athletic environment safe for all participants. Know how to handle medical emergencies!

References

Miller Brewing Co. (1983). *American attitudes toward sports*. Milwaukee, Wisconsin: Miller Brewing Co.

Suggested Readings

Smith, N.J. (Ed.). (1983). *Sports medicine: Health care for young athletes*. Evanston, IL: American Academy of Pediatrics.
Hawkins, J.D. (Ed.). (1984). *Sports medicine—A guide for youth sports*. Greensboro, NC: Sports Studies Foundation.
Micheli, L.J. (1985, August). "Preventing youth sports injuries", *Journal of Physical Education, Recreation and Dance*. Reston, VA: AAHPERD.
Micheli, L.J. (Ed.). (1984). *Pediatric and adolescent sports medicine*. Boston, MA: Little, Brown and Co.

chapter seventeen

Legal Liabilities of the Coach

John N. Drowatzky
University of Toledo

Questions to consider . . .

☐ *How do I know if I have met my legal duties when teaching sports skills to my athletes?*

☐ *Am I responsible for equipment and facilities as well as teaching the game?*

☐ *What is supervision? Am I legally responsible for supervision?*

☐ *Why should I develop unit and lesson plans? I'm a coach!*

☐ *Aren't injuries the responsibility of medical personnel?*

☐ *What records are there besides win-loss records?*

D uring the past several years, our society has been living through a revolution in knowledge, communication, and technology. This revolution has had a profound influence on all parts of our lives—educational, professional, recreational, and personal. Athletic programs, administrators, coaches, and participants have felt the influence of this revolution along with everyone else. In particular, athletic programs have been influenced by changes in conditioning and training programs, new facilities and equipment technology, increased knowledge in the scientific bases such as sport medicine, exercise physiology, and biomechanics, and changes in the physical and psychological characteristics of the participants. All of these changes have led to increased demands upon coaches, particularly in the areas of responsibility and accountability. Today, one of the first considerations athletic personnel must face, whether purchasing equipment, designing facilities, or coaching, is safety. The concept of "safety first" has arrived. Today, the name of the game is not basketball or football—it is *responsibility*.

Responsibility in athletic programs is not a new concept, especially in legal circles, but the emphasis placed upon responsibility has increased greatly in recent years. In part, developments in communication are responsible for this increased attention, as television programs weekly point out good coaching techniques and pertinent characteristics of atheletic equipment. Individuals who participate in physical activities are also partially responsible for this emphasis, as people of both genders and all ages now actively participate in competitive events. In fact, some participants have national and world class competitive experience by the time they enter high school programs. In part, increased awareness of one's legal rights and increased contact with the legal system through tort or negligence liability has increased the emphasis on responsibility in athletics. There are many reasons for the current priority placed upon safety and responsibility by coaches in atheletic programs. We cannot ignore this trend because it will not go away.

The Duty of Care

All parts of our social system, including athletics, impose legal duties upon us as we relate to other people. The general duty imposed upon us is simply the requirement that we use due care to avoid subjecting others to an unreasonable risk of harm. In other words, we must not create unreasonable risks for others.

The legal system considers the relationships existing between people as a basis for judgments. Whenever someone is in a more powerful position than those with whom he or she is dealing, a more stringent duty of care is placed on that person. Persons in charge must exercise more care to prevent the risk of harm to those people that they are directing. This view of relationships carries over into employment through that branch of law known as agency law. The employer has a duty to provide a safe working place for the employees and the employees have a duty to always act in the best interest of their employer whenever their conduct is within the scope of their employment. For example, coaches and teachers have a duty to inspect the equipment and facilities provided by their employers to make sure it is safe for use. If it is found to be unsafe, then they have a duty to report the problem to their employer and the employer has a duty to remedy the problem. In the case of school programs, courts have included anyone acting for, or paid by, the schools into the agency relationship. Officials are considered to be agents of the school paying their salary and schools have been found liable if the officials were negligent. As a consequence, aides, athletic trainers, volunteer coaches, and other persons associated with the program must be adequately supervised to avoid extra risk of liability. Thus, responsibilities flow between all parties involved in the relationship.

Responsibility for others is a part of coaching.

The focus of this chapter will be the relationship existing between the coach and the athletes. The first step will be to identify the coach's duty with regard to athletes and then to discuss how general duty applies to specific situations.

A coach must use due care to protect others from unreasonable risk of physical or mental harm and to avoid acts or omissions that might produce such harm. This duty applies particularly to the areas of instruction or coaching, supervision, equipment selection and use, facility selection and use, and handling injuries. The standard of care used to determine whether the coach has breached this duty is called the reasonable person standard. That standard is, unless he or she represents that he or she has greater or less skill or knowledge, one who undertakes to render services in the practice of a profession or trade is required to exercise the skill and knowledge normally possessed by members of that profession or trade in good standing in similar communities (American Law Institute, 1965).

Langerman and Fidel (1977) have identified several areas where duties are commonly breached by coaches:

- safety in selection and use of equipment and facilities
- use of progressive instructional and coaching methods
- matching athletes with opponents having like abilities
- providing instruction in safety procedures
- checkup procedures for past injuries

Primary reasons for negligent conduct by coaches and teachers in sport and physical education include having a careless or indifferent attitude toward the safety and interests of others, and failing to use common sense when approaching athletic situations. The following guidelines are presented to assist coaches in meeting their duty of due care with regard to instruction, supervision, equipment, facilities, and injuries.

Instruction

Instruction is teaching players any new aspect of the game.

In this chapter, instructions means that part of coaching during which the coach teaches the player new aspects of the game, whether it is skill and technique acquisition or rules and strategy. Although coaches frequently deal with performers who are physically superior to the typical person, instruction while coaching is regarded the same as instruction during a class. Adequate instruction in either classroom or coaching situations requires the following:

- teaching correct skills and techniques
- using language appropriate to the students or players
- using of progressive instructional methods
- including safety factors in instruction
- relating critical equipment characteristics to the players
- providing adequate conditioning and preliminary instruction

Review of court decisions indicate that the use of due care during instruction means the coach or teacher must include all of these components. In addition, courts have universally held that the duty for proper instruction may not be delegated to the students, athletes, or aides such as parents. Examples of critical factors in instruction emphasized by court decisions follow.

Skills and techniques. The participant must receive instruction in the skills and techniques necessary for proper performance as well as instruction regarding the rules of the game.

Safety precautions. The coaches must include the following components as a part of their instruction: the training and use of spotters where appropriate; alerting participants to the potential dangers inherent in the activity; and teaching athletes how to react to dangerous situations that may arise during participation.

Characteristics of athletes. There are a number of guidelines that the coach must consider, depending on the age, grade, and skill levels of the athletes. Advanced performers may require different techniques and instructions than beginners. Beginners may be unaware of dangers and hazards that are known to the more advanced performer. Advanced performers may attempt more dangerous activities than beginners. The athlete's health status and the nature of past injuries must be considered when asking them to perform. Differences in maturation, knowledge, and resistance to heat disorders or other injuries must be considered. Mental attitudes of the participants must be taken into account during performance. The coach must weigh the desire of the athlete to return to competition as soon as possible against the seriousness of the injury or illness that caused the athlete to miss participation and the amount of rehabilitation that may still be necessary. Highly motivated athletes often want to return to competition and practice before they are physically ready.

Clear instructions. The coach must give directions and instructions in such a manner that the students will not misunderstand. The correct method of performance must be made clear. If the athletes can interpret the task in more than one way and still be within the confines of the instructions, then the instructions are ambiguous and do not possess sufficient clarity.

Figure 1. Make sure that your instructions are clear and unambiguous.

Progressive teaching methods. Instruction must follow a logical progression with regard to difficulty and must be presented in an approved instructional method common to the subject. The practice session must be conducted within the athletes' exercise tolerance and skill level. The best way to plan for the proper sequence of material to be taught is to use unit and lesson plans. The coach should have plans that cover the season as a whole and plans for each practice session. These plans should be carefully prepared and kept on file.

Equipment characteristics. Dangerous equipment, such as the football helmet, requires special instructions. It is the manufacturer's duty to mark the equipment and provide these instructions, but it is the coach's duty to make sure that the team members receive and understand the instructions. Any time coaches use equipment that is either dangerous or unfamiliar to the athlete, they must discuss the characteristics and safety procedures associated with the equipment. Other examples of such equipment include the trampoline, springboards used in diving and gymnastics, protective equipment used in baseball or softball, and eye protection required for racquetball and similar sports. Athletes should be taught how to inspect their equipment for defects and breakage and how to properly fit their equipment. Such instructions should be a standard part of the directions given with the activity.

As an example of proper instruction, the following case is summarized. The court in Vendrell v. School District (1962) addressed the issue of adequate instruction when determining whether the coach was negligent after one of his football players became a permanent paraplegic following a neck injury. The neck injury resulted when the player charged head first into approaching tacklers in an attempt to gain extra distance. The coach and school district were found not guilty of negligence because of facts presented during the case. All potential team members were given a preparticipation physical examination by a physician and the athlete involved was found to be physically fit for participation. The athletes were put through an extensive training program that included calisthenics, instruction in physical conditioning and training, instruction in the fundamental skills required in the game, and how to use protective equipment to absorb blows. The coach had stressed proper fundamentals as an essential aspect of both successful play and self-protection. The court was impressed by the instruction and conditioning used to prepare the athletes for the shocks, blows, and other rough treatment that would be present during actual play. In cases such as this, lesson plans provide the necessary documentation to prove that adequate instruction was given.

Supervision

Teaching and coaching not only require instruction, but also continual supervision of athletes and students while changing clothes before and after practice and games, and during passing periods between activities and classes. Supervision, like instruction, is a duty that can not be delegated to others. The Ohio Revised Code (Chapter 33), for example, states that the teacher can depart the room leaving an aide in charge only after the teacher has determined that the aide will maintain the same degree of discipline and control as the teacher would, if present. The teacher is still ultimately responsible for effective supervision by the aide. Similar requirements apply to coaches. The coach must recognize the specific duties associated with supervision during the different sports activities: instruction or coaching; activity periods and practice; shower and changing periods; preparticipation warmup; and passing periods. Courts are in general agreement about the responsibility of supervision.

Supervision means protecting the athletes from harm.

The duty required during skill instruction is that of providing a reasonable amount of supervision necessary to prevent an unreasonable risk of harm to the athlete. Courts generally hold that general supervision is required on the field and in the gymnasium and locker areas. However, close, direct, and specific supervision is required during the teaching of new skills or techniques and conduct of practice. Supervision imposes the duty of ordinary care for most activities and this requires that the person in charge possess the ability to foresee the need for additional supervision. There is no hard and fast rule because the degree of supervision required will vary with the foreseeable danger or hazard present in the situation. Degree of danger of the activity is one factor influencing the amount of care required by the coach. If an activity has been declared inherently dangerous by a court, then a high standard of care has been imposed by the court. If the activity is compulsory—that is, required by the teacher or coach after an athlete has voiced some concern—then a higher standard of care is also imposed. The highest standard of care is imposed when the activity is both dangerous and required by the coach or instructor; then extraordinary efforts must be used to prevent injuries.

The coach must also consider the athletes' characteristics when determining proper supervision. Coaches must consider the comparable size, weight, strength, motor ability, and skill of the participants. Competitors must be approximately equal to minimize injuries. It would be foolish to have two teams that are greatly unequal in physical ability, size, and skill competing in contact and collision activities because the risk of injury would increase greatly. Mental abilities and developmental characteristics also determine the amount of supervision necessary. If the athletes are known to engage in horseplay, then more supervision is necessary.

Figure 2.   Supervision requires your presence.

Athletes assume only the inherent risks of sport.

There has been a recent shift in the attitude of courts toward injuries resulting from violence in sport and physical activity. Now courts are holding that a participant assumes the risk of injury during activity only from those actions that are an inherent part of the activity. Court decisions have emphasized that players do not assume the risk of injury from intentional misconduct during sport, as misconduct is not considered an inherent part of sport. Players have been found liable when their violation of rules or unnecessary roughness and intentional misconduct have produced injuries to others. If it could be shown that the coach encouraged or condoned such misconduct by his or her players and did not adequately supervise them to prevent such misconduct, the coach might well be found negligent in his or her supervision of the team. Do not allow your players to continue to play without reprimand when they flagrantly violate the rules or engage in other misconduct.

Equipment and Facilities

Participation in most sports requires the use of equipment. In some cases the equipment is furnished by the performer and in other cases the equipment is furnished by the school, club, or some other supplier. If the athlete supplies his or her own equipment, any problems resulting from the equipment are usually between the athlete and the supplier or manufacturer. Liability may fall on the manufacturers, sellers, leasors, or other providers of equipment, such as the schools, if they are negligent in the production, supply, or use of the equipment and an injury results from their negligence. Coaches may also become liable for injuries produced by athletic equipment if they are negligent in their duties related to the equipment. Typically, their negligence with equipment results from the use and selection of inappropriate equipment, failure to inspect the equipment for breakage or defects before use, and the failure to give adequate instructions and warnings regarding the use and dangers associated with the equipment. Coaches and teachers are obligated to keep up to date with their knowledge and understanding of new equipment, as well as any changes relative to the equipment that they already have and use.

Teach students and athletes to use equipment and facilities in a responsible manner.

The legal system has created duties with regard to owners and occupiers of land or premises. These duties relate to whether the injured person had permission to enter the premises, whether the owner had reason to know that trespass was occurring, or whether the person was using the premises for the owner's benefit. In any of these cases, the owner must use reasonable care to prevent undue risk to persons entering the premises. For those persons using the premises to benefit the owner, such as athletes, officials, and spectators, the owner must inspect the premises to detect and remove any hazards that may be reasonably discovered. When new safety features become available at a reasonable price and become the new standard, the facility owner should upgrade the present facilities. If unsafe conditions exist, they should be corrected. Preventive maintenance, along with frequent inspections, should be standard operating procedures. Persons on the premises who are working for or acting on behalf of the owner or possessor are subject to the same liabilities as the owner. Consequently, coaches should make inspections of the practice and game facilities before beginning to use them. If any dangerous conditions are found, coaches must use reasonable care to prevent the hazard from injuring their athletes. When organizing drills and other activities, coaches must plan so that athletes do not risk injury from the facilities. For example, coaches must allow adequate stopping areas when running toward walls or other immovable objects.

Common sense underlies responsible coaching.

Coaches must exercise common sense with regard to equipment and facilities when organizing their practices. The school or club must provide safe equipment and facilities, but it is the coach's duty to inspect the equipment and facilities

Figure 3. Inspect the facilities before use.

before use. Likewise, it is the coach's duty to order equipment that is safe and appropriate for use with the athletes. The coach must be aware of potential dangers with regard to equipment and facilities, subsequently organizing the practice sessions to eliminate or avoid those dangers. Today, one can not walk past a hazard and say that the problem belongs to someone else; coaches must take affirmative action for safety.

Injuries

Remember that the overall duty imposed upon coaches is that they must use due care to prevent an unreasonable risk of injury to athletes. Thus, the school, club, or institution must take such actions as are necessary to meet this duty. You should consider temperature, humidity, wind, and other environmental factors when scheduling practice sessions. In the case of injuries that have already occurred, the duty becomes one of preventing further injury or harm to that injured party. To accomplish this task, you should conduct a survey of the facilities and programs to determine what types of injuries are probable, and then obtain the first-aid and emergency equipment needed to meet these injuries. For example, an aquatics facility should have a backboard present to remove people with suspected back injuries from the water safely and football programs should have splints available. All personnel should be trained in first aid and appropriate emergency procedures. Coaches have been found liable for their failure to know and use adequate first aid for heat stroke and for not knowing how to move players with suspected neck or back injuries.

Use due care to prevent further injury.

The duties regarding the treatment of injuries can be summarized as follows. First, there is the duty to provide or secure reasonable medical assistance for the injured party as soon as possible. Second, if medical assistance is not immediately available at the site of the injury, then the injured party must be transported to a place where medical care can be provided as soon as possible. At least one court has defined reasonable medical assistance as the provision of reasonable facilities and equipment as well as the presence of persons with the necessary degree of skill and experience.

Require medical approval before athletes practice.

As mentioned earlier, coaches must make sure that each athlete has a properly completed preparticipation physical examination record on file. Records should be kept of injuries that occur during the season, and follow-up procedures should

Figure 4. Use common sense and consider the potential for injuries.

be developed. If the athlete suffers an injury, you should have a written copy of the doctor's permission before you allow the athlete to resume play or practice. Make sure adequate medical follow-up of serious injuries is completed and know what rehabilitation is required before the athlete returns. When in doubt, be conservative and keep the athlete off the practice field. The key to preventing liability here is fourfold.

1) Have a good working relationship with the physicians.
2) Be prepared for injuries.
3) Develop and follow reasonable procedures to deal with injuries.
4) Document how injuries occur and what is done for them.

Reduce Your Liability Potential

Perhaps the best summary for a chapter on legal issues of concern to the coach is a series of recommendations to reduce potential legal problems. The following points are suggested to help the coach avoid liability.

Plan adequately. Planning is necessary to make sure that your coaching is well organized, proper techniques are used, safety instructions are given, proper equipment is used, facilities are safe and appropriate, adequate and appropriate supervision is present, and injuries will be handled in an acceptable fashion.

Plan for safety. Believe in "safety first". Get in the habit of planning for safety when you develop your other unit and lesson plans. Make periodic and regular safety inspections a part of your routine and stress the importance of safety to your athletes and assistants. In a word, be safety conscious!

Keep records. Proper, appropriate records can help when facing a law suit, particularly if the records show that you have met your legal duties. Be sure your coaching plans are written, followed, and kept on file. Keep copies of accident reports, permission slips, preparticipation physical examinations and other pertinent records. Records should be kept with sufficient detail to show exactly what happened.

Remember that records pertaining to athletes are confidential and cannot be released to others without the athlete's or parents' written permission. Screen your records on a regular basis and remove all information that is no longer valid. Finally, if an injury is involved and a potential lawsuit exists, keep the records until the statute of limitations has expired (tolled). This time can vary from state to state, but in Ohio, for example, it tolls four years after the child reaches legal adulthood for injuries sustained any time before age 18 years. For adults the statute in most states usually tolls 4 years after the injury.

Update your education. Keep abreast of new developments and techniques in conditioning, skill instruction, safety, equipment, first aid, athletic training, and other aspects of your coaching responsibilities. Regular attendance at classes, seminars, workshops, and other similar opportunities can make a difference. Likewise, read pertinent journals and attend professional meetings to improve your skill and knowledge. Keep up to date!

Maintain communications. Communication is one of the most important parts of coaching. Keep lines of communication open with administrators, staff, athletes, parents, assistants, and medical support personnel. Not only must you communicate to others, you must also listen to their communications and be aware of what they are telling you. Good communication is understood by those with whom you are communicating.

At first appearance, the list of legal duties may seem burdensome and unreasonable. Further consideration will prove that the duties discussed are hallmarks of good, competent instruction and coaching. These duties summarize the manner in which each of us would like to be treated as a student or athlete.

In spite of the many potential law suits that exist, coaches and teachers are not often brought to court. Parents, lawyers, and judges realize that participation in any physical activity has risk and accidents can occur. A review of the cases in which teachers and coaches have been found negligent shows that each of the injuries producing liability could have been prevented if appropriate coaching or teaching methods had been followed. The threat of legal action is not as onerous as many people believe it to be.

References

Drowatzky, J. (1977). On the firing line: Negligence in physical education. *Journal of Law & Education. 6*, 481–490.

Drowatzky, J. (1984). *Legal issues in sport and physical education management.* Champaign, IL: Stipes Publishing Company.

Langerman, S. & Fidel, N. (1977). Responsibility is also part of the game. *Trial, 13*, 22–25.

Ohio Revised Code, Chapter 33.

The American Law Institute. (1965). *Restatement of torts, second: Torts 2d.* St. Paul, MN: American Law Institute Publishers.

Vendrell v. School District No. 26C, 376 P.2d 406 (1962).

Weistart, J., & Lowell, C., (1979). *The law of sports.* New York: The Bobbs-Merrill Company, Inc.

Suggested Readings

Drowatzky, J., (1984). *Legal issues in sport and physical education management.* Champaign, IL: Stipes Publishing Company.

chapter eighteen

Sports for Disabled Children

John M. Dunn
Oregon State University

18

Questions to consider . . .

☐ *How can sport enhance the lives of disabled youth?*

☐ *How do I organize a youth sport program for children with disabilities?*

☐ *Should sport experiences for disabled youth be integrated or segregated?*

☐ *What special skills and knowledge are needed to teach disabled athletes?*

☐ *Are there organizations which promote and provide information on sport experiences for disabled athletes?*

S ociety's awareness and acceptance of individuals with disabilities has improved dramatically during the past few years. This acceptance is clearly demonstrated by analyzing the progress which has been made in the provision of sport experiences for disabled individuals. This progress was highlighted during the recent Inspire '85 International Festival held in Washington, D.C. The festival was a showcase for the accomplishments of disabled Americans in sport, recreation, cultural arts, and employment. The theme of the event was to promote opportunities that contribute to equality, independence, and dignity for all Americans.

For too many years, society in general, and educators and coaches in particular, ignored the potential value of sport programs for disabled youth. This was due to the once common philosophy that education for youth with disabilities should focus on the basic educational skills. Little attention, therefore, was given to extracurricular activities such as sport programs. Some, too, may have felt that disabled youth would not benefit from sport experiences. An unfortunate but common assumption of the past was that students with impairments would not be able to successfully participate in sport programs. Today, enlightened individuals recognize that when given the opportunity, disabled youth can participate successfully and safely in a wide variety of sport activities.

Sport programs for the disabled are mandated by federal law.

Recent legislation has also reinforced the rights of disabled youth to participate in sport programs. The Education for All Handicapped Children Act of 1975, Public Law 94-142, and Section 504 of the Rehabilitation Act of 1973, Public Law 93-112, specify that physical education experiences, including intramural activities and sports, must be available to handicapped students to the same extent that these opportunities are available to nonhandicapped students. This means that youth with disabilities should not be denied equal opportunity to participate on regular school or community teams or comparable special teams.

In this chapter, information will be provided on the value of sport experiences for disabled youth, how to organize and promote sport programs for disabled individuals, the need for coaches who work with disabled youth to acquire special skills, and an overview of sport organizations for disabled individuals which provide information and support to youth coaches.

Sport programs benefit disabled youth in many ways.

Figure 1. Youth with disabilities should not be denied equal opportunity to participate on regular school or community teams or comparable special teams.

Value of Sport for Disabled Youth

The value of sport programs for disabled youth are many and varied. The benefits range from those experienced by anyone who participates in sport, for example, improved skill and fitness level, to those values which are somewhat unique to the disabled, such as fuller integration into community activities. Within this section, the value of sport for disabled youth will be discussed from the perspective of its contribution to health and fitness, normalization, psychological well-being, and, finally, sport for sport's sake.

Health and Fitness

Participation in sport makes an important contribution to the health and fitness of disabled persons. Although the amount of information is limited, studies suggest that the fitness levels of disabled youth are lower than those of their nonhandicapped peers. Some of the factors which interfere with the health and fitness of disabled persons include the following.

Nutrition. The nutritional status of some disabled youth is affected by several factors including specific disability, medication required, and behavioral influences. In a study of children with developmental disabilities, Palmer (1978) found that over 90% exhibited nutritional disorders.

Sedentary life-styles. Disabled youth frequently find opportunities to participate in activity outside of their homes or residential settings to be more restricted than for the nondisabled. This results in greater reliance on television and other forms of sedentary entertainment.

Lack of understanding of the concept of fitness. Some disabled youth, particularly those with mental impairments, fail to understand the important relationship between health and fitness.

Hereditary factors. The nature of some disabilities is such that associated health problems can lead to further deterioration in the individual's physical fitness. For example, 40% of children with Down Syndrome have a congenital heart disorder.

Fear of failure. For disabled individuals, particularly the mentally retarded, orthopedically impaired, and sensory impaired, the performance of "routine" exercises can be very difficult. The inability to grasp the technique of the exercise or to possess the coordination to perform the exercise can create a vicious cycle of failure, followed by avoidance.

Program and facility accessibility. Unfortunately, the health fitness level of many disabled people is lower than expected because of the unavailability of appropriate programs or programs that are conducted in inaccessible facilities.

Disabled youth need as many opportunities as possible to improve their health and fitness levels. Sport can play a significant role in developing the desired levels of fitness. Studies indicate that the disabled, including those who are severely mentally retarded, can be taught sport skills, thereby improving important variables such as health and physical fitness (Cuvo, Ellis, Wisotzek, Davis, Schilling, & Bechtal, 1983).

Participation in sport assists the integration of disabled youngsters into family and community activities.

Normalization

Disabled youth desire very much to be part of the society in which they live. This means access and participation in the various aspects of the community including school, church, and sport programs. Advocates of sport for the disabled recognize, too, that participation in sport will assist disabled persons to integrate more fully into family and community activities. A student who becomes a proficient swimmer can use this skill not only to compete but, perhaps, more importantly, as a way to become involved in all water activities enjoyed by his or her family.

Disabled youth can also use sport to convey that although they may be disabled, they are not ill. There is a general tendency to assume that a disabled person is weak and frail. This misconception is quickly dispelled when disabled youth are observed vigorously participating in sport programs common to the general public.

The ultimate form of integration for a youngster with a disability is to participate in an activity in which the disability does not interfere with either his or her team's performance. Many examples are found in sport where disabled and nondisabled individuals have successfully participated or competed together. Harold Connolly, one of the United States' great Olympians, won a gold medal in the hammer throw although he performed with a withered left arm. Carol Johnson, a Canadian, is a highly competent all-around gymnast even though she has only one arm. These examples, once stories worthy of national attention, are now becoming common occurrences. Many disabled youth in communities across the United States have overcome obstacles and participate successfully with their non-disabled peers.

Disabled children are not invalids.

Psychological Value

The activities of daily living, taken for granted by most individuals, can present major challenges to children with sensory, orthopedic, or neuromuscular impairments. For some disabled youth, rising from bed, dressing, and eating require

Figure 2. Many disabled youth in communities across the United States have overcome obstacles and participate successfully with their non-disabled peers.

a concerted amount of effort and organization. The continual struggle to perform routine activities successfully may prove disheartening to some disabled youth. This feeling may be reinforced by family and friends who treat the disabled individual as an invalid. An inferiority complex, characterized by anxiety, with a loss of self-confidence and self-esteem, may lead to self-pity, self-centered isolationism, and anti-social attitudes for some children with disabilities.

For disabled youth, participating in sport can often restore psychological equilibrium, counteract feelings of inferiority, and become a motivating force in the enjoyment of life (Guttman, 1976). Sport, with its emphasis on action, communicates in a very visible way that being disabled is not synonymous with being an invalid. The psychological contribution of sport, coupled with the sense of well-being generated by activity, can be used by many disabled individuals as a means of enhancing their concept of self.

Disabled athletes enjoy sport similar to others.

Sport for Sport's Sake

Disabled individuals and their advocates frequently remind others that disabled people are more similar than dissimilar to the nondisabled. This observation, applied to sport, suggests that the disabled view sport as valuable for the same reasons as do their nondisabled peers. They enjoy sport programs because they are fun, provide opportunities to socialize, and contribute to health. They stress that sport for them is a sport experience as it is for everyone and not primarily a therapeutic or rehabilitative activity. Some disabled athletes, like some nondisabled athletes, undertake rigorous training programs, emphasizing the quality of their efforts and strive for maximum performance.

Schools, community organizations, and youth clubs all have a responsibility to share in the promotion and development of sport programs for disabled youth. Public and private youth agencies must make a concerted effort to ensure that their services are coordinated and consistent with the goal of a well-rounded sport program for disabled youth. It is the responsibility of the organizations and their leaders to conduct programs which foster the same high ideals in ethics and sportsmanship that are promoted in all sports programs.

Sport programs for the disabled, as for the nondisabled, are subject to potentially negative features. Overzealous athletes and coaches can lead to situations in which the desire to win is greater than the desire to compete or cooperate fairly. Promoters and coaches of youth sport programs for the disabled must be vigilant in their effort to provide programs for novice, as well as gifted, participants.

The variance in response to sport competition among disabled youth will be no less than in the population as a whole. Programs which provide a continuum of sport participation, from developmental activities to highly organized teams, are needed. Coaches must avoid fostering an atmosphere which conveys an attitude that those who do not wish to participate are inferior to those who do and that participation in competitive sport is the most important activity in the program. For most disabled individuals, "successful" sport competition provides an opportunity to develop an optimum level of physical fitness and skill and, additionally, offers the satisfaction of gaining personal recognition and participating with peers. Schools, community organizations, and youth agencies are responsible for ensuring that disabled individuals are not deprived of this opportunity.

Organizing Sport for Disabled Youth

The first and most essential step in organizing a community based program for disabled youth is to hold an organizational meeting with parents of disabled youngsters and leaders of advocacy groups for the disabled. There are several ways to reach the desired audience. Some suggestions are outlined in the following.

Contact local agencies which promote services for the disabled. This list would include organizations such as the Association for Retarded Citizens, Association for Children with Learning Disabilities, and the United Cerebral Palsy Association.

Meet with public school officials to obtain a list of parents who serve on committees related to programs for the disabled. Many school districts have a special education advisory committee.

Contact state institutions such as the School for the Blind and School for the Deaf to obtain their assistance in identifying parents of local children who attend these institutions.

Write to the sport organizations identified in Table 1 to obtain the names of local representatives of the various sport associations for the disabled.

Meet with representatives of civic organizations such as the Lion's Club, Kiwanis, and Rotary to obtain their input and the assistance of prominent citizens.

A sports program for disabled individuals must be sensitive to diverse needs.

The purpose in meeting with parents and advocates of disabled persons is to establish the intent of the program. Parents should know that the sport program to be developed is, first and foremost, a program which in every way possible is sensitive to the needs of the population for whom it is intended. These early meetings will help to establish credibility.

Parents of disabled children will be very candid with respect to their expectations. They may be skeptical or uninformed about the value of sport for their child. Parents may also believe that their son or daughter is too severely handicapped to benefit from a sport experience. Observations such as these will allow the sport program organizer to reassure parents of the value of sport and to emphasize clearly that appropriate experiences will be developed for all children including those who are multiply handicapped.

The views of parents on various topics such as segregated programs, the nature of competition, and the importance of sport programs are essential in establishing a broad based and realistic program. From these early meetings, promoters of sport for the disabled can gain the information they will need to inform the community of the need for a sport program for youth with disabilities.

Figure 3. Meet with governmental officials to discuss your position paper on sport for disabled youth.

Parents, disabled individuals, and youth sport program providers must work together.

Preparing the Community

Efforts to inform the community about the importance and value of a sport program for disabled youth begins with the formulation of a steering committee. This committee, composed of parents, disabled individuals, advocates for the disabled, and community leaders, is given the task of designing a plan to develop sport programs for disabled youth. The responsibility of this group is to establish a foundation upon which a strong program can be built. Suggested steps in developing the plan include the following.

Review federal and state laws related to programs and services for disabled populations. Public Law 94-142, the Education for All Handicapped Children Act of 1975, and Public Law 93-112, Section 504 of the Rehabilitation Act of 1973, specify that handicapped students must be provided an equal opportunity to participate in athletic programs. The provisions of Public Law 94-142 and Public Law 93-112 pertain to agencies that accept federal assistance. This obviously would include schools and other governmental agencies such as community recreation programs.

Prepare a position paper that discusses the importance and value of sport for all. Include references to Public Law 94-142 and Public Law 93-112.

Submit the position paper to elected and appointed governmental officials from school districts and city government. Meet with the officials to discuss the paper and to respond to questions. The outcome of the meeting should clarify what is presently being offered through schools and other governmental programs. Additionally, school officials should be asked to cooperate in conducting a survey of parents of disabled youth to determine the sport programs in which their children are presently participating and their perceptions as to the need for additional services.

Meet with representatives of non-governmental community-based youth programs such as the YMCA, YWCA, Boy Scouts, and Girl Scouts to review with them the position paper on youth sport for the disabled. A similar meeting should be held with representatives of local youth sport programs such as Little League baseball, Pop Warner football, and American Youth Soccer Organization to determine the extent to which their programs serve the needs of disabled youth.

Prepare a state of the art paper based on the information obtained from the meetings with representatives from governmental and non-governmental agencies. The paper should provide a clear statement as to the services presently available, the number of disabled youth participating in sport programs, the type of programs available, and the number of disabled children requesting, but not receiving, an opportunity to participate.

Present the state-of-the-art paper to officials from governmental agencies and youth programs involved in the earlier discussions and ask for their verification as to the report's accuracy. The attempt here is to ensure that a baseline can be established which accurately assesses the level of sport programming presently available to children with disabilities. Modifications in the report should be made if new information is obtained. Caution should be exercised to avoid accusations and negative statements. The approach must be one of optimism for the future.

In meeting with government officials to discuss sport opportunities for the disabled, avoid accusations and negative statements. The approach must be one of optimism for the future.

Establish a plan with long term goals for the development of a comprehensive youth sport program for disabled persons. The plan should include timelines, with responsibilities assigned to the appropriate agency, community organization, or youth sport program. This can be accomplished by involving representatives from the designated organizations and agencies in the development of the plan. As the plan unfolds, responsibilities for carrying it out will become clear and a sense of joint ownership of the plan will become evident.

Submit the comprehensive plan and the long range goals of the youth sport program for the disabled to organization and agencies outside of the local community. Suggested agencies include the State Department of Education, the state agency responsible for school athletic programs, and national and state organizations which promote sport for the disabled. The purpose in circulating the plan is to share information and to obtain additional assistance. The plan may serve as a model to assist others in their efforts to promote sport for the disabled. State officials may perceive the plan as evidence of a group or community's effort to promote sport for the disabled and may be helpful in identifying additional resources.

Utilize the plan as the medium for a public awareness program on sport for the disabled. The plan, along with a slide presentation of disabled youth participating in sport, can be effective in meetings with civic organizations and groups. Activities such as sponsoring a wheelchair basketball game between halves of the local high school game, inviting a well known disabled athlete to address a school assembly, and staging an event in which public officials play their sport with an imposed disability, such as playing golf blindfolded, help to generate public support.

The primary objectives of the plan for implementing a youth sport program for the disabled is to objectively document the sport experiences presently available for the disabled, recommend improvements where necessary, and communicate this information effectively to the community, thus building a broad base of support for future programs. With the plan as a foundation, promoters of youth sport for the disabled can begin to focus on the individual needs of disabled children and youth.

Diverse needs require individualized programs.

Focusing on Individual Needs

Disabled youth are so diverse that developing appropriate sport experiences require careful attention to the needs of each individual. Within public schools the effort to individualize instruction for the disabled is assisted by the federal requirement that an Individualized Education Plan (IEP) be developed for each special education student. The IEP is a document which specifies educational goals and objectives and identifies timelines by which selected educational outcomes are to be achieved. Parents, teachers, and others invited by the parent or the school participate as a team in the development of the IEP.

The process for developing the IEP should be used to respond to the disabled student's right to particiate in extracurricular activities, including sport programs. Using the IEP mechanism ensures that this important aspect of the child's educational program will not be overlooked. In addition, the composition of the IEP team, including parents, teachers, and others, where appropriate, such as therapists and community service providers, creates a unique opportunity to capitalize on programs offered by the school as well as other sport experiences available within the community. Every effort must be made to coordinate services among agencies to maximize the sport opportunities available to disabled youth.

The IEP team will be faced with several important decisions concerning the educational needs of special students. In discussions related to sport programs, this will require that team members challenge some old assumptions about the nature of sport and its relevance for all students. Some of the more frequently discussed issues are presented here.

Many disabled children participate successfully in regular programs.

Segregated or integrated sport programs. Authorities agree that the first consideration in identifying an appropriate sport activity for the disabled student is to analyze the available sport programs in the community. Many disabled youngsters will be able to successfully participate with their nondisabled peers in regular sport programs. In some instances this may require minor adjustments in equipment, the rules, or coaching strategy. The extent to which special accommodations are necessary should be thoroughly discussed by the members of the IEP team. The input of parents, and the children, where appropriate, will help in making a wise decision. If, after careful study and discussions, placement in the regular sport program seems inappropriate, that is, an experience where it appears that the failure ratio will exceed the success ratio, efforts should then be directed toward identifying a special sport program. Fortunately, there are several organizations, including Special Olympics and the United States Association for Blind Athletes, which provide specialized sport experiences for disabled individuals. These organizations will be identified and described briefly later in this chapter.

Academic performance. Participation on a sport team sponsored by the schools, community, or religious organizations frequently requires that a student maintain a minimum grade point average. Although it is desirable to encourage athletes to maintain high academic standards, this rule, if administered inflexibly, may discriminate against some disabled students. For instance, it may be unrealistic to expect an educable mentally retarded individual to achieve the desired grade

Figure 4. The process for developing the IEP should be used to respond to the disabled student's right to participate in extracurricular activities including sport programs.

point average. A more equitable basis for determining eligibility might be to monitor the special student's progress toward meeting the goals and objectives identified in the individual's IEP.

This example reinforces the principle that the law mandates equal opportunity, not equal treatment. Requiring disabled students to meet the same academic standards required of nondisabled students may be equal treatment, but it denies equal opportunity.

Medical considerations. Section 504 of the Rehabilitation Act of 1973 emphasizes that agencies which receive federal assistance may not exclude students from participation in sport programs on the basis of a medical disability. This law is designed to protect the rights of individuals with various health impairments such as asthma, diabetes, epilepsy, heart disease, and leukemia. The spirit of the law should be extended to private, as well as public agencies, which serve children and youth. To exclude, for example, a child from participating on a team because of a seizure disorder focuses only on the individual's disability, and fails to consider other significant variables in the child's life.

There are many documented cases where students who have lost one of a paired organ, such as an eye or a kidney, have been automatically denied the opportunity to participate on a team. Although in some cases this may be a wise and prudent decision, categorical decisions do not allow for the recognition of individual needs. Important decisions such as these can best be made by the combined wisdom and expertise of the student's IEP team, including parents and representatives from the medical community.

Age considerations. Youth sport programs usually impose age or grade restrictions on participants. This rule is designed to protect athletes from unfair competition as well as from potential danger due to weight and size inequities. Although this is a logical rule, it tends to discriminate against the student who has been delayed in his or her development due to illness, disability, or congenital birth defect. In such cases it would be more appropriate to consider the participant's developmental level rather than chronological age. Any decision of this nature should be made by the child's IEP team in consultation with the coach of the team and the league organizers.

Definitive answers to the various issues that arise concerning the disabled individual's participation in youth sport programs are not possible. Each disabled athlete is a unique individual, with needs that may require the league codes for a particular sport to be modified. Policies which categorically discriminate against disabled persons are not acceptable. Fortunately, the IEP is an effective tool for resolving issues related to sport programs for the indivdiual with a disability.

Successful programs require sensitive and knowledgeable coaches.

Special Coaching Skills

The success of any youth sport experience is dependent, to a large extent, upon the quality of coaches in the program. This statement is equally true in sport programs which include disabled youth. In addition to the skills required of all good coaches, for example, knowledge of the activity, basic understanding of principles relative to growth and motor development, and recognition of good health and safety procedures, the coach assigned to work with disabled children must have a desire to work with disabled individuals and a willingness to develop additional expertise. Some of the specialized skills required are presented in this section.

Knowledge of Disabilities

The coach should have a practical understanding of the nature of various disabilities, particularly the disabilities of the population with which the coach is asked to work. Recognition of possible causes and characteristics of the disability and the implications of these on the participant's health and skill development will be helpful. An understanding, for example, of the various types of cerebral palsy and the variations in movement patterns associated with the athetoid type, as compared to the spastic type, will assist in developing appropriate programs.

Coaches also need to be aware of medical problems related to a particular disability. For instance, congenital heart problems are very common in children with Down Syndrome. Discussions with the child's parents and the family physician can help to develop programs that are safe, yet challenging. The book by Bleck and Nagel (1982) included in the suggested reading list is a valuable reference with useful and easy to follow information on background and medical implications for many disabling conditions.

Although coaches need to be aware of the limitations associated with various disabilities, they also need to emphasize the youth's ability level. A practical exercise which many coaches use to emphasize the disabled child's ability is to list all of the ways the individual is similar to his or her nondisabled peers. This exercise is helpful in emphasizing the disabled athlete's many strengths and serves to underline the importance of coaching strategies which stress empathy, not sympathy.

Coaches must emphasize the quality of effort rather than the outcome of that effort.

Awareness of Skill Level

The skill levels among children with disabilities will vary tremendously, depending upon the nature and severity of the disability. As explained earlier, some children will require separate, specialized sport programs, whereas others will participate successfully with minor modifications in regular programs. Regardless of the skill level, it is essential that coaches learn to appreciate the quality of the disabled athlete's effort. Some may find it helpful to experience sport in ways as similar as possible to the disabled. For example, shooting a basketball from a wheelchair requires a different level of skill than shooting from a standing position. In a contest with trained paraplegic javelin throwers, Guttman (1976) found that nondisabled javelin throwers could not throw the javelin from a seated position as well as the well trained paraplegic could. This study illustrates that training is specific: one becomes good at tasks one practices, and disabled athletes develop, through training, musculature and skill proficiency that is unique to them. Some disabled performers may never equal the records of their non-disabled peers. This, however, does not negate the relative merit of their effort. Coaches of disabled youth should recognize and reinforce good performance and help others to appreciate the quality of the disabled athlete's effort.

Development of Specialized Skills

Coaches who work with disabled youth will need to learn some specialized skills pertaining to instruction and communication. Working with the mentally retarded will require the coach to be very specific with directions, avoiding abstract statements and generalizations. Using the expression "go between the cones" may have little meaning to the participant who is uncertain of the meaning of "between" and may think of "cone" as something on which ice cream is served. Coaches working with hearing impaired students should develop some signing skills. Fortunately, many of the signs necessary for communication in sport can be quickly learned because the signed gesture, such as throw, is frequently a demonstration of the specific skill.

Visually impaired students also will require a coach who is sensitive to their special needs. Blind students, for instance, will require an orientation when they are first introduced to a new environment. Coaches and teammates will need to remember to avoid leaving equipment lying around thus creating a potentially harmful situation for the athlete with limited vision.

Coaches should also be knowledgeable about behavior management techniques if they work with students who have behavior problems. A knowledge of how to distinguish appropriate from inappropriate behavior is important in order to ensure success with these athletes.

Although some of the specialized techniques will require additional education, many of them rely primarily on good common sense. Coaches also will find the assistance of other professionals such as adapted physical educators, special educators, and therapists helpful in creating quality sport experiences for disabled youth.

Figure 5.   Coaches of disabled youth should recognize and reinforce good performance and help others to appreciate the quality of the disabled athlete's effort.

Knowledge of Sport Adaptations

Sport programs for disabled youth require coaches who are knowledgeable about a specific sport and who have the ability to modify the activity, when necessary, to assist participants with their performance. For example, the cerebral palsied athlete who wants to participate in team soccer, a sport recognized by the National Association of Sports for Cerebral Palsy, must be taught the basics of soccer and the adaptations necessary so that these movement skills can be used efficiently. An understanding of anatomy, physiology, biomechanics, and motor learning is helpful for all coaches, particularly those who work with students who have orthopedic and neurologic impairments. Guttman's text, *Sport for the Disabled*, (1976) is an excellent reference for the coach who needs additional information about scientifically oriented sport adaptations.

Indicated below are some guidelines coaches can use when modifying skills and drills to assist the child with a disability.

Activity modifications require creativity and common sense.

Adaptations of Skills, Rules, and Strategies

Modify the Rules of an Activity

Children play many games that have intricate rules which require a high degree of comprehension and reasoning ability. In baseball, for instance, some players may need a coach on the field to assist them when running the bases or fielding a ball. Other students may be successful if the size of the ball or bat is altered. Many of the modifications in rules and equipment can be made with minimal adjustments and inconvenience to the other players.

Avoiding Activities that Eliminate Participants

Many lead-up activities and drills are designed to eliminate players. The shooting game of "Horse" in basketball is an example of such an activity. These activities are particularly discouraging to disabled students who find that they are frequently eliminated first because of the effect that various disabilities have on their skill level. Elimination activities can be easily modified by changing the level of expectation. For example, in the game of "Horse" a basket is scored if the ball hits the rim. Increasing the size of the target or number of trials permitted are other ways to equate contestants who are of unequal abilities.

Accommodating Special Needs

Students with orthopedic and sensory impairments will find it impossible to participate with success in some games unless their special needs are considered. Many visually impaired students can participate with success in some skills of baseball, such as batting and running the bases, but have difficulty fielding ground or fly balls. These children can be successful if additional time to field the ball is provided and their teammates are encouraged to provide verbal assistance.

A rule modification that a runner going to first is out if the visually impaired fielder locates, pick-up, and brings the ball to the waist could be made. A throw to first would not be necessary, thus creating a situation in which a player with a disability becomes an asset to a team and not a liability.

Altering the Activity Area

Children with disabilities sometimes experience movement limitations which require that the activity area in some sports be altered. For example, in activities in which players with limited mobility serve as goalies or protectors of a certain area, the designated goal should be reduced in size, thereby enhancing the player's success as a goalie. In activities involving throwing and kicking, the distance to the target or the target size might be changed, permitting greater success. Disabled and nondisabled students find adaptations such as these acceptable if efforts are made to explain the rationale for the alteration(s) in the activity. This discussion of sport adaptations for the disabled is limited, due to space constraints. Coaches should consult the suggested reading list to obtain additional ideas.

Sport Organizations for Disabled Youth

In recent years, several national organizations have emerged to promote and encourage the participation of disabled individuals in sport programs. A significant event which encouraged this development was the passage of Public Law 95-606, the Amateur Sports Act of 1978. The enactment of this law led the United States Olympic Committee (USOC) to include within its constitution a statement of support for athletic programs and competition for disabled athletes. The USOC emphasized that whenever feasible, disabled athletes should participate in programs of athletic competition for able bodied individuals.

The United States Olympic Committee
endorses sport for disabled athletes.

To achieve this objective, the USOC established a special membership for organizations serving disabled athletes. Seven organizations promoting sport for disabled athletes have been recognized by the USOC. In addition to the competition sponsored by these groups, many of the organizations serve as referral centers which develop and share information with coaches. These organizations have developed classification systems which are used to equate the functional ability of athletes by disability. The sport organizations for disabled athletes recognized by the USOC are briefly described here. For more complete information, coaches are encouraged to write to the organization. The addresses of the USOC members and other organizations which promote sport for disabled athletes are included in Table 1.

American Athletic Association of the Deaf (AAAD). This association, organized in 1945, is composed of approximately 120 member clubs with 20,000 members. The purpose of AAAD is to foster and regulate competition, develop uniform rules, and promote interclub competition. A primary function of this organization is to select teams to participate in the World Summer and Winter Games for the Deaf and the Pan-American Games for the Deaf. Annual national tournaments are held in basketball and softball.

National Association of Sports for Cerebral Palsy (NASCP). NASCP was founded in 1978 as the national governing sport organization for individuals with cerebral palsy and similar neurological conditions. NASCP events include a few team sports such as soccer, but the majority of activities involve dual competition. Sponsored events under NASCP's auspices include archery, horseback riding, power lifting, table tennis, wheel chair and ambulent soccer, bocci, bowling, swimming, and track and field events. Outstanding athletes from local, state, and regional levels are selected to represent the United States in international competition.

The NASCP has implemented an eight category classification system that is sensitive to the participant's type of cerebral palsy, degree of involvement, and mode of ambulation. Clinics to train coaches on classification techniques and offer suggestions on coaching are available through the NASCP.

National Wheelchair Athletic Association (NWAA). The NWAA, founded in 1959, is the primary organization which promotes the conduct of competitive sport experiences for individuals with spinal cord injuries and amputees who require a wheelchair. Participants are classified on the basis of their disability into one of seven classes. The level of spinal involvement is used to determine the athlete's class with Class I designating those who are quadriplegics and Class II-V reserved for those who are paraplegics. Amputees are classified into either Class VI or VII.

The NWAA organizes and conducts competitions in seven Olympic sports: athletics (track and field, road racing), archery, air pistol and rifle shooting, swimming, weight lifting, table tennis, and fencing. Competition is also held in wheelchair slalom, an event unique to wheelchair sports. Wheelchair basketball, an extremely popular sport, is governed by the National Wheelchair Basketball Association (NWBA). This organization, founded prior to the formation of the NWAA, continues to serve as the governing organization for wheelchair basketball.

United States Association for Blind Athletes (USABA). The USABA, founded in 1976, is the national governing sport organization for blind and visually impaired individuals. The USABA organizes regional and national competitions for summer and winter events including alpine and nordic skiing, gymnastics,

Table 1.   Associations for Disabled Athletes.

American Athletic Association of the Deaf 3916 Lantern Drive Silver Spring, MD 20902	National Handicapped Sports and Recreation Association Capital Hill Station P.O. Box 18664 Denver, CO 80218
American Blind Bowler's Association 150 North Bellaire Louisville, KY 40206	National Wheelchair Athletic Association 2107 Templeton Gap Road Suite C Colorado Springs, CO 80907
American Wheelchair Bowling Association 6718 Pinehurst Drive Evansville, IN 47711	National Wheelchair Basketball Association 110 Seaton Building University of Kentucky Lexington, KY 40506
Canadian Wheelchair Sports Association 333 River Road Ottawa, Ontario, Canada K 1L B89	National Wheelchair Marathon 380 Diamond Hill Road Warwick, RI 02886
Disabled Sportsmen of America, Inc. P.O. Box 26P.O. Vinton, VA 24179	National Wheelchair Softball Association Box 737 Sioux Falls, SD 57101
International Council on Therapeutic Ice Skating P.O. Box 13 State College, PA 16801	North American Riding for the Handicapped Association Box 100 Ashburn, VA 22011
National Association of Sports for Cerebral Palsy 66 East 34th Street New York, NY 10016	Special Olympics 1701 K Street, N.W., Suite 203 Washington, DC 20006
National Beep Baseball Association 3212 Tomahawk Lawrence, KS 66044	United States Amputee Athletic Association P.O. Box 297 Fairview, TN 37062
National Foundation of Wheelchair Tennis 3857 Birch Street, Suite 411 Newport Beach, CA 92260	United States Association for Blind Athletes 55 West California Avenue Beach Haven Park, NJ 08008

These organizations provide information about local, national, and international programs for handicapped athletes.

power lifting, swimming, track and field, and wrestling. In the annual competitions which have been held since 1977, three classification categories have been utilized to permit equal competition among participants with similar visual disorders.

Special Olympics. In 1968, the Joseph P. Kennedy, Jr. Foundation, under the guidance of Eunice Kennedy Shriver, founded the Special Olympics. This organization promotes and conducts local, regional, national, and international sport experiences for mentally retarded athletes. Competition divisions, adjusted for age and ability, have been established. Fourteen official sports are recognized by Special Olympics. These include traditional activities such as track and field, swimming and diving, gymnastics, ice skating, basketball, and soccer. Unique sport forms such as poly hockey and frisbee disc are also included. Special Olympics has produced an extensive set of instructional guides to assist coaches who seek to improve the sport skill level of their athletes.

National Handicapped Sports and Recreation Association (NHSRA). NHSRA, founded in 1968, was originally known as the Amputee Skiers Association. As the organization grew and began to serve other disabilities in addition to amputees, the name was changed in 1976 to NHSRA. NHSRA is different than other organizations which promote sport for disabled athletes in that it is sport-specific and not disability-specific. The organization's primary expertise is in conducting national competition in winter sport programs, although its chapters promote year-round recreational activities and competitive sports, including water skiing and swimming. Additionally, the association sponsors a traveling physical fitness team that gives presentations and demonstrations on health and physical fitness for disabled persons.

United States Amputee Athletic Association (USAAA). A small group of amputee athletes founded the USAAA in 1981. This organization sponsors national competition annually for amputee athletes in a variety of events including air pistol, archery, standing basketball, track and field events, sit down and standing volleyball, swimming, table tennis, and weight lifting. International competition is available through the International Games for the Disabled and other sport-specific competition.

The organizations described in this section are those which are recognized by the USOC. There are, however, many other national organizations which promote sport for disabled individuals. For example, the National Foundation for Wheelchair Tennis and the National Wheel Marathon Organization may be consulted for information on developing specialized programs for wheelchair athletes. The National Beep Baseball Association has made a significant contribution in its effort to promote an exciting variation of the sport of baseball for visually impaired athletes.

Coaches may also find organizations within their states that promote or sponsor competition for children with various disabilities. In Oregon, for example, the Oregon Games for the Physically Limited are held annually. In addition to traditional track and field events, the Oregon Games incorporate creative events such as body bowling, obstacle courses, and velcro darts to ensure that all participants, regardless of disability, have the opportunity to compete and strive to perform at the highest level possible.

It's ability, not disability, that counts.

Summary

Opportunities for disabled youth to participate in sport programs have increased dramatically in recent years. A growing number of professionals, parents, and advocates recognize the significant contributions that sport can make in the lives of children with disabilities. This chapter reviewed the value of sport for disabled youth and offered suggestions for organizing an appropriate program. The importance of recognizing individual needs and differences was stressed. A discussion of the value of separate, compared to integrated, sport programs for the disabled was discussed as well as other important issues such as medical and age restrictions. Information was presented on the importance of seeking well qualified coaches and the skills that they should possess were identified. Examples of adaptations in activities were provided. National sport organizations for the disabled which interested readers and prospective coaches can contact for additional information were also identified. Youth sport programs for disabled individuals will continue to improve with the assistance of dedicated, sensitive, and empathetic coaches who remember that it's ability, not disability, that's important.

References

Bleck, E., & Nagel, D. (Eds.). (1982). *Physically handicapped children: A medical atlas for teachers* (2nd ed.). New York: Grune and Stratton.

Cuvo, A., Ellis, P., Wisotzek, I., Davis, P., Schilling, D., & Bechtal, D. (1983). Teaching athletic skills to students who are mentally retarded. *The Journal of the Association for Persons With Severe Handicaps, 8*(4), 72–81.

Guttman, L. (1976). *Textbook of sport for the disabled.* Bucks, England: HM & M Publishers. (1978).

Palmer, S. (1978) Nutrition and developmental disorders: An overview. In S. Palmer and S. Ekvall (Eds.), *Pediatric nutrition in developmental disorders.* Springfield, IL: Charles C. Thomas.

Sobsey, R. (1983). Nutrition of children with severely handicapping conditions. *The Journal of the Association for Persons With Severe Handicaps, 8*(4), 14–17.

Suggested Readings

Books

Fait, H., & Dunn, J. (1984). *Special physical education: Adapted, individualized, developmental* (5th ed.). Philadelphia: Saunders College Publishing.

Guttman, L. (1976). *Textbook of sport for the disabled.* Bucks, England: HM & M Publishers.

Owen, E. (1982). *Playing and coaching wheelchair basketball.* Urbana, IL: University of Illinois Press.

Special Olympics sport skills intructional program. Washington, DC: Joseph P. Kennedy, Jr. Foundation.

Winnick, J., & Short, F. (1985). *Physical fitness testing of the disabled.* Champaign, IL: Human Kinetics Publishers, Inc.

Magazines

Beavers, D. B. (Ed.). *Palaestra.* Published quarterly by Challenge Publications, Ltd., 549 Meadow Drive, P.O. Box 508, Macomb, IL 61455.

Crase, C., & Crase, N. (Eds.). *Sports 'N Spokes.* Published bi-monthly by the Paralyzed Veterans of America, 5201 North 19th Avenue, Suite 111, Phoenix, Arizona 85015.

chapter nineteen

What About Co-ed Competition?

Linda K. Bunker
University of Virginia

19

Questions to consider . . .

☐ *What are the advantages and problems of co-ed youth sport?*

☐ *What physiological issues should be considered in co-ed youth sport?*

☐ *What psychological issues should be considered in co-ed youth sport?*

☐ *What organizational issues should be considered in co-ed youth sport?*

☐ *How can we get girls to come out for and stay out for sports?*

The question of co ed competition is not so much should we, but how best can we provide quality co-ed experiences. Both boys and girls deserve the benefits of competition. Competing against opponents of similar skills and interests means that boys and girls will be in the same groups, especially during childhood. Because our society is one which values both cooperation and competition, and establishes many situations in which men and women must work together in both competitive and cooperative environments, it is important to start developing positive attitudes and skills early in life. Sports are an ideal way through which competition and cooperation can be taught to boys and girls.

In the past, some adults have assumed that girls receive little direct value from sport. The glory associated with sport was often a vicarious one for girls as they claimed fame through a more "feminine" activity such as cheerleading, or because of their association with male athletes (Sherif, 1978). Fortunately, this perspective is changing as adults recognize the value of direct participation in sport for both boys and girls.

Historically, coaches and parents have received little help in dealing with the issues surrounding co-ed youth sport. However, there are some basic principles which may help you interact with children of both genders in a sporting situation. There are also some guidelines for program directors which may help them provide more co-educational experiences. The relative value of co-ed competition for all children depends on four characteristics:

- how the social situation of competition is structured
- how the rules and social values are shared
- how the activities are interpreted by both the children (competitors) and significant others (peers, parents, coaches, other adults)
- what emphasis is placed on the outcome (win/lose) in comparison to the value of pure participation

Each of these four characteristics is related to at least one of the four primary questions addressed in this chapter:

- What are the physiological issues in co-ed sport?
- What are the psychological issues in co-ed sport?
- What are the organizational issues in co-ed sport?
- How do we get girls to come out and stay out for sports?

Co-ed competition, per se, is neither good nor bad. Rather, it is an opportunity for children to interact in all aspects of their social world. It is a process which allows individuals or groups to compare themselves with others. As such, it is an important aspect of our culture, and should be available to all children.

Co-ed competition provides an opportunity for boys and girls to interact in unique ways in their social world.

Is success in youth sports really important?

All children need to develop a sense of well-being and an understanding of their personal skills and abilities. Both boys and girls benefit from the opportunity to test their skills against some standard, whether it is in comparison to one's personal best in a test such as speed or strength, or in comparison to a standard set by another competitor. Matching or beating the standard is considered "success," no matter how difficult the standard.

Children who experience success at a level appropriate to their past experience and age are often rewarded by adults and peers. They receive praise and an enhanced sense of self-esteem when they have competed against a tough, but reasonable, standard. If success is a regular occurrence, the occasional failure or "off day" can be tolerated and recognized as such. However, the child whose persistent experiences are labeled as "failures" or "less than desirable" suffers from the perceived disapproval of others. This cycle of reward for positive effect and failure associated with negative effect is true for both boys and girls. Our challenge as adult leaders is to create a wide variety of experiences in which children can experience positive growth and success. To do this we must emphasize more than just winning.

Are the advantages and benefits derived from sport the same for boys and girls?

All children can benefit both emotionally and physically from quality experiences in youth sport. Opportunities to experience social interactions in a competitive situation are important to both boys and girls. Unfortunately, in the past, a sort of double-edged sword existed. A girl was often rewarded and praised for her skill, only to be called a "tomboy" by some insensitive peers or adults. Similarly a boy was sometimes encouraged to compete against "any and all comers." If he lost to another boy, the result was often followed by comments such as "nice try," or "good effort"; but if he lost to a girl, the outcome may have resulted in chiding or comments such as "How could you let a girl beat you?" Such comments do nothing but undermine the value of sport for everyone. Coaches must avoid such comparisons if boys and girls are to receive the maximum benefit from sport (Rotella and Bunker, 1987).

*Boys and girls can benefit both emotionally
and physically from quality co-ed youth sport
experiences.*

Physiological Issues in Co-Ed Sport

Many parents and coaches are concerned about physical differences between boys and girls, and their potential detrimental impact on sport experiences. These concerns are generally unfounded for children 2-12 years of age, and differences in older children can be controlled by careful program planning on the part of adult leaders.

A defensible youth sport program should structure competition to create similar groupings, and give equal access and equal protection to all children, based on skill and experience. Therefore it should make no difference in a competitive setting if the child is a boy or girl. Quality programs are based on individual needs and skills, not merely on chronological age, size, or gender. (For additional information see Chapter 13: "Equating Children for Sports Competition.")

*Defensible childrens' sport programs are based
on individual needs and skills, not on
chronological age or gender.*

Until recently, some adults have questioned whether girls and boys should compete against each other in sports. Their concerns seemed to center on physical issues related to either safety or equality of performance. Examine for yourself some of the basic questions.

Aren't boys bigger than girls?

It may surprise you to know that on the average, girls are slightly more neurologically mature at birth than boys. Between the ages of two and nine all children of the same chronological age are essentially similar in size and weight, although across all children within an age group there is tremendous variation. At about 10 years of age, girls begin a growth spurt whereby they become taller and heavier than boys. This often results in a slight advantage in some sports where speed or height are required. This growth spurt for girls generally ends by about 15-16 years of age. Boys start their growth spurt later, but have a longer growth period, continuing until about 17-18 years. This extended growth period results in heavier, larger, and taller structures on the average for boys, with the obvious advantages in speed and strength. (For additional information on growth and size, see Chapter 4: "How Children Grow and Develop.")

For the youth sport coach, the point to remember is that until both genders have completed puberty, there are probably as many differences within each gender as there are between boys and girls.

Are girls as coordinated as boys?

Prior to puberty, girls and boys have basically the same potential for fast reactions and coordinated movements. In fact, girls mature slightly sooner than boys and some may have a physiological advantage in activities that require strength and speed. Unfortunately, in the past girls often had fewer opportunities to develop specific sport skills where coordination could be developed and demonstrated. This lack of opportunity is not uncommon even among some boys, because without basic skills neither boys nor girls can improve their abilities.

Coordination is a physical attribute which develops primarily due to experience. Given equal opportunity and experience, children with the same sport history will develop similar skills independent of their gender. The key is obviously to give both boys and girls abundant opportunities to develop their skills, with lots of reinforcement for participation.

Coordination develops in both boys and girls due to past experience and reinforcement.

Are the bones of girls more fragile than those of boys?

The bone structure of boys and girls is essentially the same. However, just as small, thin boys may be more susceptible to injuries due to bodily contact or collisions, this would apply to the same sized girls, also. Some medical literature has reported that boys have a higher rate of severe injuries (primarily in ice hockey and football) while girls have a higher rate of minor injuries. These differences are probably due to the past inequities in participation and the nature of specific sports, rather than any physiological differences between the skeletal structure of boys and girls.

Boys and girls are equally sturdy when body size, skill level, and experience are equal.

Are sports dangerous to a child's reproductive system?

This question is often asked in reference to the female anatomy, when in fact, a girl's anatomy is carefully protected within her body as compared to the boy's more vulnerable external male reproductive organs. In either case, most sports

Figure 1. Within-gender differences at any given chronological age may be greater than the differences between genders.

Figure 2. Given equal opportunity and experience, children with the same sport history will develop similar skills independent of their gender.

are quite safe for children's reproductive systems. A similar question is often asked in terms of a girl's breasts. The adolescent girl may experience bruised breasts if hit with an object, but there is no evidence of serious consequences from such an event. The old tale of increased breast cancer due to injuries to the breast is unsubstantiated in medical literature.

Does sport participation delay or impede the onset of puberty?

Under most circumstances, the reverse is true. Girls who participate in regular exercise seem to have more regular cycles with less discomfort. There is, however, some recent evidence that excessive training (e.g. for marathon runs, Olympic caliber gymnastics or swimming) may disrupt the menstrual cycle, or cause a delay in puberty. Apparently it is the severe reduction in body fat and not the activity itself which alters growth and other essential body functions. The same may be true regarding the onset of puberty or secondary sex characteristics for males who engage in extreme conditioning or who attempt to manipulate their weight by withholding foods and liquids. The bottom line appears to be that moderate levels of participation and competition are good for the physical development of both boys and girls.

Should boys and girls participate in co-ed sports after puberty?

Yes, if they are organized by adults who regulate the activities on the basis of safety, skill level, and experience of the participants. The characteristics of good competition hold for all ages; competitors just become harder to match as males get bigger and stronger. Obviously in sports like golf, swimming, tennis, and track and field there are ways to equate competition based on ability, so that size or strength can be neutralized. Such organizational arrangements have nothing to do with gender, but merely provide equal opportunities for the success of all participants.

In some sports, such as basketball and football, which require high components of strength and power, the overall advantages of adolescent boys may make it difficult to have co-ed leagues with approximately equal numbers of boys and girls. However, in baseball, and probably basketball, if a girl has the necessary skills there is no reason why she shouldn't play in a co-ed league.

If boys and girls have similar skills and capacities to perform a sport, there is no reason why co-ed competition should not be promoted.

Figure 3. "Welcome to the Pine Basketball League. You have all been selected to play on this team because last Saturday you demonstrated you had similar skills. If for some reason you think you belong in the Oak or Maple League, please see us after practice today."

Do girls become more masculinized through sport participation?

There is some evidence that a child's body composition can be influenced by his or her choice of sports especially in the amount of lean and fat tissue. It is also important to recognize that certain sports place a high premium on specific motor characteristics. For example, consider agility, coordination, power, and strength. These characteristics are found in the majority of sports. Their degree of emphasis for skill attainment will vary within a sport. In sports such as gymnastics and dance, there is a high premium on agility and coordination due to the precision requirements of the skill involved. In sports such as basketball, body-building, and track and field, there is a high premium on power and strength. Each of these characteristics is specific to the activity, and not the gender of the participants.

Psychological Issues in Co-ed Sports

The psychological health of young athletes is just as important and vulnerable to injury and abuse as their physical health. For example, in any competitive situation, there are concerns expressed about helping children deal with both winning and losing. The basic self-worth of all competitors is at stake, yet competition may become a special problem when different values are applied to winning or losing, depending on whether the winner or loser is a boy or a girl.

Aren't there psychological problems when a boy loses to a girl?

This question, or fear, on the part of adults has probably done more to prevent the development of co-ed youth sport than any other issue. No one likes to lose, and losing is equally unpleasant for boys and girls. The distinction between losing to a girl or boy is something adults instill in children. If children are matched on their abilities, then it should not matter against whom they play nor should the gender of the winner or loser be of any consequence.

If adults deliver the message that boys should not lose to girls, what are we telling our children? Are we suggesting to them that somehow girls are innately less competent than boys, and boys should never lose to an incompetent opponent? Or are we telling boys that their masculinity is at stake if they lose to a female?

The notion that a boy's masculinity is at stake whenever he plays against a girl, or that somehow men must always dominate women is one of the most unhealthy attitudes a child could experience. Unfortunately, some individuals feel that way, including James Michener, author of *Sport in America*, who wrote that the need for males to dominate females in sport is an "immutable genetic inheritance" of the male. He further suggested that boys must dominate over girls in sport between the ages of 12–22 because that "conforms to some permanent psychological need of the human race." (Michener, 1976, p. 130) Yet, as our culture has evolved, so have our psychological needs.

Our culture values equality and the right for each person to become the best that they are capable of becoming. That means having opportunities to develop

Figure 4.   The gender of the winner or loser in a contest should not have an influence on how the outcome of the event is interpreted.

skill, and to test that skill against others of equal or better ability. It also means having the opportunity to develop healthy attitudes toward winning and losing, without reference to gender.

What happens to a child's ego when he/she is beaten by a member of the opposite gender?

That question in itself is an interesting comment on the male-female issues in sport. Have you ever been concerned about a girl who loses a contest just because she was beaten by a boy? Probably not. The real concern comes when parents are so worried about their son's ego when he loses to a girl that they add pressure to the situation.

An interesting case occurred in Hoboken, New Jersey, when Maria Pepe first became a pitcher for a little league team. It wasn't until she started striking everyone out that her participation became a problem. That is when the "boys only" policy was employed. Executives at the National Headquarters ordered that either Maria be eliminated, or the team would be expelled from the league. Fortunately, Maria's case was taken to court and the judge ruled that it was unfair to deny fifty percent of the population the opportunity to enjoy something as "American as apple pie." In fact, the judge ruled "there is no reason why part of Americana should be withheld from little girls. The sooner little boys begin to realize that little girls are equal and that there will be many opportunities for a boy to be bested by a girl, the closer we will be to having a healthy society." (Dworkin, 1974; p. 20)

Are "Tomboys" O.K.?

Girls who excel in sports are active, take pride in their accomplishments, and feel good about themselves. They are generally healthier and happier than inactive girls because of their participation. When the term "tomboy" is used to describe them, it should certainly be "O.K." and even desirable. We sometimes call a talented, successful boy a "star," "stud," or "jock", and mean that in a very positive way. The only parallel term for a girl is a "tomboy," and that term should also be considered to be a positive reflection of ability.

A recent survey of the top 100 women leaders in sport asked each if they had ever been characterized as a "tomboy." Eighty percent said "Yes," and they also said they were proud of it. When asked what characteristics of a tomboy they liked, they listed attributes such as dedicated, skilled, competitive, able to set goals, talented, achievement-oriented, and self-assured. Those characteristics should certainly be valued in both boys and girls.

Sometimes children become too aggressive, rather than self-assured, or become involved in unsportsmanlike acts. This type of inappropriate behavior should be judged the same way for both boys and girls. The important point to remember is that the characteristics which determine a good athlete have nothing to do with one's gender.

How do you get girls to come out and stay out for sports?

Girls will participate in sport when given the encouragement and opportunity to do so. This has recently been shown by the tremendous increase in the numbers of girls participating in all forms of sport.

In order to maximize the participation of both boys and girls, it is important to identify the needs of the children in your community. After asking them what activities they would enjoy, it may also be important to get one or two of their peer leaders involved in organizing and promoting the activity. Sometimes children will not identify a particular sport as being of interest because no one else seems to play it. That is generally due to a lack of social support, or perhaps merely because no opportunity has existed in the past.

It is also critical to provide good leadership and opportunities to develop skills and have fun. Do not automatically assume that winning is the most important goal. Girls who drop out of sports often do so because they have not been encouraged to participate, have not been taught the necessary skills to be successful, or simply have not had fun. All of these reasons can be eliminated by providing programs in which the participation of girls is valued and encouraged.

How can we encourage girls to become participants rather than spectators?

Girls often evolve into spectators because of insufficient opportunities available to them, or because of unsuccessful experiences in sport. If both boys and girls are provided with opportunities to participate and develop their skills, a certain proportion of each gender will be successful and will be reinforced for their participation. Being active is a "habit" we can all learn if we start early.

Adolescents who have not previously been active may be attracted to new or novel sports. Sports such as racquetball, synchronized swimming, and fencing may be attractive to both genders. Initially, the non-gender stereotyped sports may be the easiest to introduce, but there is no reason why most sports, especially those which are classified as "non-contact," can not be played coeducationally.

What problems can we anticipate as we first introduce co-ed sports?

Studies done on co-ed physical education classes have suggested that initially there may be some problems in participation rates. When girls are added to previously all-male programs, a few boys may stop participating, and vice versa. This participation rate will generally adjust itself to previous levels as children learn that they can compete and enjoy playing together.

Some children, generally boys, believe that their skill development is being hindered by competing with members of the opposite gender. This usually occurs in boys who may try to dominate the games, or believe that girls are innately inferior at sports. This, too, will correct itself if participants have been grouped by skill level.

In which sports are co-ed activities most desirable?

Prior to puberty, there is little reason to exclude any sport from a possible co-ed experience. This includes such activities as wrestling, football, gymnastics, and ballet. At this age, differences in strength and speed as well as coordination seem to be determined more by experience and opportunity than by gender. With equal societal support and opportunities to develop skill for both boys and girls, these differences should be minimized.

With equal societal support and opportunities to develop skill for both boys and girls, differences between genders in non-contact sports should be minimized.

However, at the inception of some co-ed programs, there may be skill differences due to previous inequities in opportunities and experience. This may be true for both boys and girls. If that is the case, be careful that grouping by skill does not become an excuse to have separate leagues for boys and girls. In this situation some children, usually girls, will be relegated to the "C" league, just because they have not previously had the opportunity or encouragement to develop their skills. To avoid this type of segregation, it is important that boys and girls have equal opportunities to develop motor skills early in life.

After puberty, the issue of playing on co-ed teams becomes a bit more complex. Due to size advantages of boys during adolescence it may be wise to consider grouping participants based on size and strength, if the sport could result in injury because of a mismatch between performers. For this reason most collision sports, such as lacrosse and football, are not recommended for co-ed teenage leagues. On the other hand, if injuries are not likely to be due to the size and strength of the competitors, then co-ed leagues should be encouraged, especially in individual sports or team sports where participants can be appropriately grouped, such as golf, volleyball, softball, racquetball, tennis, basketball, and soccer.

Aren't there psychological reasons for separate leagues?

In general, the psychological concerns for youth sport are founded on cultural influences, as previously discussed. There is, however, one area in which adolescent participants may be personally affected. If the sport involves physical contact or potential for social stigma due to "touching," then there may be reason to provide activities segregated by gender.

For the majority of sport experiences, adolescents can successfully participate in co-ed sports. This is especially true of sports which can be grouped according to skill. Such sports would include all the racquet sports, most team sports (including baseball and basketball), and almost all individual sports.

There are few sports which are innately "unsuitable" for co-ed groupings. The important aspect is to create a supportive atmosphere for all of the participants and pay attention to critical aspects of safety. It may also be important to remember that whenever boys or girls participate in activities which are non-traditional for them (e.g. girls in wrestling or boys in field hockey or dance) lead-up activities and psychological support systems should be provided.

How can we help both boys and girls be comfortable playing sports together?

If children begin to participate together at an early age, there is generally no problem with their "comfort." Children will accept each other as appropriate partners if parents and coaches accept and encourage it.

The difficulty in making older children comfortable in co-ed sports situations may be that they have already developed some societal notions about appropriate interactions. This is most easily handled when sports programs are available to young children on a co-ed basis. However, this is not always possible. If you are introducing co-ed competition to adolescents for the first time, you may wish to provide some specific assistance in the transition from single-gender to co-ed participation.

There are several ways to help ease the transition into co-ed sports. If you are part of a multi-sport system (YMCA, YWCA, Boys Club, etc.), try introducing co-ed sports in the non-gender areas first. Sports such as golf, tennis, and track and field lend themselves to co-ed participation. These sports have many available role models of both genders to use as examples. Put pictures of both genders playing the sport on the wall or in your hand-outs. Provide leadership from both genders, and be sure to group the children using sound procedures (see Chapter 13: "Equating Children for Sports Competition").

In more traditionally single-gender sports such as wrestling or field hockey, it may be important to provide active support systems for the children. There are almost always role models available. Discuss these individuals and point out the positive values they have gained from sport experiences. It may also be important to openly discuss the feelings the children are having about their participation. If you are open with them, you may be surprised at how much they are willing to share with you. Tell them how you felt the first time you competed in a co-ed league. Then explain how much you support the concept now. Encourage them to share their feelings with you.

The key points to providing good co-ed sport experiences and to easing the feelings of strangeness which may accompany their introduction to co-ed sports are to:

- provide sport experiences that are suited to the participants' ability level
- be sure that the children who compete against each other are equal in sport skills and experience
- provide examples of good role models of both genders
- be sure to keep the channels of communication open: discuss ways in which

the experience can be improved and provide an avenue for children to discuss any concerns they may have with the sporting situation
- provide leaders of both genders

Should co-ed sports be coached by men or women?

Children should be exposed to quality coaching from a wide variety of sources: young adults, older or retired individuals, and middle aged adults of both genders. If children are to realize the value of sport participation, they must see all segments of the population participating in and coaching sports.

Gender should not be the primary determinant in coaching qualifications. The competencies necessary to be a good coach are certainly equally available to men and women (see Section III: "Fundamental Skills of Coaching").

The results of a national survey show that women are more likely to be found coaching younger children or those of beginning skill levels. This is probably due to two reasons: first, men seem to prefer coaching older, more skilled participants; and second, women may in the past have lacked the fundamental understandings and skill level to coach the more advanced players (Bunker and Owens, 1984). Fortunately, both of these situations are changing.

As women have had more opportunities to participate in sports at younger ages, they have developed more skills. Their earlier participation may have also exposed them to other women coaches who have continued as role models. At the same time, men have come to appreciate the skills of women coaches, and have also discovered the joys of coaching younger children. These new attitudes are merging with the need for leagues to establish more equal representation among their coaches. The unequal numbers of males and females in coaching may gradually be adjusted.

Summary

Co-educational sports are both feasible and important to a well-rounded youth sport program. The experiences derived from sport participation are enriched when a wide variety of individuals are involved. In addition, because our culture values success in cooperative and competitive interactions, it is important to provide access to youth sport experiences for both boys and girls.

This chapter provided information about three clusters of issues in co-ed youth sports: physiological, psychological, and organizational. With careful structuring of the youth sport programs by qualified adult leaders, co-ed youth sport programs will become more popular and effective in providing benefits to young competitors.

References

Bunker, L.K., & Owens, N.D. (1984). *Trends in youth sport participation: 1965–1984*. Presented at the AAHPERD convention in Anaheim, CA.

Dworkin, S. (1984). Sexism strikes out. *Ms.*, May, p. 20.

Michener, J.A. (1976). *Sports in America*. New York: Random House, p. 130.

Suggested Readings

Martens, R., Christina, R.W., Harvey, J.S., & Sharky, B.J. (1981). *Coaching young athletes*. Champaign, IL: Human Kinetics Publishers, Inc.

Martens, R. & Seefeldt, V. (1979). *Guidelines for children's sports*. Washington, D.C.: AAHPERD Publications.

Rotella, R.J. and Bunker, L.K. (1987). *Parenting Your Superstar*. Champaign, IL: Human Kinetics.

Smith, N.J., Smith, R.E., & Smoll, F.L. (1983). *Kidsports: A survival guide for parents*. Reading, MA: Addison Wesley.

chapter twenty

Post Season Evaluation: What Did We Accomplish?

Paul G. Vogel
Michigan State University

Questions to consider . . .

- ☐ *Why should coaches conduct a post-season evaluation?*

- ☐ *What should be evaluated?*

- ☐ *Who should evaluate coaching effectiveness?*

- ☐ *What steps can be used to conduct a post-season evaluation?*

Participation in youth sports programs may result in outcomes that are beneficial and/or detrimental. As indicated in Chapter 2, "Your Role as Youth Sports Coach," the degree to which beneficial effects of participation outweigh detrimental effects is due largely to the quality of adult leadership provided (Rarick, 1969; Smith, Smoll, & Hunt, 1977). Because most of the leadership in youth sport settings is provided by the coach, it is important for every coach to ask the question, "How do I rate as a coach?"

The answer to the above question should be based on more than showing up for practices, being a good person, allowing all the children to play, working the team hard, or even having a winning season. The more important question is, "Did the players make important progress toward achieving the beneficial effects, while avoiding the potentially detrimental effects that can occur with participation in youth sports?" An overview of the beneficial and detrimental effects of participation is included in Figure 1. Chapter 1, "Benefits of Competitive Sports for Children," contains a more complete description of these effects.

Why Evaluate?

Every coach should evaluate the results of the season for the following reasons:

- both beneficial and detrimental effects of participation may occur
- the degree to which the positive effects outweigh the negative effects can be altered with effective coaching (Smith, Smoll, & Curtis, 1979)

All coaches miss the mark of coaching perfection in some of the potential outcome areas for one or more of the players on their teams. Coaches who have not benefitted from coaching education programs, have not had experience as a participant in the sport, or who have not had prior coaching experience are particularly susceptible to using ineffective coaching methods. Although beginning coaches may benefit most from conducting an end-of-season evaluation, even experienced professionals can significantly improve their coaching abilities by conducting an evaluation and acting on the findings.

All coaches can significantly improve their coaching effectiveness by completing end of season evaluations.

Because the results of participation in youth sports can be positive and/or negative, it is important to determine the degree to which both are occurring. Evaluation (determining program merit) is useful to identify which benefits ac-

BENEFICIAL EFFECTS	DETRIMENTAL EFFECTS
1 Development of appropriate skills	1 Development of inappropriate skills
2 Development of fitness	2 Injury, illness, or loss of fitness
3 Acquire knowledge of rules and strategies of play	3 Acquire incorrect knowledge of rules and strategies
4 Acquire knowledge of appropriate conditioning techniques	4 Acquire incorrect knowledge of conditioning techniques or use of contraindicated exercises
5 Develop a realistic and positive self-esteem	5 Development of unrealistic or negative self-esteem
6 Facilitate a lifetime of participation in activity	6 Avoidance of future participation in activity for self and others
7 Develop a respect for rules as facilitators of fair play	7 Learning to misuse rules for the purpose of winning
8 Enjoyment and recreation	8 Lack of enjoyment or fear of failure
9 Development of beneficial personal, social and psychological skills	9 Development of detrimental social skills or psychological injury
	10 Loss of time available for other activities

Figure 1.   Potential beneficial and detrimental effects of participation in youth sports.

tually occurred, why they occurred (or perhaps more importantly, why they did not occur), and what changes can be incorporated that will improve coaching actions in subsequent seasons. Accordingly, at least two evaluation questions should be asked:

- Was the season effective in achieving its purpose(s)?
- What changes can be made to improve the quality of coaching?

Answers to these questions can provide important information that can be used to systematically improve coaching effectiveness and, consequently, the youth sport experience for children.

Because most youth sport programs are conducted by unpaid volunteers, the coaching evaluation described in this chapter does not consider coaching pay, institutional accountability and efficiency, or other more sophisticated roles that evaluation can address. Rather, its focus is on describing a systematic, but relatively simple approach that you, as a youth sport coach, can use to estimate the accomplishments of the season and to improve your coaching effectiveness for subsequent years.

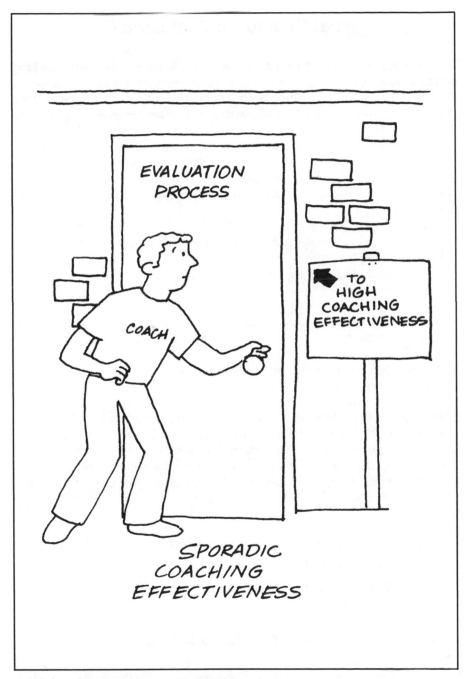

Figure 2.   Evaluation can open the door to improved coaching effectiveness.

What Should Be Evaluated?

The most important information concerning the effectiveness of your coaching activities can be obtained by determining the degree to which your players achieved the objectives established for the season. Your evaluation should include all of the players on the team and all of the season objectives. This can be accomplished by using a player evaluation form similar to the one in Figure 3.

The evaluation form contains space for evaluating players' outcomes in the skill, knowledge, fitness, and attitude areas. Within each outcome area there is space to enter season objectives that you have identified as important for your players to obtain. Using softball for an example, objectives in each outcome area include:

SKILL

hitting, running to first, running extra bases, fielding grounders . . .

KNOWLEDGE

proper stretching, warm up, rules of play, player positioning, 1 out situations, 2 out situations . . .

FITNESS

abdominal strength, aerobic capacity, grip strength, hip flexibility, upper arm strength . . .

ATTITUDE

persistence, cooperation, best effort, self control, respect for the rules of play, self esteem . . .

A player evaluation form such as that provided in Figure 3 provides a summary (vertical totals) of each player's achievement of the objectives included in your season plans. It also provides a summary (horizontal totals) of the degree to which each season objective was obtained (or not obtained) by the players on your team. Collecting, analyzing, and using the information obtained from a form like the one in Figure 3 is described later in the chapter under the heading "Evaluation Steps."

Evaluation of coaching effectiveness should be based on estimates of the degree to which players achieve appropriate outcomes.

Who Should Evaluate?

Initially, you should evaluate your own effectiveness in facilitating desired player outcomes by using a form similar to the one in Figure 3. Self evaluation is often the most important source of information for improving coaching actions.

COACH'S EVALUATION OF PLAYER OUTCOMES

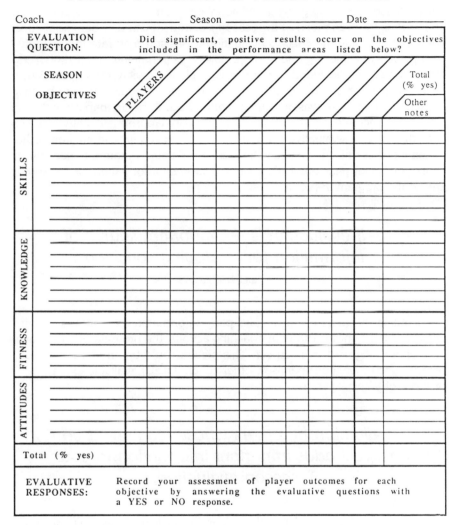

Figure 3. Coach's evaluation of player outcomes.

Some changes that are apparent to others, however, are often missed in a self evaluation. Only by gaining additional insight from others will you be able to detect all (or even most) of the season's detrimental and/or beneficial effects. For example, using the coach's evaluation form, you may rate the majority of your players as achieving one or more objectives pertaining to skill, knowledge, fitness, or attitude included in your season plans. Review by a second party, however, may reveal that you did help your players achieve your objectives, but what you thought was appropriate turned out to be an inappropriate technique, incorrect rule, contraindicated exercise, or inappropriate attitude. To prevent this type of evaluative error from occurring requires input from others. Obtaining such information demands a considerable amount of security and courage on your part, but it often yields important information for helping you and/or the program improve.

> ## *Self evaluation is an important source of information for improving coaching effectiveness.*

To obtain the most useful second party information, you should identify a person who is familiar with your coaching actions, the progress of your players, and whose judgment you respect. This person could be an assistant coach, a parent, official, league supervisor, other coach, locally available expert, or one or more of your players.

> ## *Evaluation by others whose judgement you respect adds important information to your season evaluation.*

An evaluation form similar to the one in Figure 4 provides a way for you to obtain information relative to your coaching effectiveness as perceived by others. This form can be used to estimate your effectiveness with an individual player (potential evaluators could be the player, or a parent) or with the team as a whole (potential evaluators include an assistant coach, official, supervisor, and/or local expert).

The evaluation form in Figure 4 is similar but less specific, in terms of season objectives, than the form in Figure 3. The reduction in specificity decreases the time necessary to complete the form and improves its ease of use. The purpose of the form is to reveal areas (low ratings) that need follow-up. Follow-up entails a debriefing session with the rater to determine the reasons for low ratings and

PLAYER PERFORMANCE RELATIVE TO OTHERS

Evaluator: _____   Player/team _____ Date _____

EVALUATION QUESTION:	In comparison with other players in this league, how does the player (or team) listed above perform in the areas listed below?

PERFORMANCE AREAS	PLAYER OR TEAM PERFORMANCE LEVELS						COMMENTS
	SEASON START			SEASON END			
	TOP 25%	MID 50%	BOTTOM 25%	TOP 25%	MID 50%	BOTTOM 25%	
SKILL OFFENSIVE							
DEFENSIVE							
KNOWLEDGE RULES							
STRATEGIES							
OTHER							
FITNESS STRENGTH							
ENDURANCE							
ATTITUDE PERSONAL							
SOCIAL							

INDIVIDUAL EVALUATION:
For each performance area indicate, by placing a check in the top, mid or bottom column, the beginning and ending performance level of the player.

TEAM EVALUATION:
For each performance area estimate the number of players (% or actual numbers) in the top, mid or bottom performance levels at the beginning and at the end of the season.

Figure 4. Player performance, as perceived by individuals other than the coach.

what can be done to strengthen them. Follow-up sessions with this type of focus have proven to be highly effective in identifying ways to improve programs and procedures.

In summary:

1) Participation in youth sports can result in positive and/or negative effects.
2) The degree to which positive effects outweigh negative effects is a function of your effectiveness as a coach.
3) All coaches can improve their effectiveness.
4) Evaluation is an important way to facilitate coaching improvement.
5) Both self evaluation and evaluation(s) by respected others are important aspects of a coaching evaluation.

The following sections provide a four step approach that describes how you can evaluate the season's accomplishments and how to use the results to improve your coaching effectiveness.

Evaluation Steps

There are several steps that can be used to complete an evaluation of the season. These include:

1) Identify the outcomes of the season.
2) Collect evaluation data.
3) Analyze the evaluation data.
4) Implement the needed changes.

Step 1: Identify the intended outcomes

The magnitude of your influence on player achievement is the best information you can use to determine your effectiveness as a coach. Accordingly, the outcomes (mastery or significant progress toward the achievement of the season objectives) you choose as objectives for your players must be clearly identified. The Coach's Evaluation of Player Outcomes form in Figure 3 can be used to complete this task. List the specific skills, knowledge, fitness capacities, and attitudes that you intend(ed) to teach to your players on one or more of these forms. Use the outcomes for softball that are included as an example and substitute corresponding outcomes (season objectives) for the sport you are coaching. Completion of this step clearly identifies what you believe is important for your players to achieve, and therefore, a clear indication of the outcomes upon which your players should be evaluated.

Figure 5. Clearly specifying your objectives for players will help them to understand what you are trying to teach.

The first step in conducting an evaluation of your coaching effectiveness is to clearly identify your intended outcomes.

Specification of your season objectives provides for two important evaluative actions. First, you can rate the progress of each of your players on objectives deemed important to you. Second, you can obtain information from others, whose judgement you respect, regarding the appropriateness of your season objectives for the age and experience level of your players. Suggestions for additions, deletions, or alterations in your objectives is the primary outcome of this review. Without clearly identifying the intent of your coaching actions in terms of specific objectives, it is difficult to determine the accomplishments of the season or how you can improve as a coach. Stated in another way, if you do not know where you are going, it is difficult to determine whether or not you have arrived at the appropriate destination or whether you chose the best route.

Similarly, without a clear indication of your season objectives, it is impossible for another coach, local expert, or other person to provide you with feedback regarding the appropriateness of your objectives, accomplishments of your players, or your coaching effectiveness. Clearly specifying your season objectives has two other important benefits. First, it clarifies in your own mind what your coaching focus should be, and therefore helps you plan for the coming season. Second, to the degree that you effectively communicate these season objectives to your players, it will help them understand what you are trying to teach. Research on effective instruction reveals that the clear specification of intended outcomes is strongly related to improved achievement.

Step 2: Collect the evaluation data

As suggested in the previous section entitled "Who should evaluate?," coaches should conduct a self evaluation of the season's results. An assessment of the season by selected others, in combination with a self assessment is, however, much more valuable for identifying important player outcomes and potential coaching improvements. For this reason both approaches are recommended for evaluating the accomplishments of the season.

Completing the coach's assessment of player performance. Begin the evaluation by entering your season objectives in the first column of the Coach's Evaluation of Player Performance evaluation form. Next enter the names of the players in the spaces across the top of the form. Then respond either "Yes" or "No" to the question posed on the top of the form. The evaluation question, "Did significant, positive results occur?" should be asked and answered for each player on every objective.

Your decision to enter a "Yes" or "No" requires you to define a standard. For example, all of your players may have improved in one of the season's objectives listed on the form, but you may feel that several of those players did not achieve enough to receive a "Yes." A "No," however, may also seem to be an inappropriate entry. To resolve this difficulty, it is important for you to clarify the amount of player achievement for each season's objective that you are willing to accept as evidence of a meaningful gain. For the volunteer coach there is no exact method of determining how much gain is enough. If you wish to discriminate between large and/or small gains you can use a scale to rate gains where: 0 = none, 1 = very little, 2 = little, 3 = some, 4 = large and 5 = very large. Given ratings of this type you could then establish, for example,

4 and 5 ratings as *large* enough to be categorized as a "Yes" response and ratings of 3 or less as "No" responses.

> *You must decide if your coaching actions*
> *resulted in a large majority of your players*
> *achieving significant gains on a large majority*
> *of the outcomes you intended to teach.*

It is important to remember that players who begin the season at low levels of skill have the potential for more improvement than players who have mastered an objective and are seeking to maintain or refine it. You should account for this difference in your assignment of "Yes" or "No" entries. When players at high performance levels maintain and/or gain a small increment in performance it is usually appropriate to assign a "Yes" rather than a "No" response.

> *You must be sure that your coaching acts are*
> *associated with beneficial rather than*
> *detrimental effects of participation.*

Detrimental effects of participation can be viewed as a zero or negative change in the season's objectives. Injury, loss of fitness, or development of inappropriate skills, knowledge, or attitudes are detrimental effects that can occur and should be identified. In this situation the appropriate entry is a "No" that is enhanced by circling or underlining to distinguish it from small or slight gains.

Completion of the coach's evaluation form will reveal your perception of the degree to which you helped your players achieve season objectives. By looking at one objective across all players as well as one player across all objectives you will be able to observe patterns of effectiveness across season objectives and individual players.

Obtaining information from selected other persons. To obtain information from others about your coaching effectiveness, the evaluation form in Figure 4 can be used. The form can be used for individual players or for the entire team. The estimates of performance are relative to other players of similar age and gender in the league. Where rating individual players, ask the user of the form to place a check in the appropriate column (top 25%, mid 50%, or bottom 25%) for each performance area. When rating the entire team, enter the number o the percent of players judged to be in each column.

High, low, or mixed ratings of player performance at the end of the sea

Figure 6. Discuss your coaching strengths and weaknesses with the person who completed the evaluation.

are not very useful without knowing player performance levels at the beginning of the season. It is the change in the performance levels of the players resulting from participation in the season that provides insight into your coaching effectiveness. The best way to determine change in player performance is to obtain a rating prior to the time that coaching occurred and another rating subsequent o the coaching. Two or more ratings may be difficult to obtain, however, because ˙the time it requires of your rater(s). A good alternative is to have the evaluator(s) ord changes in player performance that they have observed, using a double system. For example, if three of your players were perceived to be in the % of their peers at the beginning of the season and four additional players were elevated to that performance level by the end of the season, the net gain in this performance category would be 4. Your goal may be to have all of your players move into the top 25% category during the course of the season. Such a goal is unrealistic, however. Having 50% of your players move from the bottom to mid, or mid to top performance levels would be excellent.

It would be nice to look at your evaluation of player performance and the evaluation(s) of their performance by others and see only "Yes" responses or ratings in the top 25%. Such a set of responses, however, would not be very helpful for improving your coaching effectiveness. An excessive number of high ratings (85-100%) for either of the evaluation instruments would probably signal the use of a relaxed set of standards. All coaches vary in their effectiveness across performance areas and across individual players on the team. It is these failures that are most useful, however, in revealing principles of coaching effectiveness that are being violated. It is important, therefore, to use evaluative standards for your self-ratings (or for the ratings of others) that result in no more than 80% of the responses being "Yes" on the Coach's Evaluation of Player Performance or in the top 25% when rated by others. As you will see in Step 3, mixed ratings are an aid for you to determine areas where your effectiveness may be strengthened.

The performance of your players and reactions to your coaching methods by others can be invaluable for determining potential coaching improvements.

Use of the form "Evaluation of Player Performance Relative to Others" provides you with an estimate of changes in player performance as viewed by someone other than yourself, whose judgement you respect. The relatively broad performance areas upon which the evaluation is based do not, however, provide sufficiently detailed information for you to understand how to interpret the data obtained. Simply stated, more information is needed. This information can be obtained by using the technique of debriefing.

In a debriefing session, use the information obtained from the form as the basis for a discussion of your coaching strengths and weaknesses with the person who completed the evaluation. During the debriefing session be sure to:
1) Thank the individual for taking the time to complete the evaluation form.
2) Point out that although learning of your strengths as a coach is nice, and appreciated, the most important purpose of the debriefing session is to identify weaknesses, and how they may be improved.
3) Proceed through the performance areas and their corresponding ratings, seeking to understand why each area was rated high or low. For example,

Figure 7. We can all find ways to improve our effectiveness.

if a disproportionate number of the players were rated low relative to their peers on offensive skills, and there were very small gains from the beginning of the season to the end of the season, you need more information. Attempt to determine what offensive skills were weak, and what could be changed to help strengthen them in the coming season.

4) In your discussion, probe for the things you can do (or avoid doing) that may produce better results. Make a special attempt to identify the rationale that would support a suggested alternative action.

Compliments on coaching effectiveness are pleasing to hear, but identified deficiencies are more helpful for improving effectiveness.

5) Take careful notes during the debriefing session. Record the alternatives suggested for each deficiency, the rationale for their use, and how they might be implemented.

The data collected in this way are invaluable for helping to identify specific coaching strengths and weaknesses. More importantly, debriefing will provide you with many good ideas for increasing your ability to help players achieve next year's season's objectives.

Step 3: Analyze the data

The first step necessary to analyze the information collected on the coach's evaluation form is to total the number of "Yes" responses entered for each player across all season objectives. Divide the number of "Yes" responses by the total number of season objectives and enter the percent of "Yes" responses in the row labeled "Total" for each player. Similarly total the number of "Yes" responses across players for each season objective and enter the percent of "Yes" responses in the column labeled "Total" for each season objective.

Your goal as a dedicated coach is to have 100% of your players make significant gains on 100% of the season objectives. Rarely, however, is this possible. Most evaluators would be skeptical of such results and would claim that the high scores represent relaxed standards for making the "Yes/No" decisions. Typically, evaluators use a 80/80 rule which suggests that things have gone well if 80% of the children make important gains on 80% of the objectives.

From a coaching improvement viewpoint it is necessary to have a mixture of "Yes" and "No" responses across both the objectives and players. Although obtaining 100% of the responses in the "Yes" category would be nice, it is the "No's" that are most helpful in identifying needed coaching improvements. Accordingly, if you exceed the 80/80 rule when rating player performance, you should re-rate each row and column. In re-rating, force yourself to use 25%

"Yes" and 25% "No" responses for each season objective. Repeat the same procedure for each player. The pattern of "Yes" and "No" responses that will emerge from these forced ratings can be very helpful in identifying the season objectives for which your coaching is most and least effective. Similarly, by looking at the characteristics of the players who obtained the highest and lowest gains, you may learn that you need to be more effective with certain kinds of players.

Answer to the question, "Why did several players not make a sufficient number of meaningful improvements?" will often reveal needed coaching changes.

The real benefits of evaluating player achievement in each of the performance areas comes with evaluating the reasons why few or no players received "Yes" responses. It is the answer(s) to the "Why?" question that reveal changes you can make to improve your coaching effectiveness.

To help you determine the reasons why you were (or were not) successful with your coaching in certain player performance areas, use the "Checklist of Effective Coaching Actions" at the end of this chapter. The checklist provides a series of rateable items that may help you identify some of the reasons for ineffective coaching. For example, if John, Sue, and Tom made insufficient progress in fielding fly balls, you could review the checklist to help determine coaching actions you used (or did not use) that may be related to helping players that are similar in skill level, fitness, or character to John, Sue, and Tom. As you identify coaching actions that may have detracted from player performance, note these and then alter your subsequent coaching actions accordingly.

Sometimes it is helpful to contrast high achieving players with low achieving players on one or more season objectives. Contrasting the characteristics of players achieving at different levels will often reveal differences in player's characteristics that require different coaching approaches. Often these differences are not readily apparent when high or low achievers are educated in the absence of the other group.

Interpreting unmet expectations. The above suggestions will help you to identify ways to improve your coaching ability. There are, however, other ways to interpret lack of improved player performance. One common excuse is to blame lack of performance on lack of player interest. This reasoning is nearly always incorrect!

Figure 8.   Effective coaches significantly alter player's skill, knowledge, fitness, AND attitudes.

Be sure to consider all possibilities for self improvement before accepting other reasons for unmet expectations.

Effective coaches significantly alter player's skill, knowledge, fitness, AND attitudes all of the time, and rarely, even with below average talent, perform poorly in league competition, particularly in the latter portion of the season. The most helpful approach you can use to improve your coaching effectiveness is to assume that when results do not meet expectations, the solution to the problem will be found in your coaching actions. This may prove to be the wrong reason, but you must be absolutely sure that you have considered all possibilities for self-improvement prior to accepting other reasons for unmet expectations.

You must also evaluate the performance standards that you expect your players to attain. If you determine that poor player performance cannot be attributed to ineffective coaching actions, it is possible that the level of expectation you hold for your players is unrealistic. Remember, motivation is enhanced when players are achieving performance expectations that are self imposed or communicated by the coach. Expectations that are too high can have a negative effect on achievement. A combination of high but realistic expectations that are divided into achievable, sequential performance steps is a creative alternative that is most likely to yield appropriate and effective standards of performance.

Insufficient time for practice of the season's objectives can result in poor player achievement even when performance expectations and coaching actions are appropriate. Players must have sufficient time to attempt a task, make errors, obtain feedback, refine their attempts, and habituate abilities before it is reasonable to expect these abilities to be used within the context of a game. Attempting to cover too many skills within a limited amount of practice time is a major cause of delayed achievement. Even when the quality of coaching is excellent, player performance expectations may not be met when the amount of coaching and practice time is too short.

If the coaching actions necessary to improve coaching effectiveness are not implemented, evaluation is a waste of time.

Step 4. Act on the needed changes

The reason for conducting an evaluation of your coaching effectiveness is to learn what you can do to improve the contribution you make to your players. Most coaches would like to receive excellent ratings in all categories. Some coaches are good to excellent in most categories, but no one attains coaching perfection. We all can find ways to improve our effectiveness, whether in season or practice planning, implementation of plans, knowledge of the game, or even in our ability to evaluate ourselves. Regardless of our level of expertise, by systematically relating high and low levels of player achievement to our coaching actions, and by systematically seeking information from others, we can find ways to become more effective and more efficient. Merely identifying what changes may lead to improvements is a waste of time if the changes are not implemented.

Figure 9. By taking action on the changes that are identified, you can take a significant step toward becoming a more effective and efficient coach.

Summary

By evaluating player outcomes on the objectives of the season, you can estimate the effectiveness of your coaching actions. Limited achievement of players in some performance areas can signal the need for changes in some of your coaching actions. Use of the Checklist of Effective Coaching Actions and information obtained from others whose judgement you respect may reveal changes that you need to make. By taking action on the changes that are identified, you can take a significant step toward becoming a more effective and efficient coach.

CHECKLIST OF EFFECTIVE COACHING ACTIONS

This checklist can be used to review coaching actions that are related to player achievement of desired outcomes. It serves as an aid to identify the reason(s) why a player(s) did not achieve one or more of the expected outcomes. To use the checklist in this way, read the items in each content category and ask yourself the question. "Could my coaching actions (or inactions) implied by this item contribute to the unmet expectation?" Answer the question by responding with a 'yes' or 'no.' If you wish to rate the degree to which your actions (inactions) were consistent with the guidelines implied by the items, use the 5 point rating scale, where: 1 = strongly disagree, 2 = disagree, 3 = neutral, 4 = agree, and 5 = strongly agree. Items which result in 'no' or 'low' ratings may indicate that you are in discord with effective coaching practices. The process of seeking answers to specific concerns identified by your reaction to checklist items is an excellent way to obtain important coaching improvement information.

Item	Rating Disagree					Agree
Coaching Role						
1. The benefits (skill, knowledge, fitness, attitudes) and costs (time, money, injury, etc.) of participation were clearly in mind during planning and coaching times.	(NO) 1	2	3	4	5	(YES)
2. My primary purpose for coaching was to maximize the benefits for all of the players.	(NO) 1	2	3	4	5	(YES)
3. I communicated through actions and words that I expected each player to succeed in improving his/her level of play.	(NO) 1	2	3	4	5	(YES)
Organization						
4. I completed a written draft of season objectives to guide the conduct of my practices.	(NO) 1	2	3	4	5	(YES)
5. Performance expectations set for the players were realistic and attainable.	(NO) 1	2	3	4	5	(YES)
6. I conscientiously decided which objectives must be emphasized in the pre, early, mid and late season.	(NO) 1	2	3	4	5	(YES)
7. Objectives for developing my practices were drawn from those identified and sequenced from pre to late season.	(NO) 1	2	3	4	5	(YES)
8. The amount of total practice time allocated to each season objective was sufficient.	(NO) 1	2	3	4	5	(YES)
9. My practices would be characterized by others as orderly, safe, and enjoyable.	(NO) 1	2	3	4	5	(YES)
10. Objectives were broken down as necessary to allow players to achieve them in several small steps.	(NO) 1	2	3	4	5	(YES)

Knowledge of the Sport

11. I am familiar with the rationale for each season   (NO)   1   2   3   4   5   (YES)
objective selected and clearly communicated
its purpose and described how it is to be
executed to my players.

12. I was able to identify the key elements of   (NO)   1   2   3   4   5   (YES)
performance necessary for achievement of
each season objective.

Effective Instruction

13. I clearly communicated (by word and/or   (NO)   1   2   3   4   5   (YES)
example) the key elements to be learned for
each objective included in a practice.

14. Practice on an objective was initiated with a   (NO)   1   2   3   4   5   (YES)
rationale for why the objective is important.

15. Instruction did not continue without player   (NO)   1   2   3   4   5   (YES)
attention.

16. Practice on an objective provided each player   (NO)   1   2   3   4   5   (YES)
with many practice trials and with specific,
accurate, and positive feedback.

17. During practice I regularly grouped the players   (NO)   1   2   3   4   5   (YES)
in accordance with their different abilities on
the season's objectives.

18. I used questions to determine if the players   (NO)   1   2   3   4   5   (YES)
understood the objectives and instruction.

19. The players sensed a feeling of control over   (NO)   1   2   3   4   5   (YES)
their own learning which resulted from my
emphasis of clearly identifying what they
needed to learn and then encouraging
maximum effort.

20. My practices were pre-planned and clearly   (NO)   1   2   3   4   5   (YES)
associated the use of learning activities, drills,
and games with the season objectives.

21. I evaluated my practices and incorporated   (NO)   1   2   3   4   5   (YES)
appropriate changes for subsequent practices.

Motivation

22. My practices and games resulted in the players   (NO)   1   2   3   4   5   (YES)
achieving many of their goals for participation.

23. I taught the players how to realistically define   (NO)   1   2   3   4   5   (YES)
success in terms of effort and self
improvement.

24. An expert would agree, upon observing my   (NO)   1   2   3   4   5   (YES)
practices, that I use a positive coaching
approach.

Communication

25. There was no conflict between the verbal and   (NO)   1   2   3   4   5   (YES)
non-verbal messages I communicated to my
players.

26. I facilitated communication with the players by   (NO)   1   2   3   4   5   (YES)
being a good listener.

27. Accepted behaviors, and consequences of misbehavior, were communicated to players at the beginning of the season.   (NO) 1 2 3 4 5 (YES)

28. Players were involved in developing, or confirming, team rules.   (NO) 1 2 3 4 5 (YES)

29. Enforcement of team rules was consistent for all players throughout the season.   (NO) 1 2 3 4 5 (YES)

Involvement with Parents
30. Parents of the players were a positive, rather than negative, influence on player's achievement of the season objectives.   (NO) 1 2 3 4 5 (YES)

31. I communicated to the parents my responsibilities and the responsibilities of parents and players to the team.   (NO) 1 2 3 4 5 (YES)

Conditioning
32. The intensity, duration, and frequency of the physical conditioning I used was appropriate for the age of the players.   (NO) 1 2 3 4 5 (YES)

33. I routinely used a systematic warm-up and cool-down prior to and after practices and games.   (NO) 1 2 3 4 5 (YES)

34. The physical conditioning aspects of my practices appropriately simulated the requirement of the sport.   (NO) 1 2 3 4 5 (YES)

Injury Prevention
35. I followed all recommended safety procedures for the use of equipment and facilities.   (NO) 1 2 3 4 5 (YES)

36. I did not use any contraindicated exercises in my practices.   (NO) 1 2 3 4 5 (YES)

Care of Common Injuries
37. I established and followed appropriate emergency procedures and simple first aid as needed.   (NO) 1 2 3 4 5 (YES)

38. I had a well stocked first aid kit at each practice and game, including players' medical history information.   (NO) 1 2 3 4 5 (YES)

Rehabilitation of Injuries
39. None of the players experienced a recurrence of an injury that could be attributed to inappropriate rehabilitation.   (NO) 1 2 3 4 5 (YES)

Evaluation
40. I completed an evaluation of player improvement on the season objectives.   (NO) 1 2 3 4 5 (YES)

41. I identified the coaching actions (or inactions) that appeared most closely related to unmet player expectations.   (NO) 1 2 3 4 5 (YES)

42. I made the changes in coaching action needed to improve my coaching effectiveness.   (NO) 1 2 3 4 5 (YES)

REFERENCES

Rarick, G. L. (1969). Competitive sports for young boys: Controversial issues. *Medicine and Science in Sports, 1,* 181–184.

Smith, R. E., Smoll, F. L. & Curtis, B. (1979). Coach effectiveness training: A cognitive-behavioral approach to enhancing relationship skills in youth sport coaches. *Journal of Sport Psychology, 1,* 59–75.

Smith, R. E., Smoll, F. L. & Hunt, E. (1977). A system for the behavioral assessment of athletic coaches. *Research Quarterly, 48,* 401–407.

SUGGESTED READINGS

Baumgarten, S. (1984). It can be done! A model youth sports program. *Journal of Physical Education, Recreation and Dance, 55*(7), 55–58.

Bunker, L. K. (1981). Elementary physical education and youth sport. *Journal of Physical Education, Recreation and Dance, 52*(2), 26–28.

Fink, A. & Kosecoff, J. (1978). *An Evaluation Primer.* Beverly Hills, CA: Sage.

Lord, R. H. & Kozar, B. (1982). A test for volunteer youth sport coaches. *Journal of Sport Behavior, 5*(2), 77–82.

Wandzilak, T., Potter, G. & Ansorge, C. (1985). Reevaluating a youth sports basketball program. *Journal of Physical Education, Recreation and Dance, 56*(8), 21–23.